T H E

MATHEMATICS OF TECHNICAL ANALYSIS

APPLYING

STATISTICS

TO TRADING

STOCKS,

OPTIONS

AND

FUTURES

Clifford J. Sherry
Senior Scientist
Systems Research Laboratories Inc.

PROBUS PUBLISHING COMPANY
Chicago, Illinois
Cambridge, England

ISBN 1-55738-462-2

Printed in the United States of America

BC

4   5   6   7   8   9   0

With Love and Respect
This Book Is Dedicated to My Parents
Dorothy B. and Clifford W. Sherry

Contents

Acknowledgments

I would like to thank my wife Nancy, who helped type and edit the manuscript and render the illustrations. Without her encouragement this book would not have been possible. My children, Christopher, Jason, and Lori Beth also helped make this book possible by allowing me the time to work on it without interruption.

No book is the product of one mind, but is based on the interactions of the author with family, friends, colleagues, and students. Many people helped shape the ideas discussed in this book. They include Drs. Heinz Von Foerster, W.R. Klemm, D.L. Barrow, T.J. Marczynski, G. Karmos, D.J. Wolf, and Mr. S. Brudno, who all acted as sounding boards for the many ideas discussed in this book. They also provided advice, counsel, and constructive criticism during the initial development of the many techniques originally designed for the study of information processing in the nervous system. Mr. John Sweeney helped in the transition of these techniques to the study of economically important time series.

I would also like to thank all of the people at Probus Publishing Company for making the publication of this, my first book, such a pleasant experience.

Foreword

Almost by default, market technicians have found themselves the only innovative investigators of the underpinnings of modern market theory. Though our knowledge of how markets truly work is abysmal, academia has spent most of the last thirty years building evidence for the efficient markets theory. Only the astounding misvaluations of the 1980s, apparent to all, brought "street reality" to these finance theorists.

Even so, academics haven't changed their statistical tools and, so, are going to have a difficult time detecting what their tools cannot perceive: stationarity, independence and true randomness (or the lack of it) in market data.

Now it must be said that academics are ahead of traders in this respect: they are studying the fundamental questions. I would guess that fewer than one of a thousand traders has heard of stationarity, dependence or randomness or has considered their usefulness. Nevertheless, all technical trading comes down to this: (1) Do the processes which generate market prices change on one or can you count on their remaining consistent? (2) If they are consistent, do they generate random values or not? (3) Are the prices generated related to previous prices? Technicians have argued for years that (a) crowd behavior is consistent (if complex) over centuries; (b) pricing is clearly not random, else it would be far different day to day or minute to minute; and (c) past values are precisely those the crowd uses in its first estimate of today's price.

Fortunately, a researcher capable of taking a fresh look at these issues showed up at *Technical Analysis of Stocks and Commodities* in the late 1980s. Over several years, Cliff Sherry applied a variety of sophisticated techniques for time series analysis to prices time series. He did this with pencil and paper, methodically working through the conceptual bases and intricate details mathematically and graphically.

   As the Editor, I was privileged to watch this innovative process and even participate peripherally in trying to understand it well enough to publish the material. To boot, Cliff would apply the techniques to real world data, usually arriving at results surpising to my training in finance. It was really quite exciting to see data suggesting the complexity of the order in market behavior because, if there were order, then there would be ideas for research and the potential for constructing a true theory of market behavior. These tasks were and are far beyond my ability or per- haps even Cliff's, but they remain a delightful prospect and I believe Cliff's work will be a truly seminal contribution.

   Having been through the homework, I must say that what you face in this book is not a rose garden, but it is substantive. After ten years of reviewing, editing, using and reading trading "literature," I can only say that of four or five ideas. The statistical techniques described here are not buzzwords—they are hard work and valuable. They are also innovative— and I can only say that of two ideas I've seen, the other being John Ehlers' cycle work. Unfortunately, these techniques aren't yet programmed so as to be easily accessible to every trader. You cannot buy a canned program and turn it loose on your database to pre-process the data for the statisti- cal characteristics Cliff has described, but this would be an excellent proj- ect for some skilled reader. Perhaps, if he or she succeeded, a broader discussion of the issues of market order could get under way based on a solid statistical underpinning.

                                        John Sweeney
                                        Editor,
                                        Technical Analysis of
                                        Stocks and Commodities

Introduction   1

What determines the price of a stock, commodity, or index? What impact do past prices have on the current price and what impact does the current price have on future prices? The answer to these questions depends on whom you ask.

A fundamental analyst would probably try to find the appropriate earnings multiplier(s) to use to determine if a stock is over- or under-priced. In order to do this, they use a variety of sources of information to evaluate a firm's management and its financial position, as well as the *ambient* conditions, such as the general state of the economy (i.e., a recession, an inflationary period, etc.) or social and political conditions (i.e., an election year, a war going on, etc.). If asked, they would probably say that the past history of prices or *price changes* has little or no impact on the current price, and the current price, in turn, has little or no impact on future prices.

Technical analysts, on the other hand, would probably say that most of the available information about future price or *price change* can be obtained by studying the past history of prices or *price changes*. Technicians use a variety of charts and other techniques to study the time series that represents the past history of prices.

But, both of these groups tend to make these judgments based on philosophy or belief, rather than on empirical evidence. Which group is right? The answer turns, to a great extent, on whether the prices or *price changes* of a stock or other investment media are generated by a random walk or not. The random walk model assumes that sequential prices are determined randomly and independently. Unfortunately, the distinction between these two terms and the concepts they represent is often blurred, and in some cases they are used as if they are interchangeable. But, these two concepts are not interchangeable; they describe two very distinct characteristics of a time series (see Chapters 3 and 4).

The distinction between these two concepts can be clarified by considering a simple example—flipping a *fair* coin. It is random because the probability of a head or a tail, in the long run, is 50:50 and is determined by chance. (See Chapter 4 for a detailed discussion of randomness.) It is independent because the outcome of the current flip is not impacted by any past flip and the current flip has no impact on the outcome of any succeeding flip. (See Chapter 3 for a detailed discussion of independence.)

Another way to look at the distinction between randomness and independence is shown in Figure 1-1. We can think of a time series, such as the closing price of a specific stock, as a series of *bins*. Each day, one of the bins will be filled in with the closing price of the stock on that day. If you examine the top half of this figure, you will note that randomness refers to the filling of an individual bin, while independence refers to the sequential relationships between the bins and their contents.

There is a third characteristic of a time series that is generally overlooked in most discussions of the random walk model: stationarity. It is a bit more difficult to describe than randomness or independence. Basically, a time series is stationary if the underlying rules that generate it do not change over time. (See Chapter 2 for a detailed discussion of stationarity.) In the case of our *fair* coin, for example, the probability of a head or a tail is 50:50 (one example of an underlying rule), whether you flip the coin today or a hundred years from today.

The question as to whether the prices or *price changes* of stocks and other investment media are generated by a random walk has been the subject of debate since the turn of the century when Louis Bachelier published one of the first, if not the first, papers dealing with this topic. This paper, "Theory Of Speculation," published in *Ann. Sci. Ecole Norm Sup* 1900, *3*, number 1018 which was his doctoral dissertation, assumes that the reader has a strong background in mathematics and probability theory. Fortunately, this paper and many of the other papers dealing with the random walk model have been republished in a book edited by Paul Cootner, *The Random Character of Stock Prices* (M.I.T. Press, Cambridge, Massachusetts, 1964). Proponents of the random walk model generally use one or more different types of evidence to support the validity of this model.

Harry V. Roberts provides one basic type of evidence in his paper "Stock Market 'Patterns' and Financial Analysis: Methodological Suggestions" (*Journal of Finance,* 1959, *14*, 1-10, *see* Cootner). He used a random

Figure 1–1

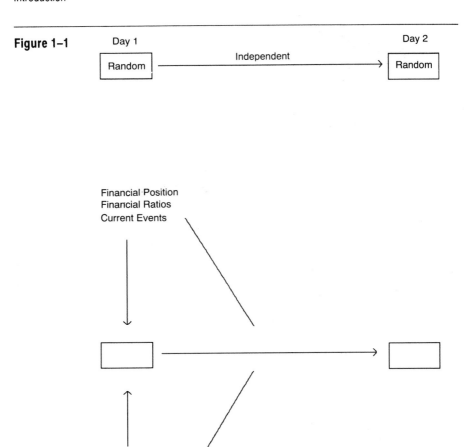

number table to generate a time series that "looks" very much like the Dow Jones Industrial Index closing prices for 1958. Does the way a plot of a time series "looks" tell us whether it was generated by random walk model or not? If we have two plots, such as those shown in Figures 1–2 and 1–3, can we determine if one represents the closing prices of a particular stock and the other a time series constructed using a random number table or a roulette wheel? Or do both represent the closing prices of real stocks? Or do they represent artificial *prices* generated by a random number table? In this case, one is generated from a random number table and the other represents the closing prices of a particular stock. Can you tell which is which? Are you really sure? Although it would be beyond the

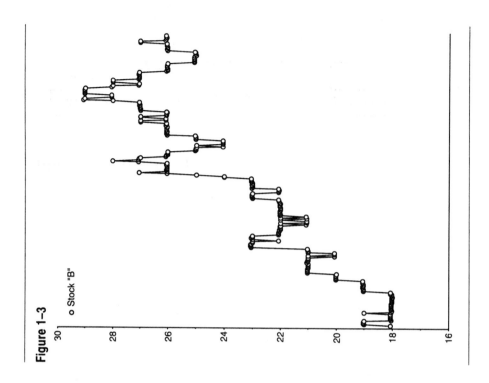

Figure 1-2

o Stock "A"

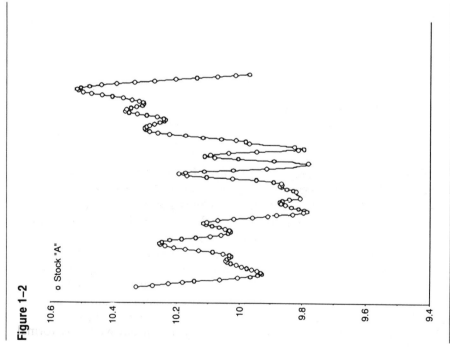

Figure 1-3

o Stock "B"

scope of this book to prove conclusively, most, if not all, statisticians (and probability theorists) would argue that the fact that plots of two time series resemble each other (even if they are virtually identical) does not prove that they were generated in the same manner.

Let us take this argument one step further and use the two time series to construct two individual probability density functions. These probability density functions can be compared with specific theoretical distributions, such as the normal distribution or Poisson distribution, etc. Again, most theorists would argue that the fact that if a probability density function is similar (or even identical) to a known theoretical distribution, this does not prove that it or its underlying time series was generated in some specific manner. It is important to realize that once we plot a probability density function, we disrupt any serial dependencies that might be present. Therefore, it would be difficult to argue that a (one dimensional) probability density function can tell us anything about independence.

Eugene F. Fama (*Journal of Finance*, 1970, pp. 383-420, *see* Cootner) provides another form of evidence—lag-1 serial correlation coefficients generated from the closing prices of a variety of stocks tend to be low. Further, the correlation coefficients tend to decrease in size with increasing lag values. This finding has been confirmed by other investigators (including plots shown in Chapter 5).

But, there is a problem with this type of evidence (the details of how serial- and auto-correlograms are constructed, as well as the problems associated with using each are discussed in detail in Chapter 5). Briefly, serial- or auto-correlograms each test for one, rather restricted, form of serial dependency. If the specific form of serial dependency is present, the correlation coefficient will be high. If it is not present, then the correlation coefficient will be low. However, it is important to note that, if the correlation coefficient is low, this does not mean that the time series does not contain significant serial dependencies; it merely means that the time series does not contain the type of serial dependencies that correlation tests for.

Two other sorts of evidence are also commonly used to argue that prices or *price changes* are generated by a random walk. They are runs tests and filter rules. One problem with runs tests is that statisticians cannot seem to agree whether runs tests test for divergence from randomness or independence (see Chapter 6). Filter rules are not discussed in this book, but a variety of other pattern detection techniques are.

How can you decide if the past prices or *price changes* of a stock, commodity, or index have been generated by a random walk? By formal hypothesis testing! The remaining chapters of this book will provide you with the methods and techniques to determine if the time series that you are interested in is stationary or nonstationary, and whether it is random or nonrandom and/or independent or dependent.

If you use these methods and techniques and find that your time series is not stationary, it is probably best to stop and think carefully about your investment strategy. Nonstationarity implies that the underlying rules that "generated" your time series change from time to time without warning. Therefore, you are dealing with maximum uncertainty about the potential outcome of your investment. As described in some detail in Chapter 8, the level of uncertainty may be a good metric to evaluate risk. The more uncertain, the greater the risk! Further, although it is not possible to prove conclusively at this point, it is likely that if your time series is not stationary, it would be difficult to use other techniques, such as fundamental analysis, to make rational (and profitable) buy-sell decisions.

On the other hand, if you find that your time series is stationary, then it would be appropriate to test to determine if it is random or nonrandom and/or independent or dependent. It is important to note that a time series can potentially be random and independent, random and dependent, nonrandom and independent, and nonrandom and dependent. If you find that it is dependent, then you can use the techniques described in Chapter 3 to potentially determine the duration of the serial dependencies. Further, if you find that your time series is either nonrandom and/or dependent, it means that the level of uncertainty is less than if the time series were random and/or independent. If you decrease the level of uncertainty, you potentially decrease the risk. Does the fact that a particular stock, commodity, or index displayed specific characteristics in the past guarantee that it will do so in the future? **NO!** But, it is certainly suggestive.

Many of the techniques that are discussed in this book, particularly those discussed in Chapters 2-4, I developed over the last 10-15 years with input from a variety of colleagues. They were developed in an entirely different context, the study of how the nervous system processes information. The original descriptions of these techniques were published in a number of refereed scientific journals, such as Brain Research, International Journal of Neuroscience, Brain Research Bulletin, etc. Before they were published in these journals, they underwent considerable scrutiny by the respective editors and referees. Since they were published, they have been scrutinized by other scientists working in the same and related areas and have not received any adverse comment.

When I discovered that people interested in investments were interested in many of the same questions that I was dealing with in my study of information processing, and because of comments received on these articles, I decided to write this book.

Stationarity $\quad$ 2

Background

Even if you are not technically oriented, you probably have seen plots like the one shown in Figure 2-1. It is a graph of the daily closing prices of the Standard & Poor's 500 Composite Stock Index for 1988. If you are technically oriented, you are probably very familiar with moving-average plots, as shown in Figure 2-2. You might also be familiar with serial correlograms such as those shown in Figures 2-3 and 2-4, which show the lag-1 and lag-10 serial correlograms, respectively.

Each of these graphs can provide important information about the S&P 500 time series. But, there are a variety of other characteristics of time series like the S&P 500 that can provide us with important information that can help us make reasoned and profitable buy-sell decisions.

Stationarity is not a concept that we are likely to encounter in our daily life. It is, however, one of the most important characteristics of a time series. A stationary time series is one in which the underlying *rules* that generate the time series do not change over time.

Consider a simple example, the probability theorist's favorite tool, a small urn filled with different colored balls (for example, 100 white, 50 blue, 50 red, and 25 black). We can use this urn and its contents to construct a "model" time series. Shake the urn and remove one ball; note its color, return it to the urn, shake, remove another, and continue this process several hundred times. This "model" time series is stationary because the underlying *rules* that we used to generate it (in this case the relative distribution of colored balls) did not change over time. Now, if someone came along and removed 50 white balls (without us knowing about it)

Figure 2–1

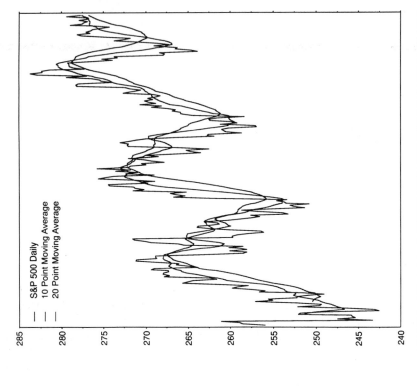

o S&P 500 Daily

Figure 2–2

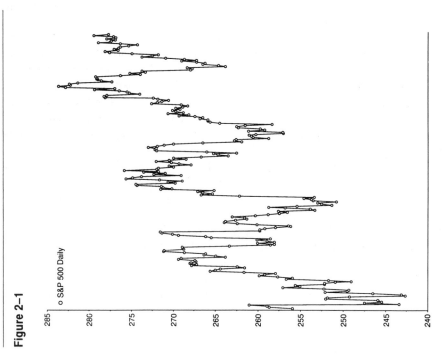

S&P 500 Daily
10 Point Moving Average
20 Point Moving Average

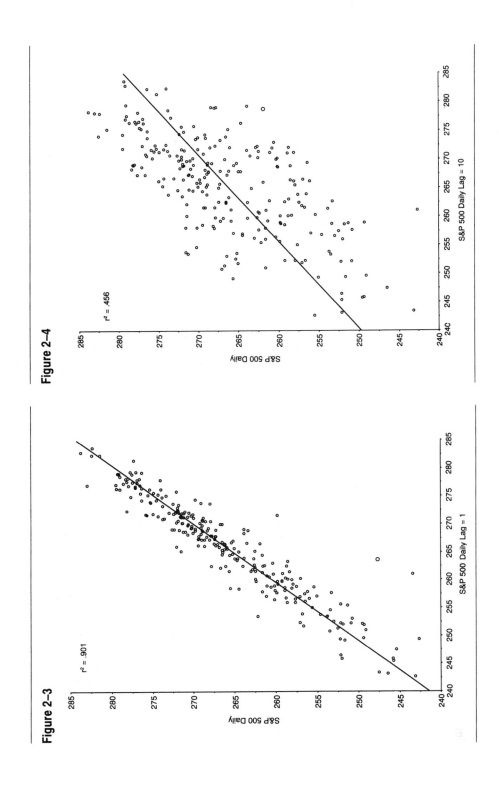

Figure 2–3

r² = .901

S&P 500 Daily

S&P 500 Daily Lag = 1

Figure 2–4

r² = .456

S&P 500 Daily

S&P 500 Daily Lag = 10

while we were constructing our "model" time series, it would no longer be stationary because the underlying *rules* (the relative distribution of balls) changed. If our time series is stationary, then we can examine it using a variety of statistical or pattern detection methods to try and determine what the underlying *rules* are and how we can use this information to make reasoned (and ultimately profitable) buy-sell decisions. If our time series is not stationary, it means that the *rules* change over time, often without warning or external sign. Most statistical methods, even relatively simple ones like moving averages will not really work, especially in the long run.

It is important to realize that we can define an economic time series, like the past history of prices of a particular stock or commodity, in a number of different ways. For example, if we are intra-day traders, we might find that the "click to click" prices or *price changes* are stationary. But, if we decide to trade on an inter-day basis, we might find that the inter-day or weekly closing prices or *price changes* are not stationary. So, it is important to test for stationarity on the same data and within the same time frame that we will be making our trading decisions. Also, it is important to realize that a time series may be stationary and then slip into nonstationarity or vice versa. So, we must test our data periodically to be sure that no changes have occurred.

Basic Procedures

The first step in testing for stationarity is to obtain a listing of the prices or *price changes* of our stock or commodity in the same time frame that we are planning to trade. For example, if we are inter-day traders, we might want to use the daily closing prices (or the daily high or low price). In general, when we do statistics, the more data points we have, the better. And, in general, the same *rule* holds here, with one important proviso: If our time series "flip-flops" into and out of stationarity, and if we include too many nonstationary periods, we might miss the period when it is stationary. So, we should begin with the longest period that is convenient. But, if we use a very long time period and find that it is not stationary, we might want to repeat the tests using only the most recent data available.

We will use the artificial "prices" shown in Table 2-1 to illustrate the basic methods used in this chapter and in each succeeding chapter. The summary statistics for the artificial prices are shown in Table 2-2. We could divide this data into halves, thirds, quarters, or whatever we choose, as long as we do it by some unvarying rule. In this case, divide the

Table 2-1

	Artificial Prices	Delta-1		Artificial Prices	Delta-1
1	9.000	1.000	35	2.000	13.000
2	10.000	−6.000	36	15.000	−4.000
3	4.000	11.000	37	11.000	−3.000
4	15.000	−9.000	38	8.000	−4.000
5	6.000	−2.000	39	4.000	4.000
6	4.000	−1.000	40	8.000	7.000
7	3.000	10.000	41	15.000	−1.000
8	13.000	−1.000	42	14.000	−2.000
9	12.000	−11.000	43	12.000	−7.000
10	1.000	2.000	44	5.000	7.000
11	3.000	1.000	45	12.000	−2.000
12	4.000	11.000	46	10.000	−1.000
13	15.000	−2.000	47	9.000	6.000
14	13.000	−12.000	48	15.000	−3.000
15	1.000	3.000	49	12.000	1.000
16	4.000	4.000	50	13.000	−11.000
17	8.000	5.000	51	2.000	4.000
18	13.000	−9.000	52	6.000	7.000
19	4.000	−2.000	53	13.000	−4.000
20	2.000	10.000	54	9.000	−4.000
21	12.000	−3.000	55	5.000	10.000
22	9.000	3.000	56	15.000	−4.000
23	12.000	−11.000	57	11.000	3.000
24	1.000	3.000	58	14.000	−3.000
25	4.000	10.000	59	11.000	−10.000
26	14.000	−13.000	60	1.000	6.000
27	1.000	14.000	61	7.000	−2.000
28	15.000	−9.000	62	5.000	1.000
29	6.000	5.000	63	6.000	8.000
30	11.000	1.000	64	14.000	−6.000
31	12.000	−4.000	65	8.000	−6.000
32	8.000	6.000	66	2.000	2.000
33	14.000	−3.000	67	4.000	1.000
34	11.000	−9.000	68	5.000	3.000

Table continues

Table 2-1   Continued

	Artificial Prices	Delta-1		Artificial Prices	Delta-1
69	8.000	5.000	103	8.000	2.000
70	13.000	-11.000	104	10.000	-8.000
71	2.000	-1.000	105	2.000	11.000
72	1.000	7.000	106	13.000	-12.000
73	8.000	4.000	107	1.000	5.000
74	12.000	-6.000	108	6.000	-4.000
75	6.000	3.000	109	2.000	7.000
76	9.000	6.000	110	9.000	-6.000
77	15.000	-5.000	111	3.000	4.000
78	10.000	-2.000	112	7.000	-6.000
79	8.000	1.000	113	1.000	3.000
80	9.000	-6.000	114	4.000	10.000
81	3.000	-1.000	115	14.000	-6.000
82	2.000	7.000	116	8.000	1.000
83	9.000	1.000	117	9.000	-7.000
84	10.000	5.000	118	2.000	6.000
85	15.000	-5.000	119	8.000	4.000
86	10.000	-4.000	120	12.000	-2.000
87	6.000	5.000	121	10.000	-9.000
88	11.000	-9.000	122	1.000	10.000
89	2.000	-1.000	123	11.000	3.000
90	1.000	11.000	124	14.000	-2.000
91	12.000	-3.000	125	12.000	-11.000
92	9.000	3.000	126	1.000	13.000
93	12.000	-11.000	127	14.000	-10.000
94	1.000	7.000	128	4.000	7.000
95	8.000	7.000	129	11.000	-9.000
96	15.000	-13.000	130	2.000	7.000
97	2.000	6.000	131	9.000	-1.000
98	8.000	1.000	132	8.000	5.000
99	9.000	6.000	133	13.000	-4.000
100	15.000	-1.000	134	9.000	-4.000
101	14.000	-2.000	135	5.000	6.000
102	12.000	-4.000	136	11.000	1.000

Table continues

Table 2-1   Continued

	Artificial Prices	Delta-1		Artificial Prices	Delta-1
137	12.000	−6.000	169	9.000	−6.000
138	6.000	3.000	170	3.000	12.000
139	9.000	−4.000	171	15.000	−5.000
140	5.000	6.000	172	10.000	2.000
141	11.000	−2.000	173	12.000	−9.000
142	9.000	−6.000	174	3.000	4.000
143	3.000	1.000	175	7.000	−1.000
144	4.000	8.000	176	6.000	7.000
145	12.000	1.000	177	13.000	−10.000
146	13.000	−7.000	178	3.000	−2.000
147	6.000	−1.000	179	1.000	5.000
148	5.000	10.000	180	6.000	−5.000
149	15.000	−13.000	181	1.000	8.000
150	2.000	12.000	182	9.000	−2.000
151	14.000	−13.000	183	7.000	−6.000
152	1.000	5.000	184	1.000	5.000
153	6.000	−1.000	185	6.000	−1.000
154	5.000	6.000	186	5.000	3.000
155	11.000	−6.000	187	8.000	4.000
156	5.000	−1.000	188	12.000	−7.000
157	4.000	4.000	189	5.000	1.000
158	8.000	−2.000	190	6.000	2.000
159	6.000	−4.000	191	8.000	2.000
160	2.000	3.000	192	10.000	4.000
161	5.000	4.000	193	14.000	−1.000
162	9.000	−6.000	194	13.000	2.000
163	3.000	−2.000	195	15.000	−5.000
164	1.000	10.000	196	10.000	1.000
165	11.000	−5.000	197	11.000	−10.000
166	6.000	5.000	198	1.000	1.000
167	11.000	−4.000	199	2.000	4.000
168	7.000	2.000			

Table 2–2   X1 : Artificial Prices

Mean	Std. Dev.	Std. Error	Variance	Coef. Var.	Count
7.925	4.397	.312	19.333	55.484	199

Minimum	Maximum	Range	Sum	Sum of Sqr.	# Missing
1	15	14	1577	16325	0

# < 10th %	10th %	25th %	50th %	75th %	90th %
18	2	4	8	12	14

# > 90th %	Mode	Geo. Mean	Har. Mean	Kurtosis	Skewness
14	•	6.214	4.175	–1.199	–.047

data into halves, using the first hundred artificial prices as the first half and the second hundred prices as the second half. The summary statistics for each half are shown in Table 2-3. We will construct two frequency histograms, one for each half of the data. It is relatively easy to construct a frequency histogram. Take a piece of graph paper and label the horizontal axis, price and create 15 bins, labeled 1 through 15, as shown in Figure 2-5. Label the vertical axis, frequency.

The first price in the artificial data is "9," so write a one in "bin-9." The second price is "10," so write a two in "bin-10." The next price is "4," represented by the three in "bin-4." The fourth and fifth prices are "15" and "6" and are represented by the four and five in "bins-15 and 6," respectively. The sixth price is a "4," so write a six immediately above the three in "bin-4." Continue this process until you reach the last price in this half and write 100 at the top of "bin-15."

If you examine this histogram, you will note that the frequency count in "bin-1" is 8. That means that there are eight "1"s in this half of the data: "price" numbers 10, 15, 24, 27, 60, 72, 90, and 94. If you were generating these histograms on a computer, the finished frequency histogram should resemble the one shown in Figure 2-6. Create another histogram like that shown in Figure 2-7, using the same method. The first price in the second half is "14," so write a one in "bin-14." The next "price" is "12," so write a

Table 2–3   Artificial Prices

Half 1

Mean	Std. Dev.	Std. Error	Variance	Coef. Var.	Count
8.38	4.541	.454	20.622	54.19	100

Minimum	Maximum	Range	Sum	Sum of Sqr.	# Missing
1	15	14	838	9064	0

# < 10th %	10th %	25th %	50th %	75th %	90th %
8	2	4	9	12	15

# > 90th %	Mode	Geo. Mean	Har. Mean	Kurtosis	Skewness
0	15	6.603	4.42	−1.223	−.151

Half 2

Mean	Std. Dev.	Std. Error	Variance	Coef. Var.	Count
7.45	4.2	.42	17.644	56.382	100

Minimum	Maximum	Range	Sum	Sum of Sqr.	# Missing
1	15	14	745	7297	0

# < 10th %	10th %	25th %	50th %	75th %	90th %
10	1.5	4	7.5	11	13

# > 90th %	Mode	Geo. Mean	Har. Mean	Kurtosis	Skewness
9	6	5.845	3.968	−1.138	.042

Figure 2–5   Stationarity 1st Half

1	2	3	4	5	6	7	8	9	10	11	12	13	14	15
														100
							98				93			96
							95	99			91			85
94	97	67					79	92			74			77
90	89	39					73	83			49			56
72	82	25		87			69	80		88	45	70		48
60	71	19		75			65	76	86	59	43	53	64	41
27	66	16	68	63			40	54	84	57	31	50	58	36
24	51	81	12	62	52		38	47	78	37	23	18	42	28
15	35	11	6	55	29		32	22	46	34	21	14	33	13
10	20	7	3	44	5	61	17	1	2	30	9	8	26	4

two in "bin-12"...the last price is "6," so write 100 at the top of "bin-6." The completed histogram should resemble Figure 2-8.

The next step is to convert the two frequency histograms into two separate probability density functions by dividing the frequency of each price by the total number of prices in the histogram (100), Table 2-4, a and b. The frequency in "bin-1" is 8 which is divided by 100 which equals 0.08, as shown in Table 2-4a. The frequency in "bin-2" is also 8, so its probability is also 0.08. The probability density function for the first half of the data is shown in Table 2-4a, column 4. Then convert the probability density function into a cumulative probability density function by summing over the individual probabilities. The probability of "bin-1" is 0.08 and for "bin-2" is also 0.08, so the cumulative probability in "bin-2" is 0.16 (i.e., 16%). The probability in "bin-3" is 0.03, so the cumulative probability of "bin-3" is 0.19 (0.16 + 0.03). The cumulative probability density function for the first half of the data is shown in Table 2-4a, column 5 and in Figure 2-9 (circles). Note that the cumulative probability should sum to 100. Proceed in exactly the same fashion with the second half of the data, shown in Table 2-4b, column 5. The completed cumulative probability density function for the second half of the data is shown in Figure 2-9 (squares).

In Figure 2-9, note that the two cumulative probability density functions are quite similar and therefore, it is likely that our artificial prices are

Figure 2–6

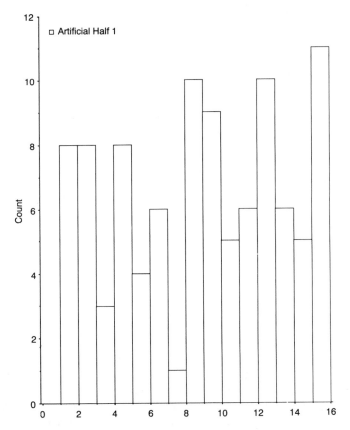

stationary. There are a number of other ways to compare these two cumulative probability density functions. For example, plot the deciles (10%, 20%, 30%, etc.) associated with each price in both halves of the time series, as shown in the insert in Figure 2-9. If the plotted deciles lie on or near the diagonal line, then the two cumulative probability density functions are very similar or identical. If this is the case, then the underlying time series (the artificial prices) is stationary. Or, determine if the time series is stationary using quantile analysis and a Chi-square test, as described in detail below.

Often the absolute prices are not stationary because of a significant trend upwards or downwards. One way to "detrend" a time series is to use *price changes* rather than prices. One way to obtain *price changes* is to

Figure 2–7   Stationarity 2nd Half

1	2	3	4	5	6	7	8	9	10	11	12	13	14	15
				100										
98				90										
84				85			82							
81			89	80			69		97					
79	99		86	76		91	62		67	88				
64	60	78	61	66		87	42		65	73				
52	50	74	56	59		58	39	96	55	45	94	93		
26	30	70	57	54	53	83	32	34	92	41	37	77	27	95
22	18	63	44	48	47	75	19	31	72	36	25	46	24	71
13	9	43	28	40	38	68	16	17	21	29	20	33	15	51
7	2	11	14	35	8	12	3	10	4	23	2	6	1	49

subtract the first price from the second, the second from the third, the third from the fourth, etc., as shown in Table 2-1, column 2. We will call these *price changes*—delta-1. Delta-2 would be obtained by subtracting the first price from the third, the second from the fourth, the third from the fifth, etc. A positive delta-1 means that there was a price increase; a negative delta-1 indicates a price decrease. The summary statistics are shown in Table 2-5.

In this case, create a histogram with 31 bins labeled -15, -14, -13 ... -1, 0, +1, +2, ... +15, on the horizontal axis. The first *price change* is "+1," so write a one over "bin +1"; the next *price change* is "-6," so write a two over "bin -6"; the third *price change* is "+11," so write a three over "bin +11," etc. The completed frequency histograms are shown respectively in Figures 2-10 and 2-11 for the first and second half of delta-1 *price changes* and in Table 2-6, a and b. These histograms are converted to probability density functions and cumulative probability density functions as described above. The cumulative probability density functions are shown in Table 2-6, a and b, column 5 and in Figure 2-12 (circles—first half, squares—second half). Note that all of the percentiles fall on the diagonal line (insert Figure 2-12). This means that the delta-1 *price changes* are stationary.

Figure 2–8

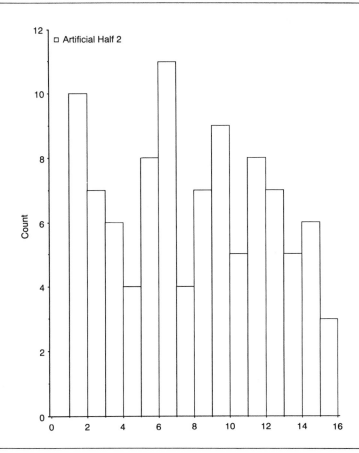

Real Data

This section deals with real data. Figure 2-1 and Table 2-7 show the closing prices for the Standard & Poor's 500 Composite Stock Index for 1988, while the summary statistics are shown in Table 2-8. We proceed with these data in the same manner as described above when we used the artificial data.

Divide the data into two equal halves. In this case, one half would have 126 and the other half 127 data points. Use each half to construct two separate frequency histograms. The completed histogram should resemble those shown in Figures 2-13 and 2-14 for the first and second halves, respectively, and the summary statistics are shown in Table 2-9, a and b.

Table 2–4a   Artificial Half 1

From (≥)	To (<)	Count	Percent	Percent
0	1	0	0%	0%
1	2	8	8%	8%
2	3	8	8%	16%
3	4	3	3%	19%
4	5	8	8%	27%
5	6	4	4%	31%
6	7	6	6%	37%
7	8	1	1%	38%
8	9	10	10%	48%
9	10	9	9%	57%
10	11	5	5%	62%
11	12	6	6%	68%
12	13	10	10%	78%
13	14	6	6%	84%
14	15	5	5%	89%
15	16	11	11%	100%

Table 2–4b   Artificial Half 2

From (≥)	To (<)	Count	Percent	Percent
0	1	0	0%	0%
1	2	10	10%	10%
2	3	7	7%	17%
3	4	6	6%	23%
4	5	4	4%	27%
5	6	8	8%	35%
6	7	11	11%	46%
7	8	4	4%	50%
8	9	7	7%	57%
9	10	9	9%	66%
10	11	5	5%	71%
11	12	8	8%	79%
12	13	7	7%	86%
13	14	5	5%	91%
14	15	6	6%	97%
15	16	3	3%	100%

Figure 2–9

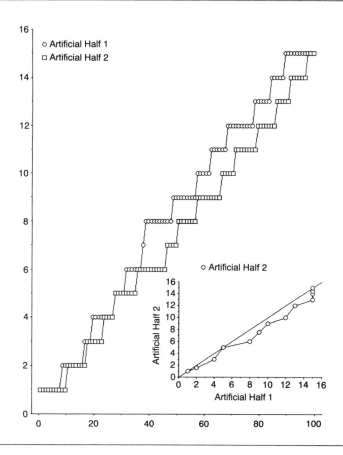

Use these frequency histograms to construct two probability density functions. Remember, do this by dividing each column in our frequency histogram by the total number of data points in the histogram, as described above. The two probability density functions are used to construct two cumulative probability density functions, as shown in Figure 2-15. Based on an examination of the two cumulative probability density functions (main part of figure) and the percentile comparison (insert), it is clear that the two probability density functions are different from each other. This difference is probably due to the noticeable upward trend in the prices as shown in Figure 2-1. However, the insert shows that the percentile comparisons lie on a line parallel to the diagonal line. This suggests that despite the upward trend, the prices may still be stationary.

Table 2-5

Artificial Delta–1 Half 1

Mean	Std. Dev.	Std. Error	Variance	Coef. Var.	Count
.061	6.462	.649	41.751	10661.527	99

Minimum	Maximum	Range	Sum	Sum of Sqr.	# Missing
–13	14	27	6	4092	1

# < 10th %	10th %	25th %	50th %	75th %	90th %
9	–9	–4	1	5	7.6

# > 90th %	Mode	Geo. Mean	Har. Mean
10	1	•	•

Artificial Delta–1 Half 2

Mean	Std. Dev.	Std. Error	Variance	Coef. Var.	Count
–.081	6.17	.62	38.075	–7635.99	99

Minimum	Maximum	Range	Sum	Sum of Sqr.	# Missing
–13	13	26	–8	3732	1

# < 10th %	10th %	25th %	50th %	75th %	90th %
10	–8.6	–5	1	4	7.6

# > 90th %	Mode	Geo. Mean	Har. Mean
10	–6	•	•

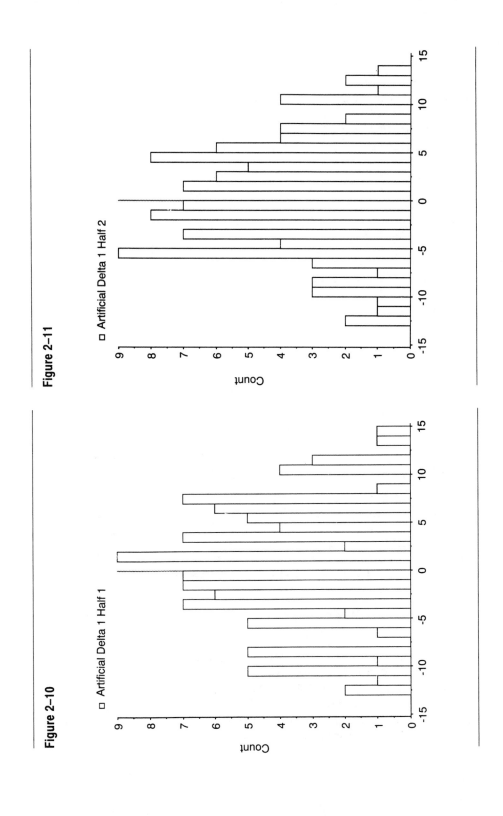

Figure 2-10

Figure 2-11

Table 2–6a   Artificial Delta-1 Half 1

From (≥)	To (<)	Count	Percent	Cum. Percent
−15	−14	0	0%	0%
−14	−13	0	0%	0%
−13	−12	2	2.02%	2.02%
−12	−11	1	1.01%	3.03%
−11	−10	5	5.051%	8.081%
−10	−9	1	1.01%	9.091%
−9	−8	5	5.051%	14.141%
−8	−7	0	0%	14.141%
−7	−6	1	1.01%	15.152%
−6	−5	5	5.051%	20.202%
−5	−4	2	2.02%	22.222%
−4	−3	7	7.071%	29.293%
−3	−2	6	6.061%	35.354%
−2	−1	7	7.071%	42.424%
−1	0	7	7.071%	49.495%
0	1	0	0%	49.495%
1	2	9	9.091%	58.586%
2	3	2	2.02%	60.606%
3	4	7	7.071%	67.677%
4	5	4	4.04%	71.717%
5	6	5	5.051%	76.768%
6	7	6	6.061%	82.828%
7	8	7	7.071%	89.899%
8	9	1	1.01%	90.909%
9	10	0	0%	90.909%
10	11	4	4.04%	94.949%
11	12	3	3.03%	97.98%
12	13	0	0%	97.98%
13	14	1	1.01%	98.99%
14	15	1	1.01%	100%

We will "detrend" these data by subtracting the first price from the second, the second from the third, the third from the fourth, etc. We will call this data set the S&P 500—delta-1, and it is shown in Table 2-7, column 2. We will divide the list of S&P 500—delta-1 *price changes* in half and generate a frequency histogram, a probability density function (see Figures 2-16 and 2-17), for each half, as described above. The summary statis-

Table 2–6b   Artificial Delta-1 Half 2

From (≥)	To (<)	Count	Percent	Cum. Percent
−15	−14	0	0%	0%
−14	−13	0	0%	0%
−13	−12	2	2.02%	2.02%
−12	−11	1	1.01%	3.03%
−11	−10	1	1.01%	4.04%
−10	−9	3	3.03%	7.071%
−9	−8	3	3.03%	10.101%
−8	−7	1	1.01%	11.111%
−7	−6	3	3.03%	14.141%
−6	−5	9	9.091%	23.232%
−5	−4	4	4.04%	27.273%
−4	−3	7	7.071%	34.343%
−3	−2	0	0%	34.343%
−2	−1	8	8.081%	42.424%
−1	0	7	7.071%	49.495%
0	1	0	0%	49.495%
1	2	7	7.071%	56.566%
2	3	6	6.061%	62.626%
3	4	5	5.051%	67.677%
4	5	8	8.081%	75.758%
5	6	6	6.061%	81.818%
6	7	4	4.04%	85.859%
7	8	4	4.04%	89.899%
8	9	2	2.02%	91.919%
9	10	0	0%	91.919%
10	11	4	4.04%	95.96%
11	12	1	1.01%	96.97%
12	13	2	2.02%	98.99%
13	14	1	1.01%	100%

tics are shown in Table 2-10. The cumulative probability density functions for the first (circles) and second (squares) halves of the S&P 500—delta-1 are shown in Figure 2-18. In Figure 2-18, note that these two cumulative probability density functions are very similar and the percentile comparisons (see insert) fall on the diagonal line. Based on our examination, we can tentatively conclude that the S&P 500—delta-1 *price changes* are sta-

Figure 2–12

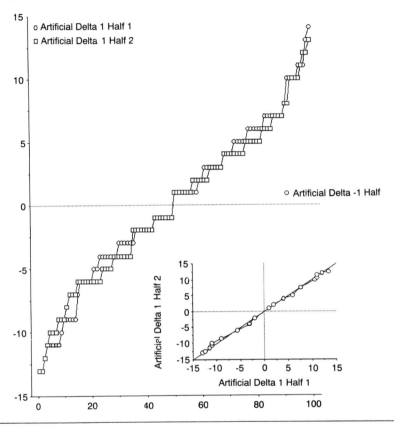

tionary. But are they? One way to determine if the differences in the two cumulative probability density functions are not significantly different from each other (i.e., the underlying time series S&P 500—delta-1 is stationary) is to use a quantile Chi-square test. Use the cumulative probability density functions as shown in Figure 2-18 or the tabled value for the same histogram as shown in Table 2-11, a and b. If there are relatively few data points and if the range of *price changes* is relatively small, it is probably easier to use the tabled values to make these calculations. If there are

Table 2-7

	S&P 500 Daily-1988	S&P 500 Delta-1		S&P 500 Daily-1988	S&P 500 Delta-1
1	255.940	•	37	264.430	-.590
2	258.630	2.690	38	261.580	-2.850
3	258.890	.260	39	262.460	.880
4	261.070	2.180	40	267.820	5.360
5	243.400	-17.670	41	267.220	-.600
6	247.490	4.090	42	267.980	.760
7	245.420	-2.070	43	267.880	-.100
8	245.810	.390	44	267.300	-.580
9	245.880	.070	45	267.380	.080
10	252.050	6.170	46	269.430	2.050
11	251.880	-.170	47	269.060	-.370
12	249.320	-2.560	48	263.840	-5.220
13	242.630	-6.690	49	264.940	1.100
14	243.140	.510	50	266.370	1.430
15	246.500	3.360	51	266.130	-.240
16	252.170	5.670	52	268.650	2.520
17	249.570	-2.600	53	271.220	2.570
18	249.380	-.190	54	271.120	-.100
19	252.290	2.910	55	268.740	-2.380
20	257.070	4.780	56	268.840	.100
21	255.040	-2.030	57	268.910	.070
22	255.570	.530	58	263.350	-5.560
23	252.210	-3.360	59	258.510	-4.840
24	252.210	0	60	258.060	-.450
25	250.960	-1.250	61	260.070	2.010
26	249.100	-1.860	62	258.070	-2.000
27	251.720	2.620	63	258.890	.820
28	256.660	4.940	64	260.140	1.250
29	255.950	-.710	65	258.510	-1.630
30	257.630	1.680	66	265.490	6.980
31	259.830	2.200	67	266.160	.670
32	259.210	-.620	68	269.430	3.270
33	257.910	-1.300	69	270.160	.730
34	261.610	3.700	70	271.370	1.210
35	265.640	4.030	71	271.570	.200
36	265.020	-.620	72	259.750	-11.820

Table continues

Table 2–7   Continued

	S&P 500 Daily–1988	S&P 500 Delta–1		S&P 500 Daily–1988	S&P 500 Delta–1
73	259.770	.020	109	265.170	−1.880
74	259.210	−.560	110	271.520	6.350
75	257.920	−1.290	111	270.200	−1.320
76	256.130	−1.790	112	271.260	1.060
77	256.420	.290	113	271.430	.170
78	260.140	3.720	114	274.300	2.870
79	262.460	2.320	115	274.450	.150
80	263.930	1.470	116	269.770	−4.680
81	263.800	−.130	117	270.680	.910
82	262.610	−1.190	118	268.940	−1.740
83	261.330	−1.280	119	271.670	2.730
84	261.560	.230	120	275.660	3.990
85	263.000	1.440	121	274.820	−.840
86	260.320	−2.680	122	273.780	−1.040
87	258.790	−1.530	123	269.060	−4.720
88	257.480	−1.310	124	272.310	3.250
89	256.540	−.940	125	270.980	−1.330
90	257.620	1.080	126	273.500	2.520
91	253.310	−4.310	127	271.780	−1.720
92	253.850	.540	128	275.810	4.030
93	256.780	2.930	129	272.020	−3.790
94	258.710	1.930	130	271.780	−.240
95	255.390	−3.320	131	270.020	−1.760
96	251.350	−4.040	132	270.550	.530
97	252.570	1.220	133	267.850	−2.700
98	253.020	.450	134	269.320	1.470
99	250.830	−2.190	135	270.260	.940
100	253.510	2.680	136	272.050	1.790
101	253.760	.250	137	270.510	−1.540
102	254.630	.870	138	268.470	−2.040
103	253.420	−1.210	139	270.000	1.530
104	262.160	8.740	140	266.660	−3.340
105	266.690	4.530	141	263.500	−3.160
106	265.330	−1.360	142	264.680	1.180
107	266.450	1.120	143	265.190	.510
108	267.050	.600	144	262.500	−2.690

Table continues

Table 2–7   Continued

	S&P 500 Daily–1988	S&P 500 Delta–1		S&P 500 Daily–1988	S&P 500 Delta–1
145	266.020	3.520	181	268.820	−1.830
146	272.020	6.000	182	269.730	.910
147	272.210	.190	183	270.160	.430
148	272.060	−.150	184	269.180	−.980
149	272.980	.920	185	269.760	.580
150	271.930	−1.050	186	268.880	−.880
151	271.150	−.780	187	268.260	−.620
152	269.980	−1.170	188	269.080	.820
153	266.490	−3.490	189	272.590	3.510
154	261.900	−4.590	190	271.910	−.680
155	262.750	.850	191	271.380	−.530
156	262.550	−.200	192	270.620	−.760
157	258.690	−3.860	193	271.860	1.240
158	260.560	1.870	194	272.390	.530
159	260.770	.210	195	278.070	5.680
160	261.030	.260	196	278.240	.170
161	260.240	−.790	197	277.930	−.310
162	256.980	−3.260	198	273.980	−3.950
163	257.090	.110	199	275.220	1.240
164	261.130	4.040	200	275.500	.280
165	259.180	−1.950	201	276.410	.910
166	259.680	.500	202	279.380	2.970
167	262.330	2.650	203	276.970	−2.410
168	262.510	.180	204	282.880	5.910
169	261.520	−.990	205	283.660	.780
170	258.350	−3.170	206	282.280	−1.380
171	264.480	6.130	207	282.380	.100
172	265.590	1.110	208	281.380	−1.000
173	265.870	.280	209	277.288	−4.100
174	265.880	.010	210	278.530	1.250
175	266.840	.960	211	278.970	.440
176	266.470	−.370	212	279.060	.090
177	267.430	.960	213	279.060	0
178	269.310	1.880	214	279.200	.140
179	268.130	−1.180	215	276.310	−2.890
180	270.650	−2.520	216	273.930	−2.380

Table continues

Table 2-7   Continued

	S&P 500 Daily–1988	S&P 500 Delta–1		S&P 500 Daily–1988	S&P 500 Delta–1
217	275.150	1.220	236	277.590	2.660
218	273.330	−1.820	237	278.130	.540
219	273.690	.360	238	276.590	−1.540
220	267.920	−5.770	239	277.030	.440
221	267.720	−.200	240	276.520	−.510
222	268.340	.620	241	276.310	−.210
223	263.820	−4.520	242	275.310	−1.000
224	264.600	.780	243	274.280	−1.030
225	266.470	1.870	244	276.290	2.010
226	266.220	−.250	245	278.910	2.620
227	267.210	.990	246	277.470	−1.440
228	269.000	1.790	247	277.380	−.090
229	267.230	−1.770	248	276.870	−.510
230	268.640	1.410	249	277.870	1.000
231	270.910	2.270	250	276.830	−1,040
232	273.700	2.790	251	277.088	.250
233	272.490	−1.210	252	279.400	2.320
234	271.810	−.680	253	277.720	−1.680
235	274.930	3.120			

Table 2-8

x_1 : S&P 500 Daily—1988

Mean	Std. Dev.	Std. Error	Variance	Coef. Var.	Count
265.892	8.705	.547	75.776	3.274	253

Minimum	Maximum	Range	Sum	Sum of Sqr.	# Missing
242.63	283.66	41.03	67270.67	17905827.06	0

# < 10th %	10th %	25th %	50th %	75th %	90th %
25	253.398	259.733	267.22	271.915	276.982

# > 90th %	Mode	Geo. Mean	Har. Mean	Kurtosis	Skewness
25	•	265.749	265.604	−.378	−.406

Figure 2–13

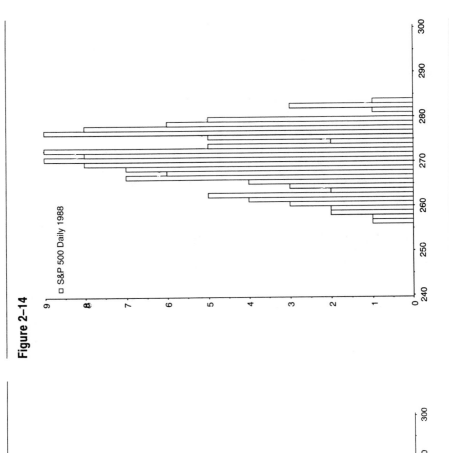

□ S&P 500 Daily 1988

Figure 2–14

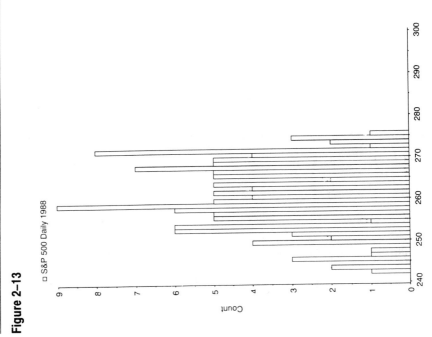

□ S&P 500 Daily 1988

Table 2–9a

x_1 : S&P 500 Daily

Mean	Std. Dev.	Std. Error	Variance	Coef. Var.	Count
260.897	7.998	.712	63.963	3.065	126

Minimum	Maximum	Range	Sum	Sum of Sqr.	# Missing
242.63	275.66	33.03	32872.97	8584441.115	0

# < 10th %	10th %	25th %	50th %	75th %	90th %
13	250.843	255.39	260.23	267.82	271.256

# > 90th %	Mode	Geo. Mean	Har. Mean	Kurtosis	Skewness
13	•	260.774	260.652	–.768	–.209

Table 2–9b

x_2 : Column 2

Mean	Std. Dev.	Std. Error	Variance	Coef. Var.	Count
270.793	6.19	.551	38.312	2.286	126

Minimum	Maximum	Range	Sum	Sum of Sqr.	# Missing
256.98	283.66	26.68	34119.98	9244257.546	0

# < 10th %	10th %	25th %	50th %	75th %	90th %
13	261.943	266.49	270.78	276.31	278.501

# > 90th %	Mode	Geo. Mean	Har. Mean	Kurtosis	Skewness
13	•	270.723	270.652	–.653	–.182

Figure 2–16

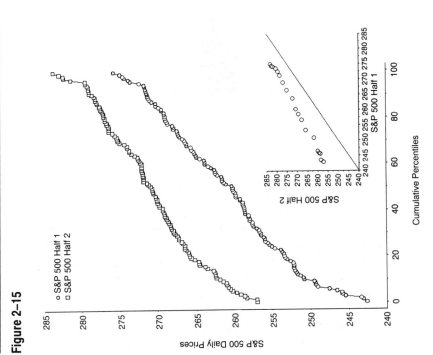

Figure 2–15

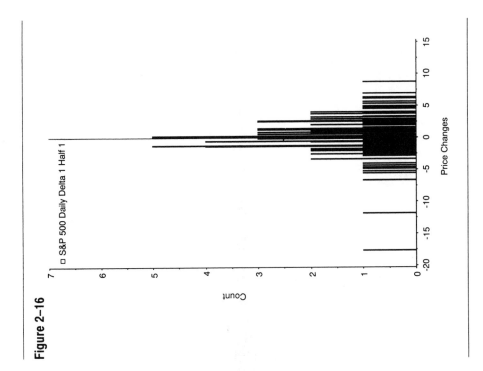

Figure 2–17

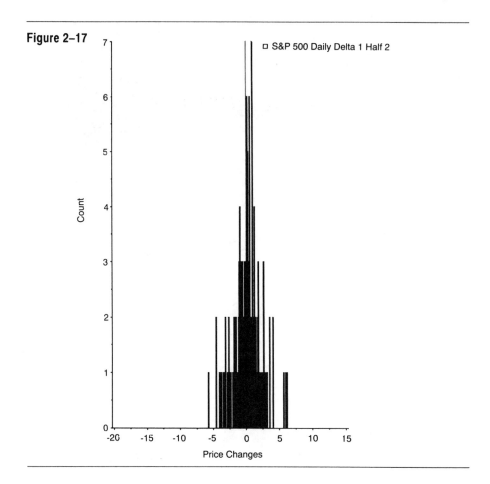

a large number of data points or if the range is large, then it is probably easier to use the figure. In this case, we will use the tabled values.

Examine Table 2-11a and find the bin that is closest to 10%. In this case, it is 10.317%. Then, determine the *price change* that is associated with it, which is, in this case, –2.8. Now, look for the bin closest to 20%. In this case, it is 20.238% and the *price change* associated with it is –1.6. Repeat this process for the remaining deciles (i.e., 30%, 40%, etc.), Table 2-12, column 1 and 2.

Now examine Table 2-11b and find the first *price change* (that is, –2.8) and determine the percentage associated with it (that is, 10.4%). Repeat

Table 2–10

x_1 : S&P 500 Half 1 Delta-1

Mean	Std. Dev.	Std. Error	Variance	Coef. Var.	Count
.14	3.282	.294	10.77	2336.138	125

Minimum	Maximum	Range	Sum	Sum of Sqr.	# Missing
−17.67	8.74	26.41	17.56	1337.978	1

# < 10th %	10th %	25th %	50th %	75th %	90th %
12	−2.85	−1.302	.17	2.02	3.72

# > 90th %	Mode	Geo. Mean	Har. Mean	Kurtosis	Skewness
12	−.62	•	•	7.074	−1.425

x_2 : S&P 500 Half 2 Delta-1

Mean	Std. Dev.	Std. Error	Variance	Coef. Var.	Count
.061	2.167	.194	4.694	3554.126	125

Minimum	Maximum	Range	Sum	Sum of Sqr.	# Missing
−5.77	6.13	11.9	7.62	582.537	1

# < 10th %	10th %	25th %	50th %	75th %	90th %
12	−2.89	−1.043	.17	1.127	2.65

# > 90th %	Mode	Geo. Mean	Har. Mean	Kurtosis	Skewness
12	•	•	•	.756	.184

Figure 2–18

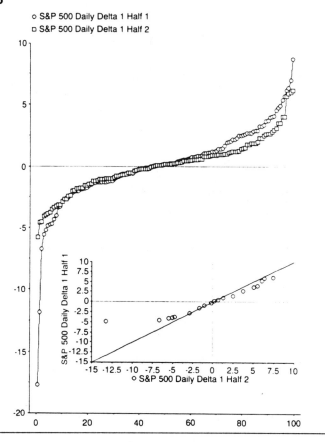

this process for each of the other *price changes* as shown in Table 2-12, column 4. The formula for Chi-square is as follows:

$$x^2 = \sum_{1}^{n} \frac{(\text{Observed}-\text{Expected})^2}{\text{Expected}}$$

where n is the number of deciles

The expected decile is shown in Table 2-12, column 3 and the observed decile is shown in column 5. To find the Chi-square, subtract the first expected decile (9.92) from the first observed decile (8.0) = 1.92.

Table 2–11a

x₁ : S&P 500 Daily Delta-1 Half 1

From (≥)	To (<)	Cumul	Percent
−14	−13.9	1	.397%
−13.9	−13.8	1	.397%
−13.8	−13.7	1	.397%
−13.7	−13.6	1	.397%
−13.6	−13.5	1	.397%
−13.5	−13.4	1	.397%
−13.4	−13.3	1	.397%
−13.3	−13.2	1	.397%
−13.2	−13.1	1	.397%
−13.1	−13	1	.397%
−13	−12.9	1	.397%
−12.9	−12.8	1	.397%
−12.8	−12.7	1	.397%
−12.7	−12.6	1	.397%
−12.6	−12.5	1	.397%
−12.5	−12.4	1	.397%
−12.4	−12.3	1	.397%
−12.3	−12.2	1	.397%
−12.2	−12.1	1	.397%
−12.1	−12	1	.397%
−12	−11.9	1	.397%
−11.9	−11.8	2	.794%
−11.8	−11.7	2	.794%
−11.7	−11.6	2	.794%
−11.6	−11.5	2	.794%
−11.5	−11.4	2	.794%
−11.4	−11.3	2	.794%
−11.3	−11.2	2	.794%
−11.2	−11.1	2	.794%
−11.1	−11	2	.794%
−11	−10.9	2	.794%
−10.9	−10.8	2	.794%
−10.8	−10.7	2	.794%
−10.7	−10.6	2	.794%
−10.6	−10.5	2	.794%

Table continues

Table 2–11a Continued

x_1 : S&P 500 Daily Delta-1 Half 1

From (≥)	To (<)	Cumul	Percent
–10.5	–10.4	2	.794%
–10.4	–10.3	2	.794%
–10.3	–10.2	2	.794%
–10.2	–10.1	2	.794%
–10.1	–10	2	.794%
–10	–9.9	2	.794%
–9.9	–9.8	2	.794%
–9.8	–9.7	2	.794%
–9.7	–9.6	2	.794%
–9.6	–9.5	2	.794%
–9.5	–9.4	2	.794%
–9.4	–9.3	2	.794%
–9.3	–9.2	2	.794%
–9.2	–9.1	2	.794%
–9.1	–9	2	.794%
–9	–8.9	2	.794%
–8.9	–8.8	2	.7.4%
–8.8	–8.7	2	.794%
–8.7	–8.6	2	.794%
–8.6	–8.5	2	.794%
–8.5	–8.4	2	.794%
–8.4	–8.3	2	.794%
–8.3	–8.2	2	.794%
–8.2	–8.1	2	.794%
–8.1	–8	2	.794%
–8	–7.9	2	.794%
–7.9	–7.8	2	.794%
–7.8	–7.7	2	.794%
–7.7	–7.6	2	.794%
–7.6	–7.5	2	.794%
–7.5	–7.4	2	.794%
–7.4	–7.3	2	.794%
–7.3	–7.2	2	.794%
–7.2	–7.1	2	.794%
–7.1	–7	2	.794%

Table continues

Table 2–11a Continued

x_1 : S&P 500 Daily Delta-1 Half 1

From (≥)	To (<)	Cumul	Percent
−7	−6.9	2	.794%
−6.9	−6.8	2	.794%
−6.8	−6.7	2	.794%
−6.7	−6.6	3	1.19%
−6.6	−6.5	3	1.19%
−6.5	−6.4	3	1.19%
−6.4	−6.3	3	1.19%
−6.3	−6.2	3	1.19%
−6.2	−6.1	3	1.19%
−6.1	−6	3	1.19%
−6	−5.9	3	1.19%
−5.9	−5.8	3	1.19%
−5.8	−5.7	4	1.587%
−5.7	−5.6	4	1.587%
−5.6	−5.5	5	1.984%
−5.5	−5.4	5	1.984%
−5.4	−5.3	5	1.984%
−5.3	−5.2	6	2.381%
−5.2	−5.1	6	2.381%
−5.1	−5	6	2.381%
−5	−4.9	6	2.381%
−4.9	−4.8	7	2.778%
−4.8	−4.7	8	3.175%
−4.7	−4.6	9	3.571%
−4.6	−4.5	11	4.365%
−4.5	−4.4	11	4.365%
−4.4	−4.3	12	4.762%
−4.3	−4.2	12	4.762%
−4.2	−4.1	12	4.762%
−4.1	−4	14	5.556%
−4	−3.9	15	5.952%
−3.9	−3.8	16	6.349%
−3.8	−3.7	17	6.746%
−3.7	−3.6	17	6.746%
−3.6	−3.5	17	6.746%

Table continues

Table 2–11a   Continued

x₁ : S&P 500 Daily Delta-1 Half 1

From (≥)	To (<)	Cumul	Percent
−3.5	−3.4	18	7.143%
−3.4	−3.3	21	8.333%
−3.3	−3.2	22	8.73%
−3.2	−3.1	24	9.524%
−3.1	−3	24	9.524%
−3	−2.9	24	9.524%
−2.9	−2.8	26	10.317%
−2.8	−2.7	26	10.317%
−2.7	−2.6	29	11.508%
−2.6	−2.5	31	12.302%
−2.5	−2.4	32	12.698%
−2.4	−2.3	34	13.492%
−2.3	−2.2	34	13.492%
−2.2	−2.1	35	13.889%
−2.1	−2	38	15.079%
−2	−1.9	40	15.873%
−1.9	−1.8	44	17.46%
−1.8	−1.7	49	19.444%
−1.7	−1.6	51	20.238%
−1.6	−1.5	54	21.429%
−1.5	−1.4	55	21.825%
−1.4	−1.3	60	23.81%
−1.3	−1.2	66	26.19%
−1.2	−1.1	69	27.381%
−1.1	−1	73	28.968%
−1	− .9	78	30.952%
− .9	− .8	80	31.746%
− .8	− .7	84	33.333%
− .7	− .6	89	35.317%
− .6	− .5	96	38.095%
− .5	− .4	97	38.492%
− .4	− .3	100	39.683%
− .3	− .2	104	41.27%
− .2	− .1	110	43.651%
− .1	0	113	44.841%

Table continues

Table 2–11a   Continued

x₁ : S&P 500 Daily Delta-1 Half 1

From (≥)	To (<)	Cumul	Percent
0	.1	121	48.016%
.1	.2	130	51.587%
.2	.3	140	55.556%*
.3	.4	142	56.349%
.4	.5	146	57.937%
.5	.6	155	61.508%
.6	.7	158	62.698%
.7	.8	162	64.286%
.8	.9	167	66.27%
.9	1	175	69.444%
1	1.1	178	70.635%
1.1	1.2	182	72.222%
1.2	1.3	189	75%
1.3	1.4	189	75%
1.4	1.5	194	76.984%
1.5	1.6	195	77.381%
1.6	1.7	196	77.778%
1.7	1.8	198	78.571%
1.8	1.9	201	79.762%
1.9	2	202	80.159%
2	2.1	205	81.349%
2.1	2.2	206	81.746%
2.2	2.3	208	82.54%
2.3	2.4	210	83.333%
2.4	2.5	210	83.333%
2.5	2.6	214	84.921%
2.6	2.7	220	87.302%
2.7	2.8	222	88.095%
2.8	2.9	223	88.492%
2.9	3	226	89.683%
3	3.1	226	89.683%
3.1	3.2	227	90.079%
3.2	3.3	229	90.873%
3.3	3.4	230	91.27%
3.4	3.5	230	91.27%

Table continues   *–Mode

Table 2–11a Continued

x_1 : S&P 500 Daily Delta-1 Half 1

From (≥)	To (<)	Cumul	Percent
3.5	3.6	232	92.063%
3.6	3.7	232	92.063%
3.7	3.8	234	92.857%
3.8	3.9	234	92.857%
3.9	4	235	93.254%
4	4.1	239	94.841%
4.1	4.2	239	94.841%
4.2	4.3	239	94.841%
4.3	4.4	239	94.841%
4.4	4.5	239	94.841%
4.5	4.6	240	95.238%
4.6	4.7	240	95.238%
4.7	4.8	241	95.635%
4.8	4.9	241	95.635%
4.9	5	242	96.032%
5	5.1	242	96.032%
5.1	5.2	242	96.032%
5.2	5.3	242	96.032%
5.3	5.4	243	96.429%
5.4	5.5	243	96.429%
5.5	5.6	243	96.429%
5.6	5.7	245	97.222%
5.7	5.8	245	97.222%
5.8	5.9	245	97.222%
5.9	6	246	97.619%
6	6.1	247	98.016%
6.1	6.2	249	98.81%
6.2	6.3	249	98.81%
6.3	6.4	250	99.206%
6.4	6.5	250	99.206%
6.5	6.6	250	99.206%
6.6	6.7	250	99.206%
6.7	6.8	250	99.206%
6.8	6.9	250	99.206%
6.9	7	251	99.603%

Table continues

Table 2–11a   Continued

x_1 : S&P 500 Daily Delta-1 Half 1

From (≥)	To (<)	Cumul	Percent
7	7.1	251	99.603%
7.1	7.2	251	99.603%
7.2	7.3	251	99.603%
7.3	7.4	251	99.603%
7.4	7.5	251	99.603%
7.5	7.6	251	99.603%
7.6	7.7	251	99.603%
7.7	7.8	251	99.603%
7.8	7.9	251	99.603%
7.9	8	251	99.603%
8	8.1	251	99.603%
8.1	8.2	251	99.603%
8.2	8.3	251	99.603%
8.3	8.4	251	99.603%
8.4	8.5	251	99.603%
8.5	8.6	251	99.603%
8.6	8.7	251	99.603%
8.7	8.8	252	100%
8.8	8.9	252	100%
8.9	9	252	100%
9	9.1	252	100%
9.1	9.2	252	100%
9.2	9.3	252	100%
9.3	9.4	252	100%
9.4	9.5	252	100%
9.5	9.6	252	100%
9.6	9.7	252	100%
9.7	9.8	252	100%
9.8	9.9	252	100%
9.9	10	252	100%

Table 2–11b

x_2 : S&P 500 Daily Delta-1 Half 2

From (≥)	To (<)	Cumul	Percent
−20	−19.9	0	0%
−19.9	−19.8	0	0%
−19.8	−19.7	0	0%
−19.7	−19.6	0	0%
−19.6	−19.5	0	0%
−19.5	−19.4	0	0%
−19.4	−19.3	0	0%
−19.3	−19.2	0	0%
−19.2	−19.1	0	0%
−19.1	−19	0	0%
−19	−18.9	0	0%
−18.9	−18.8	0	0%
−18.8	−18.7	0	0%
−18.7	−18.6	0	0%
−18.6	−18.5	0	0%
−18.5	−18.4	0	0%
−18.4	−18.3	0	0%
−18.3	−18.2	0	0%
−18.2	−18.1	0	0%
−18.1	−18	0	0%
−18	−17.9	0	0%
−17.9	−17.8	0	0%
−17.8	−17.7	0	0%
−17.7	−17.6	0	0%
−17.6	−17.5	0	0%
−17.5	−17.4	0	0%
−17.4	−17.3	0	0%
−17.3	−17.2	0	0%
−17.2	−17.1	0	0%
−17.1	−17	0	0%
−17	−16.9	0	0%
−16.9	−16.8	0	0%
−16.8	−16.7	0	0%
−16.7	−16.6	0	0%
−16.6	−16.5	0	0%

Table continues

Table 2–11b   Continued

x_2 : S&P 500 Daily Delta-1 Half 2

From (≥)	To (<)	Cumul	Percent
−16.5	−16.4	0	0%
−16.4	−16.3	0	0%
−16.3	−16.2	0	0%
−16.2	−16.1	0	0%
−16.1	−16	0	0%
−16	−15.9	0	0%
−15.9	−15.8	0	0%
−15.8	−15.7	0	0%
−15.7	−15.6	0	0%
−15.6	−15.5	0	0%
−15.5	−15.4	0	0%
−15.4	−15.3	0	0%
−15.3	−15.2	0	0%
−15.2	−15.1	0	0%
−15.1	−15	0	0%
−15	−14.9	0	0%
−14.9	−14.8	0	0%
−14.8	−14.7	0	0%
−14.7	−14.6	0	0%
−14.6	−14.5	0	0%
−14.5	−14.4	0	0%
−14.4	−14.3	0	0%
−14.3	−14.2	0	0%
−14.2	−14.1	0	0%
−14.1	−14	0	0%
−14	−13.9	0	0%
−13.9	−13.8	0	0%
−13.8	−13.7	0	0%
−13.7	−13.6	0	0%
−13.6	−13.5	0	0%
−13.5	−13.4	0	0%
−13.4	−13.3	0	0%
−13.3	−13.2	0	0%
−13.2	−13.1	0	0%
−13.1	−13	0	0%

Table continues

Table 2–11b   Continued

x$_2$: S&P 500 Daily Delta-1 Half 2

From (≥)	To (<)	Cumul	Percent
−13	−12.9	0	0%
−12.9	−12.8	0	0%
−12.8	−12.7	0	0%
−12.7	−12.6	0	0%
−12.6	−12.5	0	0%
−12.5	−12.4	0	0%
−12.4	−12.3	0	0%
−12.3	−12.2	0	0%
−12.2	−12.1	0	0%
−12.1	−12	0	0%
−12	−11.9	0	0%
−11.9	−11.8	0	0%
−11.8	−11.7	0	0%
−11.7	−11.6	0	0%
−11.6	−11.5	0	0%
−11.5	−11.4	0	0%
−11.4	−11.3	0	0%
−11.3	−11.2	0	0%
−11.2	−11.1	0	0%
−11.1	−11	0	0%
−11	−10.9	0	0%
−10.9	−10.8	0	0%
−10.8	−10.7	0	0%
−10.7	−10.6	0	0%
−10.6	−10.5	0	0%
−10.5	−10.4	0	0%
−10.4	−10.3	0	0%
−10.3	−10.2	0	0%
−10.2	−10.1	0	0%
−10.1	−10	0	0%
−10	−9.9	0	0%
−9.9	−9.8	0	0%
−9.8	−9.7	0	0%
−9.7	−9.6	0	0%
−9.6	−9.5	0	0%

Table continues

Table 2–11b   Continued

x_2 : S&P 500 Daily Delta-1 Half 2

From (≥)	To (<)	Cumul	Percent
−9.5	−9.4	0	0%
−9.4	−9.3	0	0%
−9.3	−9.2	0	0%
−9.2	−9.1	0	0%
−9.1	−9	0	0%
−9	−8.9	0	0%
−8.9	−8.8	0	0%
−8.8	−8.7	0	0%
−8.7	−8.6	0	0%
−8.6	−8.5	0	0%
−8.5	−8.4	0	0%
−8.4	−8.3	0	0%
−8.3	−8.2	0	0%
−8.2	−8.1	0	0%
−8.1	−8	0	0%
−8	−7.9	0	0%
−7.9	−7.8	0	0%
−7.8	−7.7	0	0%
−7.7	−7.6	0	0%
−7.6	−7.5	0	0%
−7.5	−7.4	0	0%
−7.4	−7.3	0	0%
−7.3	−7.2	0	0%
−7.2	−7.1	0	0%
−7.1	−7	0	0%
−7	−6.9	0	0%
−6.9	−6.8	0	0%
−6.8	−6.7	0	0%
−6.7	−6.6	0	0%
−6.6	−6.5	0	0%
−6.5	−6.4	0	0%
−6.4	−6.3	0	0%
−6.3	−6.2	0	0%
−6.2	−6.1	0	0%
−6.1	−6	0	0%

Table continues

Table 2–11b   Continued

x₂ : S&P 500 Daily Delta-1 Half 2

From (≥)	To (<)	Cumul	Percent
–6	–5.9	0	0%
–5.9	–5.8	0	0%
–5.8	–5.7	1	.8%
–5.7	–5.6	1	.8%
–5.6	–5.5	1	.8%
–5.5	–5.4	1	.8%
–5.4	–5.3	1	.8%
–5.3	–5.2	1	.8%
–5.2	–5.1	1	.8%
–5.1	–5	1	.8%
–5	–4.9	1	.8%
–4.9	–4.8	1	.8%
–4.8	–4.7	1	.8%
–4.7	–4.6	1	.8%
–4.6	–4.5	3	2.4%
–4.5	–4.4	3	2.4%
–4.4	–4.3	3	2.4%
–4.3	–4.2	3	2.4%
–4.2	–4.1	3	2.4%
–4.1	–4	4	3.2%
–4	–3.9	5	4%
–3.9	–3.8	6	4.8%
–3.8	–3.7	7	5.6%
–3.7	–3.6	7	5.6%
–3.6	–3.5	7	5.6%
–3.5	–3.4	8	6.4%
–3.4	–3.3	9	7.2%
–3.3	–3.2	10	8%
–3.2	–3.1	12	9.6%
–3.1	–3	12	9.6%
–3	–2.9	12	9.6%
–2.9	–2.8	13	10.4%
–2.8	–2.7	13	10.4%
–2.7	–2.6	15	12%
–2.6	–2.5	15	12%

Table continues

Table 2–11b   Continued

x_2 : S&P 500 Daily Delta-1 Half 2

From (≥)	To (<)	Cumul	Percent
−2.5	−2.4	16	12.8%
−2.4	−2.3	17	13.6%
−2.3	−2.2	17	13.6%
−2.2	−2.1	17	13.6%
−2.1	−2	18	14.4%
−2	−1.9	19	15.2%
−1.9	−1.8	21	16.8%
−1.8	−1.7	23	18.4%
−1.7	−1.6	23	18.4%
−1.6	−1.5	25	20%
−1.5	−1.4	26	20.8%
−1.4	−1.3	27	21.6%
−1.3	−1.2	28	22.4%
−1.2	−1.1	30	24%
−1.1	−1	33	26.4%
−1	−.9	37	29.6%
−.9	−.8	38	30.4%
−.8	−.7	41	32.8%
−.7	−.6	44	35.2%
−.6	−.5	47	37.6%
−.5	−.4	47	37.6%
−.4	−.3	49	39.2%
−.3	−.2	52	41.6%
−.2	−.1	55	44%
−.1	3.639E-17	56	44.8%
3.639E-17	.1	59	47.2%
.1	.2	65	52%
.2	.3	70	56%
.3	.4	71	56.8%
.4	.5	74	59.2%
.5	.6	80	64%
.6	.7	81	64.8%
.7	.8	83	66.4%
.8	.9	85	68%
.9	1	92	73.6%

Table continues

Table 2–11b   Continued

x_2 : S&P 500 Daily Delta-1 Half 2

From (≥)	To (<)	Cumul	Percent
1	1.1	93	74.4%
1.1	1,2	95	76%
1.2	1.3	99	79.2%
1.3	1.4	99	79.2%
1.4	1.5	101	80.8%
1.5	1.6	102	81.6%
1.6	1.7	102	81.6%
1.7	1.8	104	83.2%
1.8	1.9	107	85.6%
1.9	2	107	85.6%
2	2.1	108	86.4%
2.1	2.2	108	86.4%
2.2	2.3	109	87.2
2.3	2.4	110	88%
2.4	2.5	110	88%
2.5	2.6	111	88.8%
2.6	2.7	114	91.2%
2.7	2.8	115	92%
2.8	2.9	115	92%
2.9	3	116	92.8%
3	3.1	116	92.8%
3.1	3.2	117	93.6%
3.2	3.3	117	93.6%
3.3	3.4	117	93.6%
3.4	3.5	117	93.6%
3.5	3.6	119	95.2%
3.6	3.7	119	95.2%
3.7	3.8	119	95.2%
3.8	3.9	119	95.2%
3.9	4	119	95.2%
4	4.1	121	96.8%
4.1	4.2	121	96.8%
4.2	4.3	121	96.8%
4.3	4.4	121	96.8%
4.4	4.5	121	96.8%

Table continues

Table 2–11b   Continued

x_2 : S&P 500 Daily Delta-1 Half 2

From (≥)	To (<)	Cumul	Percent
4.5	4.6	121	96.8%
4.6	4.7	121	96.8%
4.7	4.8	121	96.8%
4.8	4.9	121	96.8%
4.9	5	121	96.8%
5	5.1	121	96.8%
5.1	5.2	121	96.8%
5.2	5.3	121	96.8%
5.3	5.4	121	96.8%
5.4	5.5	121	96.8%
5.5	5.6	121	96.8%
5.6	5.7	122	97.6%
5.7	5.8	122	97.6%
5.8	5.9	122	97.6%
5.9	6	123	98.4%
6	6.1	124	99.2%
6.1	6.2	125	100%
6.2	6.3	125	100%
6.3	6.4	125	100%
6.4	6.5	125	100%
6.5	6.6	125	100%
6.6	6.7	125	100%
6.7	6.8	125	100%
6.8	6.9	125	100%
6.9	7	125	100%
7	7.1	125	100%
7.1	7.2	125	100%
7.2	7.3	125	100%
7.3	7.4	125	100%
7.4	7.5	125	100%
7.5	7.6	125	100%
7.6	7.7	125	100%
7.7	7.8	125	100%
7.8	7.9	125	100%
7.9	8	125	100%

Table continues

Table 2–11b   Continued

x_2 : S&P 500 Daily Delta-1 Half 2

From ($\geq$)	To ($<$)	Cumul	Percent
8	8.1	125	100%
8.1	8.2	125	100%
8.2	8.3	125	100%
8.3	8.4	125	100%
8.4	8.5	125	100%
8.5	8.6	125	100%
8.6	8.7	125	100%
8.7	8.8	125	100%
8.8	8.9	125	100%
8.9	9	125	100%
9	9.1	125	100%
9.1	9.2	125	100%
9.2	9.3	125	100%
9.3	9.4	125	100%
9.4	9.5	125	100%
9.5	9.6	125	100%
9.6	9.7	125	100%
9.7	9.8	125	100%
9.8	9.9	125	100%
9.9	10	125	100%

Square the result $(1.92)^2 = 3.69$. Divide the squared value (3.69) by the expected decile (9.92) and write the result (0.372) in Table 2-12, column 9. Repeat this process for each decile. The running sum in column 9, row 8 is 2.351, the value of the Chi-square. This sum is less than 18.48, which is the critical value for the Chi-square (degrees of freedom is 8 -1 = 7; $p \leq 0.01$), so the two cumulative probability density functions are not significantly different from each other and, therefore, the underlying time series S&P 500—delta-1 is stationary. If the sum had been larger than 18.48, then the two cumulative probability density functions would have been significantly different from each other and the underlying time series would not be stationary.

Table 2-12

Percentile1	Price1	Expected	Percentile2	Observed	Observed-Expected	(Observed-Expected)^2	(Observed-Expected)^2/Expected	Σ
10.317	-2.8		10.4	8.0	1.92	3.69	0.372	0.372
20.238	-1.6	9.92	18.4	11.20	-0.49	0.240	0.022	0.394
30.952	-0.9	10.71	29.6	9.6	-0.87	0.757	0.087	0.481
39.683	-0.3	8.73	39.2	12.80	-0.900	0.810	0.068	0.549
51.587	0.2	11.90	52	12.00	-2.08	4.326	0.436	0.985
61.508	0.6	9.92	64	9.60	-1.66	2.756	0.347	1.332
69.444	1.0	7.94	73.6	12.00	-1.68	2.822	0.273	1.605
79.762	1.9	10.32	85.6	7.20	2.72	7.398	0.746	2.351
89.683	3.1	9.92	92.8					

Figure 2–19

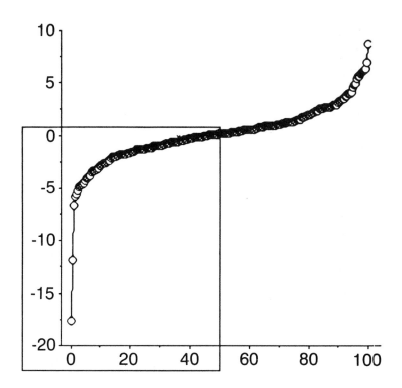

If you want to use the second method, examine Figure 2-19. This is a plot of the first half of S&P 500—delta-1. Draw a perpendicular line from the horizontal axis (10%) to the cumulative probability density function. Then, draw a perpendicular line from this line to the vertical axis. Estimate the value of the S&P 500—delta-1 *price change* at this point. Repeat this process for each decile (20%, 30%, 40%, etc.) and calculate the Chi-square as described above.

The closing prices for General Motors common stock for 1988 are shown in Figure 2-20 and Table 2-13, column 1, while the summary statistics for half 1 and 2 are shown in Table 2-14. Statisticians report that if the average ± its standard deviation of two sets of prices overlap, then the two groups of prices are not significantly different from each other. (The

Figure 2–20

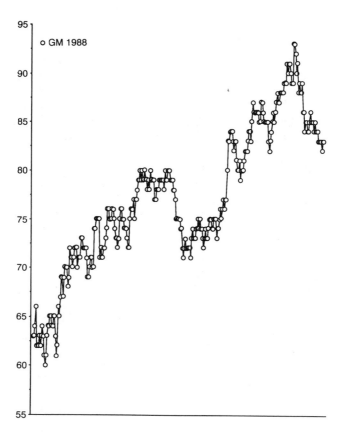

method used to calculate the standard deviation and its meaning are discussed in Chapter 7.) In this case, the average (72.636) ± its standard deviation (5.546) is 67.090 to 78.182 for the first half of the GM prices. The second half average (81.522) ± its standard deviation (5.9920) is 75.530 to 87.514. The two sets of values overlap, which means that the prices in the first half are not significantly different from the prices in the second half, despite the noticeable upward trend seen in Figure 2-20. But, it is important to realize that the fact that the prices do not differ significantly does not necessarily mean that they are stationary.

For example, if you examine the two cumulative probability density functions shown in Figure 2-21, you will note that they are different (see also the insert for this figure). This means that the underlying time series

Table 2-13

	GM 1988	GM Delta-1		GM 1988	GM Delta-1
1	63.020	•	37	70.000	−.010
2	63.060	.040	38	68.050	−1.950
3	64.020	.960	39	69.010	.960
4	66.020	2.000	40	72.020	3.010
5	62.000	−4.020	41	71.010	−1.010
6	62.060	.060	42	71.010	0
7	62.040	−.020	43	70.060	−.950
8	63.030	.990	44	71.040	.980
9	62.030	−1.000	45	72.000	.960
10	63.030	1.000	46	72.060	.060
11	64.030	1.000	47	72.040	−.020
12	63.000	−1.030	48	70.020	−2.020
13	61.030	−1.970	49	71.060	1.040
14	60.040	−.990	50	71.060	0
15	61.040	1.000	51	71.060	0
16	63.040	2.000	52	73.060	2.000
17	64.070	1.030	53	73.040	−.020
18	64.010	−.060	54	72.000	−1.040
19	65.040	1.030	55	72.000	0
20	65.060	.020	56	72.020	.020
21	64.070	−.990	57	72.030	.010
22	64.030	−040	58	71.000	−1.030
23	65.030	1.000	59	69.020	−1.980
24	65.040	.010	60	69.040	.020
25	63.010	−2.030	61	70.070	1.030
26	61.020	−1.990	62	71.020	.950
27	62.070	1.050	63	71.030	.010
28	66.010	3.940	64	70.030	−1.000
29	65.050	−.960	65	70.050	.020
30	67.010	1.960	66	74.000	3.950
31	69.020	2.010	67	74.010	.010
32	69.000	−.020	68	75.020	1.010
33	67.040	−1.960	69	75.020	0
34	69.010	1.970	70	75.060	.040
35	70.050	1.040	71	75.030	−.030
36	70.010	−.040	72	71.050	−3.980

Table continues

Table 2–13   Continued

	GM 1988	GM Delta–1		GM 1988	GM Delta–1
73	72.060	1.010	109	75.040	–1.960
74	71.070	–.990	110	77.050	2.010
75	71.060	–.010	111	77.030	–.020
76	72.020	.960	112	78.020	.990
77	72.010	–.010	113	79.030	1.010
78	73.030	1.020	114	79.050	.020
79	74.050	1.020	115	80.010	.960
80	76.050	2.000	116	79.000	–1.010
81	76.060	.010	117	80.010	1.010
82	75.040	–1.020	118	79.040	–.970
83	75.000	–.040	119	79.070	.030
84	75.060	.060	120	80.050	.980
85	76.070	1.010	121	79.070	–.980
86	76.000	–.070	122	79.080	.010
87	75.060	–.940	123	78.040	–1.040
88	74.030	–1.030	124	79.010	.970
89	73.060	–.970	125	78.050	–.960
90	73.030	–.030	126	80.010	1.960
91	72.050	–.980	127	79.060	–.950
92	73.000	.950	128	79.070	.010
93	75.020	2.020	129	79.000	–.070
94	76.060	1.040	130	79.000	0
95	76.040	–.020	131	77.060	–1.940
96	75.000	–1.040	132	77.030	–.030
97	75.000	0	133	78.070	1.040
98	74.050	–.950	134	78.070	0
99	74.050	0	135	78.030	–.040
100	74.010	–.040	136	79.040	1.010
101	73.030	–.980	137	79.050	.010
102	72.070	–.960	138	79.000	–.050
103	72.060	–.010	139	79.020	.020
104	75.010	2.950	140	79.050	.030
105	76.070	1.060	141	78.050	–1.000
106	76.020	–.050	142	80.000	1.950
107	76.020	0	143	79.030	–.970
108	77.000	.980	144	79.020	–.010

Table continues

Table 2–13   Continued

	GM 1988	GM Delta–1		GM 1988	GM Delta–1
145	80.000	.980	181	74.030	−1.000
146	80.010	.010	182	74.020	−.010
147	80.000	−.010	183	73.070	−.950
148	79.020	−.980	184	72.060	−1.010
149	79.060	.040	185	73.050	.990
150	79.020	−.040	186	74.010	.960
151	78.010	−1.010	187	73.050	−.960
152	78.000	−.010	188	73.030	−.020
153	77.020	−.980	189	74.040	1.010
154	75.060	−1.960	190	75.000	.960
155	75.070	.010	191	75.010	.010
156	75.060	−.010	192	75.000	−.010
157	75.030	−.030	193	74.040	−.960
158	75.000	−.030	194	74.010	−.030
159	74.000	−1.000	195	75.050	1.040
160	74.060	.060	196	75.050	0
161	72.000	−2.060	197	75.020	−.030
162	71.010	−.990	198	73.070	−1.950
163	72.020	1.010	199	74.040	.970
164	73.000	.980	200	74.050	.010
165	72.030	−.970	201	75.000	.950
166	72.000	−.030	202	76.070	1.070
167	72.050	.050	203	75.070	−1.000
168	72.070	.020	204	76.070	1.000
169	72.070	0	205	77.000	.930
170	71.070	−1.000	206	76.060	−.940
171	73.030	1.960	207	77.050	.990
172	74.020	.990	208	77.050	0
173	73.060	−.960	209	80.040	2.990
174	73.050	−.010	210	83.070	3.030
175	73.020	−.030	211	83.030	−.040
176	74.010	.990	212	84.000	.970
177	74.050	.040	213	84.070	.070
178	75.020	.970	214	84.050	−.020
179	74.060	−.960	215	83.030	−1.020
180	75.030	.970	216	82.040	−.990

Table continues

Table 2–13   Continued

	GM 1988	GM Delta–1		GM 1988	GM Delta–1
217	83.000	.960	253	83.040	−1.980
218	83.000	0	254	82.020	−1.020
219	81.070	−1.930	255	83.070	1.050
220	80.070	−1.000	256	84.010	.940
221	80.030	−.040	257	85.060	1.050
222	81.010	.980	258	86.010	.950
223	79.020	−1.990	259	85.050	−.960
224	80.000	.980	260	86.030	.980
225	80.010	.010	261	87.050	1.020
226	80.050	.040	262	88.000	.950
227	81.030	.980	263	87.070	−.930
228	82.020	.990	264	87.030	−.040
229	82.010	−.010	265	88.030	1.000
230	82.020	.010	266	88.040	.010
231	83.070	1.050	267	88.030	−.010
232	84.020	.950	268	88.030	0
233	84.040	.020	269	89.040	1.010
234	83.050	−.990	270	89.070	.030
235	85.060	2.010	271	89.040	−.030
236	87.020	1.960	272	91.020	1.980
237	86.030	−.990	273	90.050	−.970
238	86.000	−.030	274	91.030	.980
239	86.040	.040	275	91.010	−.020
240	86.040	0	276	90.030	−.980
241	86.030	−.010	277	89.020	−1.010
242	86.000	−.030	278	89.040	.020
243	85.050	−.950	279	93.070	4.030
244	85.060	.010	280	93.030	−.040
245	87.060	2.000	281	92.070	−.960
246	87.000	−.060	282	90.030	−2.040
247	86.010	−.990	283	91.060	1.030
248	85.060	−.950	284	88.050	−3.010
249	85.010	−.050	285	89.030	.980
250	85.030	.020	286	88.070	−.960
251	85.020	−.010	287	88.050	−.020
252	85.020	0	288	89.000	.950

Table continues

Table 2–13   Continued

	GM 1988	GM Delta–1		GM 1988	GM Delta–1
289	86.060	–2.940	301	84.060	–.980
290	86.060	0	302	85.030	.970
291	84.020	–2.040	303	84.060	–.970
292	85.010	.990	304	84.030	–.030
293	85.030	.020	305	84.040	.010
294	84.040	–.990	306	83.050	–.990
295	84.070	.030	307	83.000	–.050
296	85.030	.960	308	83.000	0
297	86.030	1.000	309	83.000	0
298	85.040	–.990	310	82.070	–.930
299	85.020	–.020	311	83.010	.940
300	85.040	.020	312	83.040	.030

is not stationary. You can "detrend" this time series by finding the delta-1 *price changes*, as shown in Table 2-13, column 2. Cumulative probability density functions are shown in Figure 2-22 and summary statistics are shown in Table 2-15. If you examine this figure, note that the cumulative probability density functions are essentially identical, which is supported by the insert. This means that the delta-1 *price changes* are stationary.

The closing prices for Comex gold for 1988 are shown in Table 2-16, column 1 and *price changes* for the first and second halves are shown in columns 2 and 3, respectively. The summary statistics for half 1 and 2 are shown in Table 2-17. These data are used to generate two frequency histograms and probability density functions, as described above. The two cumulative probability density functions are shown in Figure 2-23. It is clear that these two cumulative probability density functions are different, and this is confirmed by examining the insert of the figure. You can find the delta-1 *price changes* as described above. The summary statistics are shown in Table 2-18, while the two cumulative probability density functions are shown in Figure 2-24. It is clear by examining this figure and its insert, that the Comex gold delta-1 *price changes* are probably stationary.

Earlier in this chapter, it was determined that the Standard & Poor's 500 Composite Stock Index was stationary. The other major *gauge* of stock market performance is the Dow Jones Industrial Average. The weekly closing prices for 1950 to 1988 are shown in Figure 2-25. There is a noticeable upward trend in this time series and the cumulative probability den-

Table 2–14

x_1 : GM 1988 Half 1

Mean	Std. Dev.	Std. Error	Variance	Coef. Var.	Count
72.636	5.546	.444	30.763	7.636	156

Minimum	Maximum	Range	Sum	Sum of Sqr.	# Missing
60.04	80.05	20.01	11331.2	827820.176	156

# < 10th %	10th %	25th %	50th %	75th %	90th %
16	63.155	70.005	73.06	77.53	79.05

# > 90th %	Mode	Geo. Mean	Har. Mean	Kurtosis	Skewness
14	75.06	72.418	72.194	−.724	−.563

x_2 : GM 1988 Half 2

Mean	Std. Dev.	Std. Error	Variance	Coef. Var.	Count
81.522	5.992	.48	35.908	7.351	156

Minimum	Maximum	Range	Sum	Sum of Sqr.	# Missing
71.01	93.07	22.06	12717.44	1042317.61	156

# < 10th %	10th %	25th %	50th %	75th %	90th %
14	73.05	75.015	83.045	86.02	89.018

# > 90th %	Mode	Geo. Mean	Har. Mean	Kurtosis	Skewness
16	83	81.3	81.075	−1.204	−.222

Figure 2–21

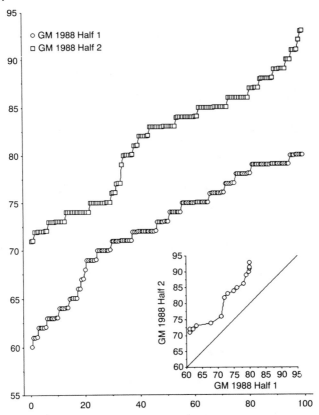

sity functions for the two halves of the Dow Jones are shown in Figure 2-26. It is clear that these two cumulative probability density functions are not similar, so the Dow Jones Industrial is not stationary. We can generate the delta-1 *price changes* for the Dow Jones Industrial. The two cumulative probability density functions are shown in Figure 2-27, while the summary statistics are shown in Table 2-19. If you examine Figure 2-27 and its insert, you will find that the two cumulative probability density functions are somewhat similar, but it is not clear if they are stationary or not. Therefore, it is appropriate to test for stationarity using the quantile Chi-square methodology as previously described. First, determine what *price change* is associated with each decile in the first cumulative probability density function. Then find this *price change* in the second probability den-

Table 2–15

x_1 : GM 1988 Half 1 Delta-1

Mean	Std. Dev.	Std. Error	Variance	Coef. Var.	Count
.078	1.217	.098	1.481	1566.885	155

Minimum	Maximum	Range	Sum	Sum of Sqr.	# Missing
−4.02	3.95	7.97	12.04	229.066	157

# < 10th %	10th %	25th %	50th %	75th %	90th %
15	−1.03	−.958	0	.98	1.06

# > 90th %	Mode	Geo. Mean	Har. Mean	Kurtosis	Skewness
15	0	•	•	1.567	.032

x_2 : GM 1988 Half 2 Delta-1

Mean	Std. Dev.	Std. Error	Variance	Coef. Var.	Count
.052	1.065	.086	1.134	2060.618	155

Minimum	Maximum	Range	Sum	Sum of Sqr.	# Missing
−3.01	4.03	7.04	8.01	175.043	157

# < 10th %	10th %	25th %	50th %	75th %	90th %
13	−1	−.95	0	.967	1.01

# > 90th %	Mode	Geo. Mean	Har. Mean	Kurtosis	Skewness
15	0	•	•	1.257	.171

Figure 2–22

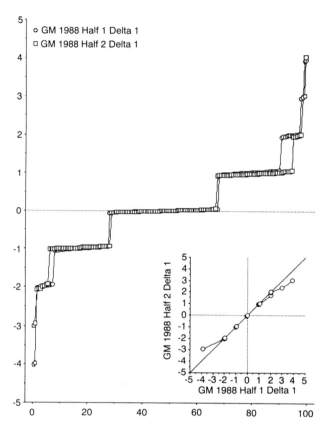

sity function and determine the percentile associated with it. Then find the expected percentiles by subtracting the first decile from the second, the second from the third, etc., (Table 2-20, column 3) and the observed percentiles by subtracting the percentiles associated with the second probability density function (Table 2-20, column 3) and then comparing these expected and observed percentiles with Chi-square. The running sum shown in Table 2-20, column 8, row 17 is 21.27 which is higher than the critical value for the Chi-square, 18.475 (df = 8 - 1 = 7, p 0.01). Therefore, the Dow Jones Industrial is not stationary.

Table 2–16

	Comex Gold 1988	Gold Delta–1 Half 1	Gold Delta–1 Half 2
1	4002.000	−210.000	228.000
2	3792.000	−20.000	137.000
3	3772.000	98.000	−125.000
4	3870.000	−28.000	132.000
5	3842.000	−67.000	−29.000
6	3775.000	−83.000	−35.000
7	3692.000	−66.000	−108.000
8	3626.000	−202.000	18.000
9	3424.000	−192.000	80.000
10	3232.000	−75.000	−78.000
11	3157.000	65.000	−7.000
12	3222.000	55.000	3.000
13	3277.000	238.000	39.000
14	3515.000	112.000	−48.000
15	3627.000	−105.000	43.000
16	3522.000	90.000	−74.000
17	3612.000	−265.000	23.000
18	3347.000	−15.000	63.000
19	3332.000	53.000	−20.000
20	3385.000	−133.000	36.000
21	3252.000	−65.000	11.000
22	3187.000	65.000	137.000
23	3252.000	−165.000	−5.000
24	3087.000	−37.000	−16.000
25	3050.000	77.000	−156.000
26	3127.000	158.000	37.000
27	3285.000	185.000	−22.000
28	3470.000	162.000	101.000
29	3632.000	−203.000	−12.000
30	3429.000	18.000	−22.000
31	3447.000	−67.000	7.000
32	3380.000	485.000	−9.000
33	3865.000	315.000	−19.000
34	4180.000	370.000	−15.000

Table continues

Table 2–16   Continued

	Comex Gold 1988	Gold Delta–1 Half 1	Gold Delta–1 Half 2
35	4550.000	−20.000	34.000
36	4530.000	−115.000	11.000
37	4415.000	−105.000	17.000
38	4310.000	−290.000	−61.000
39	4020.000	310.000	−43.000
40	4330.000	−5.000	75.000
41	4325.000	−45.000	13.000
42	4280.000	−48.000	2.000
43	4232.000	−57.000	134.000
44	4175.000	−195.000	122.000
45	3980.000	196.000	14.000
46	4176.000	−116.000	−35.000
47	4060.000	352.000	−131.000
48	4412.000	−55.000	−61.000
49	4357.000	13.000	67.000
50	4370.000	87.000	1.000
51	4457.000	112.000	52.000
52	4569.000	81.000	47.000
53	4650.000	182.000	49.000
54	4832.000	18.000	−87.000
55	4850.000	87.000	−97.000
56	4937.000	48.000	74.000
57	4985.000	60.000	11.000
58	5045.000	−10.000	14.000
59	5035.000	−388.000	−28.000
60	4647.000	−522.000	37.000
61	4125.000	80.000	−23.000
62	4205.000	12.000	−19.000
63	4217.000	−100.000	23.000
64	4117.000	30.000	−18.000
65	4147.000	65.000	46.000
66	4212.000	153.000	−66.000
67	4365.000	5.000	49.000
68	4370.000	−78.000	−22.000

Table continues

Table 2–16   Continued

	Comex Gold 1988	Gold Delta–1 Half 1	Gold Delta–1 Half 2
69	4292.000	20.000	58.000
70	4312.000	100.000	0
71	4412.000	−25.000	15.000
72	4387.000	−15.000	114.000
73	4372.000	−257.000	78.000
74	4115.000	−3.000	163.000
75	4112.000	43.000	11.000
76	4155.000	80.000	−13.000
77	4235.000	−73.000	359.000
78	4162.000	98.000	−11.000
79	4260.000	−38.000	103.000
80	4222.000	13.000	30.000
81	4235.000	−15.000	30.000
82	4220.000	−123.000	−53.000
83	4097.000	27.000	−115.000
84	4124.000	53.000	−85.000
85	4177.000	−7.000	−97.000
86	4170.000	5.000	72.000
87	4175.000	−28.000	0
88	4147.000	−92.000	−200.000
89	4055.000	75.000	−46.000
90	4130.000	−80.000	49.000
91	4050.000	−76.000	30.000
92	3974.000	13.000	33.000
93	3987.000	−45.000	−56.000
94	3942.000	−65.000	143.000
95	3877.000	−67.000	−15.000
96	3810.000	10.000	137.000
97	3820.000	−68.000	−157.000
98	3752.000	5.000	5.000
99	3757.000	250.000	21.000
100	4007.000	−120.000	−53.000
101	3887.000	−115.000	24.000
102	3772.000	33.000	61.000

Table continues

Table 2–16   Continued

	Comex Gold 1988	Gold Delta–1 Half 1	Gold Delta–1 Half 2
103	3805.000	10.000	5.000
104	3815.000	−63.000	22.000
105	3752.000	−20.000	−41.000
106	3732.000	−20.000	119.000
107	3712.000	−12.000	24.000
108	3700.000	131.000	129.000
109	3831.000	−55.000	61.000
110	3776.000	45.000	245.000
111	3821.000	136.000	−55.000
112	3957.000	−30.000	−37.000
113	3927.000	72.000	169.000
114	3999.000	−72.000	−34.000
115	3927.000	−34.000	−155.000
116	3893.000	−8.000	25.000
117	3885.000	−83.000	19.000
118	3802.000	−10.000	−64.000
119	3792.000	57.000	−49.000
120	3849.000	−57.000	21.000
121	3792.000	−27.000	−15.000
122	3765.000	−40.000	59.000
123	3725.000	31.000	27.000
124	3756.000	86.000	92.000
125	3842.000	95.000	16.000
126	3937.000	−77.000	−41.000
127	3860.000	−180.000	−45.000
128	3680.000	62.000	−21.000
129	3742.000	−12.000	113.000
130	3730.000	−198.000	−49.000
131	3532.000	−82.000	19.000
132	3450.000	−30.000	1.000
133	3420.000	−68.000	−75.000
134	3352.000	140.000	77.000
135	3492.000	−25.000	32.000
136	3467.000	53.000	53.000

Table continues

Table 2-16   Continued

	Comex Gold 1988	Gold Delta-1 Half 1	Gold Delta-1 Half 2
137	3520.000	−20.000	−17.000
138	3500.000	−18.000	−88.000
139	3482.000	−85.000	49.000
140	3397.000	15.000	8.000
141	3412.000	23.000	108.000
142	3435.000	2.000	97.000
143	3437.000	1.000	73.000
144	3438.000	−49.000	−125.000
145	3389.000	6.000	5.000
146	3395.000	−19.000	25.000
147	3376.000	55.000	−1.000
148	3431.000	37.000	−36.000
149	3468.000	−18.000	−41.000
150	3450.000	−47.000	−182.000
151	3403.000	−113.000	−163.000
152	3290.000	−20.000	19.000
153	3270.000	−45.000	−7.000
154	3225.000	−115.000	−125.000
155	3110.000	−27.000	14.000
156	3083.000	−52.000	100.000
157	3031.000	11.000	10.000
158	3042.000	38.000	90.000
159	3080.000	−92.000	51.000
160	2988.000	48.000	−75.000
161	3036.000	−38.000	69.000
162	2998.000	42.000	−77.000
163	3040.000	−56.000	4.000
164	2984.000	−112.000	−62.000
165	2872.000	38.000	67.000
166	2910.000	•	•
167	2927.000	•	•
168	3155.000	•	•
169	3292.000	•	•
170	3167.000	•	•

Table continues

Table 2–16   Continued

	Comex Gold 1988	Gold Delta–1 Half 1	Gold Delta–1 Half 2
171	3299.000	•	•
172	3270.000	•	•
173	3235.000	•	•
174	3127.000	•	•
175	3145.000	•	•
176	3225.000	•	•
177	3147.000	•	•
178	3140.000	•	•
179	3143.000	•	•
180	3182.000	•	•
181	3134.000	•	•
182	3177.000	•	•
183	3103.000	•	•
184	3126.000	•	•
185	3189.000	•	•
186	3169.000	•	•
187	3205.000	•	•
188	3216.000	•	•
189	3353.000	•	•
190	3348.000	•	•
191	3332.000	•	•
192	3176.000	•	•
193	3213.000	•	•
194	3191.000	•	•
195	3292.000	•	•
196	3280.000	•	•
197	3258.000	•	•
198	3265.000	•	•
199	3256.000	•	•
200	3237.000	•	•
201	3222.000	•	•
202	3256.000	•	•
203	3267.000	•	•
204	3284.000	•	•

Table continues

Table 2–16   Continued

	Comex Gold 1988	Gold Delta–1 Half 1	Gold Delta–1 Half 2
205	3223.000	•	•
206	3180.000	•	•
207	3255.000	•	•
208	3268.000	•	•
209	3270.000	•	•
210	3404.000	•	•
211	3526.000	•	•
212	3540.000	•	•
213	3505.000	•	•
214	3374.000	•	•
215	3313.000	•	•
216	3380.000	•	•
217	3381.000	•	•
218	3433.000	•	•
219	3480.000	•	•
220	3529.000	•	•
221	3442.000	•	•
222	3345.000	•	•
223	3419.000	•	•
224	3430.000	•	•
225	3444.000	•	•
226	3416.000	•	•
227	3453.000	•	•
228	3430.000	•	•
229	3411.000	•	•
230	3434.000	•	•
231	3416.000	•	•
232	3462.000	•	•
233	3396.000	•	•
234	3445.000	•	•
235	3423.000	•	•
236	3481.000	•	•
237	3481.000	•	•
238	3496.000	•	•

Table continues

Table 2–16   Continued

	Comex Gold 1988	Gold Delta–1 Half 1	Gold Delta–1 Half 2
239	3610.000	•	•
240	3688.000	•	•
241	3851.000	•	•
242	3862.000	•	•
243	3849.000	•	•
244	4208.000	•	•
245	4197.000	•	•
246	4300.000	•	•
247	4330.000	•	•
248	4360.000	•	•
249	4307.000	•	•
250	4192.000	•	•
251	4107.000	•	•
252	4010.000	•	•
253	4082.000	•	•
254	4082.000	•	•
255	3882.000	•	•
256	3836.000	•	•
257	3885.000	•	•
258	3915.000	•	•
259	3948.000	•	•
260	3892.000	•	•
261	4035.000	•	•
262	4020.000	•	•
263	4157.000	•	•
264	4000.000	•	•
265	4005.000	•	•
266	4026.000	•	•
267	3973.000	•	•
268	3997.000	•	•
269	4058.000	•	•
270	4063.000	•	•
271	4085.000	•	•
272	4044.000	•	•

Table continues

Table 2-16   Continued

	Comex Gold 1988	Gold Delta–1 Half 1	Gold Delta–1 Half 2
273	4163.000	•	•
274	4187.000	•	•
275	4316.000	•	•
276	4377.000	•	•
277	4622.000	•	•
278	4567.000	•	•
279	4530.000	•	•
280	4699.000	•	•
281	4665.000	•	•
282	4510.000	•	•
283	4535.000	•	•
284	4554.000	•	•
285	4490.000	•	•
286	4441.000	•	•
287	4462.000	•	•
288	4447.000	•	•
289	4506.000	•	•
290	4533.000	•	•
291	4625.000	•	•
292	4641.000	•	•
293	4600.000	•	•
294	4555.000	•	•
295	4534.000	•	•
296	4647.000	•	•
297	4598.000	•	•
298	4617.000	•	•
299	4618.000	•	•
300	4543.000	•	•
301	4620.000	•	•
302	4652.000	•	•
303	4705.000	•	•
304	4688.000	•	•
305	4600.000	•	•
306	4649.000	•	•

Table continues

Table 2–16   Continued

	Comex Gold 1988	Gold Delta–1 Half 1	Gold Delta–1 Half 2
307	4657.000	•	•
308	4765.000	•	•
309	4862.000	•	•
310	4935.000	•	•
311	4810.000	•	•
312	4815.000	•	•
313	4840.000	•	•
314	4839.000	•	•
315	4803.000	•	•
316	4762.000	•	•
317	4580.000	•	•
318	4417.000	•	•
319	4436.000	•	•
320	4429.000	•	•
321	4304.000	•	•
322	4318.000	•	•
323	4418.000	•	•
324	4428.000	•	•
325	4518.000	•	•
326	4569.000	•	•
327	4494.000	•	•
328	4563.000	•	•
329	4486.000	•	•
330	4490.000	•	•
331	4428.000	•	•
332	4495.000	•	•
333	4549.000	•	•

Table 2–17

Gold Half 1

Mean	Std. Dev.	Std. Error	Variance	Coef. Var.	Count
3814.235	475.048	36.871	225670.799	12.455	166

Minimum	Maximum	Range	Sum	Sum of Sqr.	# Missing
2872	5045	2173	633163	2452268119	167

# < 10th %	10th %	25th %	50th %	75th %	90th %
17	3190.5	3435	3807.5	4170	4371.8

# > 90th %	Mode	Geo. Mean	Har. Mean	Kurtosis	Skewness
17	3792	3784.913	3755.682	−.372	.221

Gold Half 2

Mean	Std. Dev.	Std. Error	Variance	Coef. Var.	Count
3907.837	584.472	45.364	341607.095	14.956	166

Minimum	Maximum	Range	Sum	Sum of Sqr.	# Missing
2927	4935	2008	648701	2591383167	167

# < 10th %	10th %	25th %	50th %	75th %	90th %
17	3189.2	3332	3960.5	4494	4646.4

# > 90th %	Mode	Geo. Mean	Har. Mean	Kurtosis	Skewness
17	•	3864.25	3821.041	−1.556	.072

Figure 2–23

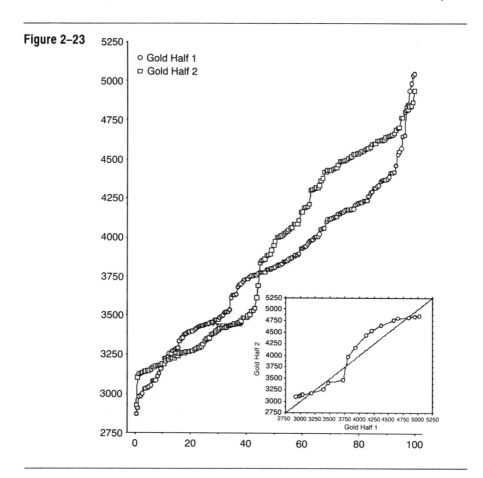

What Does It All Mean?

Why should you care if our time series (prices, *price changes*) is stationary or not? Because, if a time series is not stationary, the underlying *rules* that generate the time series change from time to time, usually without warning or external sign. Most pattern detection techniques, even relatively simple ones like moving averages, and statistical techniques, like auto- or serial-correlations, assume that the underlying time series is stationary. Violation of this assumption will generally yield results that are meaningless. Further, it means that any *patterns* that you happen to detect are spurious.

Table 2–18

Gold Delta–1 Half 1

Mean	Std. Dev.	Std. Error	Variance	Coef. Var.	Count
−6.618	123.527	9.617	15259.042	−1866.487	165

Minimum	Maximum	Range	Sum	Sum of Sqr.	# Missing
−522	485	1007	−1092	2509710	168

# < 10th %	10th %	25th %	50th %	75th %	90th %
16	−116	−67	−15	53	112

# > 90th %	Mode	Geo. Mean	Har. Mean	Kurtosis	Skewness
16	−20	•	•	3.639	.174

Gold Delta–1 Half 2

Mean	Std. Dev.	Std. Error	Variance	Coef. Var.	Count
9.503	79.82	6.214	6371.252	839.944	165

Minimum	Maximum	Range	Sum	Sum of Sqr.	# Missing
−200	359	559	1568	1059786	168

# < 10th %	10th %	25th %	50th %	75th %	90th %
16	−85	−36.25	11	49.5	108

# > 90th %	Mode	Geo. Mean	Har. Mean	Kurtosis	Skewness
16	•	•	•	2.107	.48

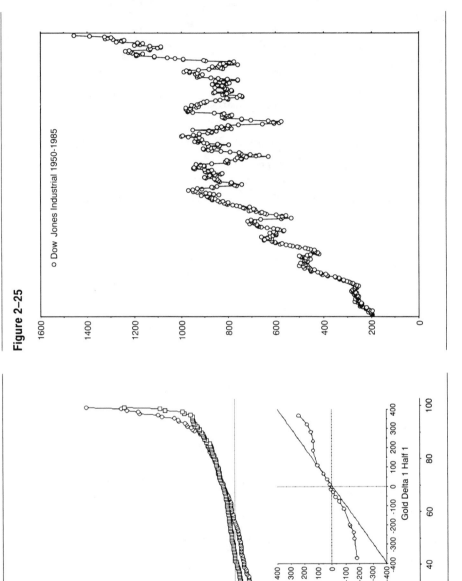

Figure 2-24

o Gold Delta 1 Half 1
□ Gold Delta 1 Half 2

Figure 2-25

o Dow Jones Industrial 1950-1985

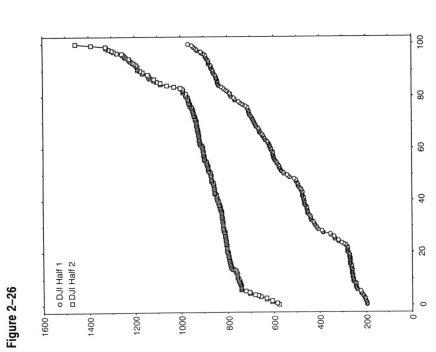

Figure 2–26

Figure 2–27

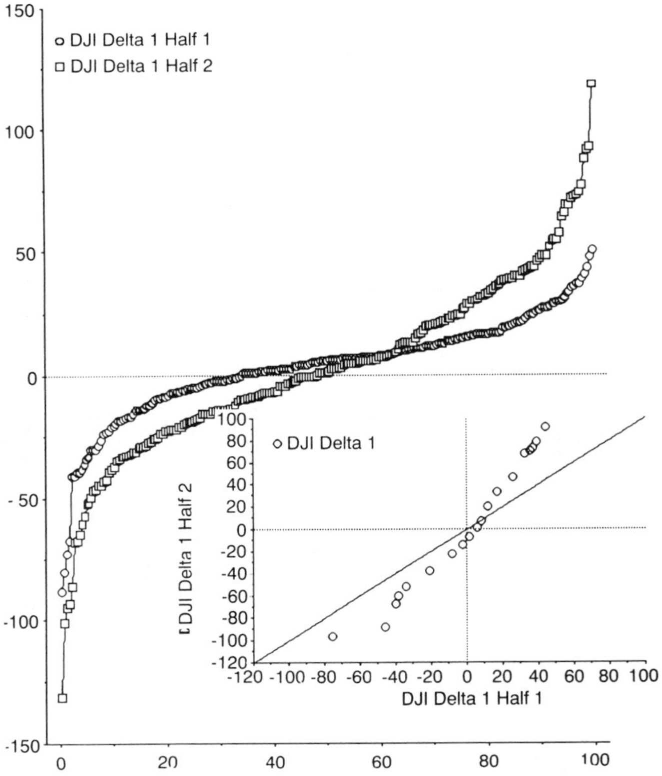

Table 2–19

x_1 : DJI Delta–1 Half 1

Mean	Std. Dev.	Std. Error	Variance	Coef. Var.	Count
3.049	20.313	1.382	412.626	666.148	216

Minimum	Maximum	Range	Sum	Sum of Sqr.	# Missing
–88.4	50.23	138.63	658.66	90723.114	216

# < 10th %	10th %	25th %	50th %	75th %	90th %
22	–20.616	–4.885	5.685	14.61	25.825

# > 90th %	Mode	Geo. Mean	Har. Mean	Kurtosis	Skewness
22	•	•	•	3.524	–1.201

x_2 : DJI Delta–1 Half 2

Mean	Std. Dev.	Std. Error	Variance	Coef. Var.	Count
2.802	36.337	2.478	1320.37	1296.798	215

Minimum	Maximum	Range	Sum	Sum of Sqr.	# Missing
–131.1	118.13	249.23	602.44	284247.261	217

# < 10th %	10th %	25th %	50th %	75th %	90th %
21	–37.36	–18.847	.98	24.402	46.98

# > 90th %	Mode	Geo. Mean	Har. Mean	Kurtosis	Skewness
21	20.65	•	•	1.063	–.10

Table 2-20

Decile 1	Price Change	Decile 2	Observed	(Observed -10)	(Observed -10)^2	(Observed -10)^2	Sum
10.223	-19.7	21.259					
			15.111	5.111	26.122	2.612	2612
20	-8.1	36.37					
			6.223	-3.777	14.266	1.427	4.039
30.268	-2.5	42.593					
			6.481	-3.519	12.383	1.238	5.277
40.465	1.9	49.07					
			7.8	-2.13	4.537	0.453	5.73
50.698	5.7	56.944					
			2.778	-7.222	52.157	5.216	10.946
60	7.9	59.722					
			2.315	-7.685	59.059	5.906	16.852
70.233	11.9	62.037					
			3.704	-6.296	39.64	3.964	20.816
80.93	16.7	65.741					
			7.87	-2.13	4.537	0.454	21.27
90.233	25.9	73.611					

For example, suppose you want to trade GM common stock and you want to use the past history of GM prices or *price changes* to develop a trading strategy. If the prices are not stationary, then any strategy that you develop will really not work in the long run, because you do not know if or when the *rules* change or when the change occurs. If you do not know if and/or when the *rules* change, it means that you cannot alter your trading strategy to take this change into account. Therefore, you are depending on luck to make your trading decisions. In other words, if the *patterns* you are using to make your trading decisions are spurious, then they do not provide valid information. Therefore, you could use the flip of a coin or roll of a die to make your trading decisions (see Chapter 9 and Appendix 2).

On the other hand, if your time series is stationary, then you can use any appropriate pattern detection or statistical technique to find some aspect of the behavior of your time series that you can use as a trading signal. If the times series is stationary, then this signal should be valid over time, and therefore, you are minimizing the effect of luck on your trading decisions.

Independence   3

Background

Like stationarity, independence is not a concept likely to be encountered in daily life. But, it is one of the most important characteristics of a time series, such as the past history of prices or *price changes*.

If you examine the ball-filled urn (described in Chapter 2), probability theorists indicate that the model time series (made by drawing one ball at a time out of the urn, noting its color, and then returning it to the urn) is independent, because the selection of the current ball is not determined or *controlled* by any previous selection. Further, the current selection does not have any impact on any future selection.

Consider another example—flipping a *fair* coin. It is independent because the outcome of the first flip has no effect on the outcome of any succeeding flip. Suppose that you flip the coin 20 times and it comes up heads each time. Will this run of heads have an impact on the outcome of the 21st flip? Common sense tells us that it should and that Providence or Mother Nature (or whoever or whatever "controls" such things) would *adjust* the outcome of the 21st flip to favor tails. So many people believe that this is true that the phenomenon is given a name, the Gambler's Paradox. Unfortunately, for gamblers and everyone else, if the process is truly independent (that is, if it is a *fair* coin and you have not inadvertently biased the outcome in some way), the probability of heads or tails is still 50:50. The previous 20 flips have no impact on the outcome of the 21st flip.

If you believe that the past history of prices or *price changes* of a stock or commodity contain useful information; that is, information that you can use to develop a trading strategy, you are making the tacit (and probably untested) assumption that the prices or *price changes* are not independent. You assume that if you know the price of a stock or commodity today, you can use this information to help you predict what the price will be tomorrow, next week, next month, or next year. Or you may not believe that you can predict the precise price but that you can predict the direction and/or magnitude of the price change. If you believe this and it is not true, then you are involved in a Gambler's Paradox type situation. If this is the case, then any system that you develop will not work in the long run and you are depending on luck rather than skill to make your trading decisions. And everyone knows just how fickle luck can be.

It is important to realize that you can make money, especially in the short run, with an independent (and stationary) process. Otherwise, gambling establishments would have long since gone out of business. Roulette (assuming you have a *fair* wheel) or craps (assuming that you have *fair* dice) are examples of independent processes. Despite the belief of countless gamblers, the number or color that comes up on the current spin of the roulette wheel was not affected by the color or number on any previous spin and will not affect the outcome of any succeeding spin. So, if you are having a winning streak, you should stop, take your winnings, and leave. This is an example of how the "law of large numbers" that probability theorists talk about works. If you continue to play for a long time period, you **will** lose! This is virtually guaranteed by the fact that the "house" adjusts the payoff so that it is slightly smaller than the real probability. For example, if you bet on a single number (either any of the numbers from 1 to 35 or 0 and 00), the payoff is 35 to 1. This gives this house an advantage of about 2/38 of 100 or 5 5/19% (about $0.26 on a $5 bet).

Procedures

The differential spectrum is a method that allows you to make one pass through the time series and determine if the entire time series is independent or not. The choice of the "bin-width" for the individual "bins" in the differential spectrum is somewhat arbitrary, but it affects both the sensitivity and computational effort. In general, as the bin-width increases, the sensitivity of the differential spectrum decreases, and the probability of detecting divergence from independence, if it actually exists, also decreases. The bin-width should not be smaller than the minimum *price change* that can occur. For example, if the minimum *price change* that can occur is $0.10 (that is, the price can "jump" from $1.00 to $1.10 but not from $1.00 to $1.06 or $1.08), then the minimum bin-width should not be less that $0.10. But, if you use this bin width you might have many bins, which would mean you (or your computer) would have to make many calculations to find the value of Chi-square. So, you might want to increase the size of the bin to $0.50 or $1.00 to minimize your computational burden. In general, it is best to start with a relatively large bin size and determine if the Chi-square is significant. If it is, this means that the time series is not independent; decrease the bin size and repeat. A good rule of thumb is to choose a bin width that will allow you to detect divergence from independence (if it exists), while keeping the number of calculations you must make within reasonable limits.

We will use the *price changes* in Table 2-1, column 2 in Chapter 2 as our data set. We will collect these *price changes* into the differential spectrum histogram with 31 bins on the horizontal axis, labeled -15, -14, -13, ..., 0, +1, +2, ..., +15, as shown in Figure 3-1. The first *price change* is a "+1," so increase the frequency of "bin-(+1)" from 0 to 1 (represented by the 1 in that bin). The next *price change* is "-6," so increase the frequency of "bin-(-6)" from 0 to 1 (represented by the 2 in that bin). Continue this process until you reach the last *price change* which is a "+4," so you increase the frequency in "bin-(+4)" from 11 to 12. *Note:* This bin contains 12 *price changes*—the 16th, 39th, 51st, 73rd, 111th, 119th, 157th, 161st, 174th, 187th, 192nd, and 199th. If we generated the differential spectrum with a computer, it should resemble Figure 3-2.

Basic probability theory states that if the *price changes* are independent, then the distribution of the *price changes* around the zero point should be symmetrical. If they are not symmetrical, then the *price changes* are not independent; that is, they contain some type of serial dependencies. We can examine Figure 3-2 and attempt to determine if the relative distribution of *price changes* is symmetrical or not by examination. But, it is better to use a statistical test, such as Chi-square, which has the following form:

$$\chi^2 = \sum_1^n \frac{(\text{Observed}-\text{Expected})^2}{\text{Expected}}$$

where E is the expected frequency of occurrence of a *price change*, 0 is the observed frequency of occurrence of the same *price change* with the opposite sign, and n is the number of bins in the histogram/2.

Figure 3-1

Differential Spectrum Artificial Data

The figure is a triangular array of numbers plotted against a horizontal axis running from −14 to 14. Each column (x value) contains a vertical stack of values. Below is the data reconstructed column by column (each column listed top to bottom).

x	values (top → bottom)
−14	26
−13	14
−12	93, 9
−11	188, 146, 117, 43
−10	177, 127, 59
−9	70, 197, 50, 23, 9
−8	151, 149, 96, 106
−7	173, 129, 121, 88, 34, 28, 18, 4
−6	123, 91, 58, 48, 37, 33, 21
−5	195, 180, 171, 165, 159, 85, 77
−4	183, 169, 162, 155, 142, 137, 115, 112, 110, 80, 74, 65, 64, 2
−3	171, 167, 163, 139, 134, 133, 108, 102, 86, 56, 54, 53, 38, 36, 31
−2	182, 178, 163, 158, 141, 120, 101, 78, 61, 45, 42, 19, 13, 5
−1	193, 185, 175, 156, 153, 147, 131, 100, 89, 81, 71, 46, 41, 8, 6
0	198, 196, 189, 160, 145, 143, 136, 116, 98, 83, 79, 67, 62, 49, 30, 11, 1
1	194, 191, 190, 172, 168, 124, 103, 66, 10
2	186, 160, 138, 113, 92, 75, 68, 57, 24, 22, 15
3	199, 192, 187, 174, 161, 157, 119, 111, 73, 51, 39, 16
4	184, 179, 166, 152, 132, 107, 87, 84, 69, 29, 17
5	176, 154, 140, 135, 118, 99, 97, 76, 60, 47, 32
6	130, 128, 109, 95, 94, 82, 72, 52, 44, 40
7	181, 144, 63
8	
9	
10	164, 148, 122, 114, 55, 25, 20, 7
11	125, 105, 90, 12, 3
12	170, 150
13	126, 35
14	27

Figure 3–2

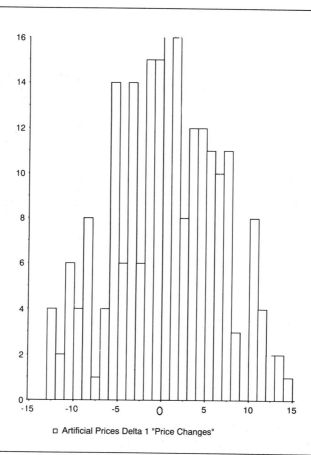

□ Artificial Prices Delta 1 "Price Changes"

For convenience, we will use the positive *price changes* as our expected frequencies and the negative *price changes* as our observed frequencies. The number of bins is 30/2 = 15.

In order to do the Chi-square analysis, we will need a table with seven columns labeled in the following manner: *price change* 1—15, observed, expected, (observed - expected), (observed - expected)^2, observed - expected)^2/ expected, and sum, as shown in Table 3-1. The first step is to list the *price change* frequencies obtained in Figure 3-1 in the second and third columns of Table 3-1. For example, a *price change* of "+1" occurred 17 times, so the first entry in row 1, column 2 of this table is 17. The next entry is 9, then 11, etc., as shown in Table 3-1. A *price change* of "–1"

Table 3–1

Price Change	Observed	Expected	Observed-Expected	(Observed-Expected)^2	(Observed-Expected)^2/Expected	Σ
1	17	15	2	4	.2667	0.2667
2	9	14	−5	25	1.786	2.053
3	11	7	4	16	2.286	4.339
4	12	15	−3	9	0.600	4.939
5	11	7	4	16	2.286	7.225
6	10	14	−4	16	1.143	8.368
7	11	4	7	49	12.25	20.618
8	3	1	2	4	4.00	24.618
9	0	8	−8	64	8.00	32.618
10	8	4	4	16	4.00	36.618
11	5	5	0	0	—	36.618
12	2	2	0	0	—	36.618
13	2	4	−2	4	1	37.618
14	1	0	1	1	—	37.618
15	0	0	0	0	—	37.618

occurred 15 times, so the first entry in row 1, column 3 of this table is 15. The next entry is 14, then 7, etc., as shown in the table.

Calculating the Chi-square is relatively straightforward. As indicated in Table 3-1, the first step in calculating the Chi-square is to subtract the expected frequency (15) from the observed frequency (17) and enter the result, 2, as the first entry in row 1, column 4 of this table. Square this value 2^2 and enter the result, 4, as the first value in row 1, column 5 of the table. Divide this value 4 by the expected frequency 15 and enter the result 0.2667 as the first entry in row 1, column 6 and 7 of the table. In the second row, 9 - 14 = -5, so we enter this value in row 2, column 4, square this value -5^2 and enter the result, 25, in row 2, column 5. Divide this value by the expected value (25/14) and enter the result 1.786 in row 2, column 6 and add this result to the first entry in row 1, column 7 and enter the result 2.053 in row 2, column 7. Repeat this process for the remaining 13 rows in the table and the running sum in column 7, row 15 is 37.618, which is the value of the Chi-square. The critical value for the Chi-square (df = 15 - 1 = 14; p 0.01) is 27.688. Our calculated Chi-square exceeds this critical value, which means that the underlying time series is not independent.

Real Data—Differential Spectrum

The differential spectrum for *price changes* for the Standard & Poor's 500 Stock Index for 1988 are shown in Figure 3-3. In this case, the bin width is $1.00; that is, all the *price changes* from $0.01 to $1.00 are collected into the first bin labeled 0—1, all *price changes* from $1.01 to $2.00 are collected into the second bin labeled 1—2, etc., as shown in Figure 3-3 and columns 2 and 3 in Table 3-2. If you examine Figure 3-3, note that a *price change* of "+1" occurred 40 times and a *price change* of "–1" occurred 62 times. The difference between these two frequencies, 40 – 62 is –22 and this value is entered in row 1, column 4 and squared – 22^2 and the result, 484, is entered in row 1, column 5. This value is divided by the expected frequency 484/62 and the result 7.806 is entered in row 1, column 6 and 7, respectively. We continue this process for the remaining 11 rows in this table. The running sum shown in row 12, column 7 is 19.04, which is the value of the Chi-square statistic. For 12 – 1 or 11 degrees of freedom, this value is not statistically significant ($p \leq 0.005$), which means that the distribution of *price changes* of the Standard & Poor's 500 Stock Index, when considered in "jumps" of $1.00 is independent.

A bin-width of $1.00 is relatively large, so we will decrease the size of the bin-width to $0.25. In this case, the horizontal axis of the differential spectrum histogram will have 48 bins labeled -6.00, -5.75, -5.00, ..., 0, +0.25, +0.50, +0.75, ..., +5.75, +6.00, as shown in Figure 3-4 and Table 3-3. The Chi-square calculations are also shown in Table 3-3. The running sum in row 24, column 7 is 55.70, which is highly significant (df 24 - 1 = 23, $p \leq 0.005$), which means that the Standard & Poor's Stock Index diverges from independence.

Or we could choose a smaller bin-width such as $0.05. In this case, we would have a differential spectrum histogram with 400 bins, labeled -20, -19.95, -19.90, -19.85, ... 0, +0.05, +0.10, ..., +19.95, +20.00, and this differential spectrum should resemble Figure 3-5. For the sake of illustration, the Chi-square calculation for the first 40 bins is given (that is, *price changes* ranging from -2.00 to +2.00) as shown in Table 3-4. The running sum in row 40, column 7 is 108.108 which is statistically significant (df 40-1 = 39, $p \leq 0.005$).

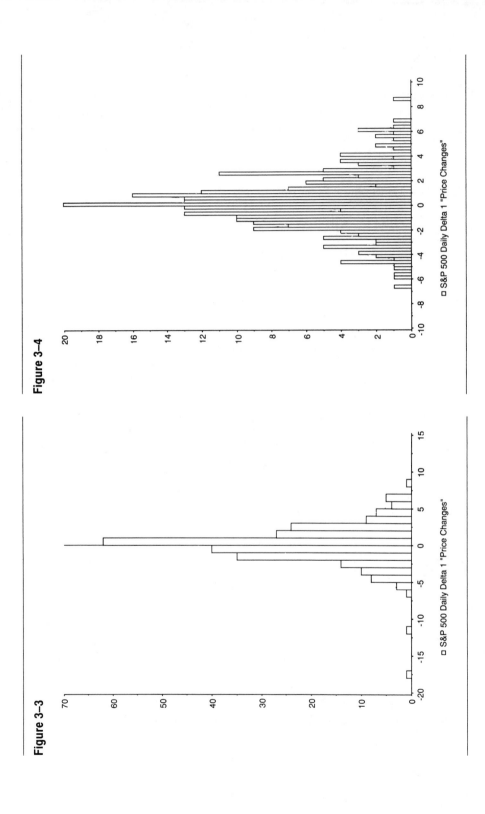

Figure 3-3

Figure 3-4

Table 3-2   S&P 500 Daily Delta-1

Price Change	Observed	Expected	Observed-Expected	(Observed-Expected)^2	(Observed-Expected)^2/Expected	Σ
1	40	62	22	484	7.806	7.806
2	35	27	8	64	2.370	10.177
3	14	24	10	100	4.167	14.434
4	10	9	1	1	0.111	14.45
5	8	7	1	1	0.143	14.59
6	3	4	1	1	0.250	14.84
7	1	5	4	16	3.20	18.04
8	0	0	0	0	0	18.04
9	0	1	1	1	1	19.04
10	0	0	0	0	0	19.04
11	0	0	0	0	0	19.04
12	1	0	1	0	0	19.04

Does the Standard & Poor's 500 Stock Index diverge from independence over a longer time frame than one year? We can answer this question by examining the monthly average of the Standard & Poor's Stock Index for 1947 to 1987. Start with a bin-width of $1.00 as we did above. In this case, you would have a differential spectrum histogram with 35 bins, labeled –17, –16, –15, ..., 0, +1, +2, ..., +17, as shown in Figure 3-6. The Chi-square calculations are shown in Table 3-5 and the running sum in row 17, column 7 in this table is 49.280 (df 17 – 1 = 16, p ≤ 0.005). The differential spectrum for the bin-width of $0.50 is shown in Figure 3-7. The Chi-square calculations are shown in Table 3-6 where the running total is 65.060, which is significant. This means that the monthly average of the Standard & Poor's Stock Index for 1947 to 1987 are not independent and contain serial dependencies.

Basic Methods—Relative Price Changes

The differential spectrum is a valuable technique because it allows you to determine if a time series is independent or not. But it does not allow you to determine what type of serial dependencies are present.

Table 3–3

Price Change	Observed	Expected	Observed-Expected	(Observed-Expected)^2	(Observed-Expected)^2/ Expected	Σ
.25	13	20	−7	49	2.45	2.45
.5	4	13	−9	81	6.23	8.68
.75	13	13	0	0	0	8.68
1.0	10	16	−6	36	2.25	10.93
1.25	10	12	−2	4	0.33	11.26
1.5	9	7	2	4	0.33	11.59
1.75	7	2	5	25	12.50	24.09
2.0	9	6	3	9	1.5	25.59
2.25	4	5	1	1	0.20	25.79
2.5	3	3	0	0	0	25.79
2.75	5	11	6	36	3.27	29.06
3.0	2	5	−3	9	1.8	30.86
3.25	2	1	1	1	1	31.86
3.5	5	3	2	4	1.33	33.19
3.75	0	4	4	16	4	37.19
4.0	3	1	2	4	4	41.19
4.25	2	4	2	4	1	42.19
4.5	1	0	1	1	1	43.19
4.75	4	1	3	9	9	52.19
5.0	1	2	1	1	.5	52.69
5.25	1	0	1	1	1	53.69
5.5	0	1	1	1	1	54.69
5.75	1	0	1	1	1	55.69
6.0	1	1	0	0	0	55.69

The relative price change method, on the other hand, allows you to determine if serial dependencies exist and to describe them. It also allows you to determine the duration of a "temporal window" during which the prices or *price changes* are not independent.

In order to use the relative price change method, you will need a listing of the prices or *price changes* in the same time frame you are planning to trade in. We will use the artificial prices (Table 2-1, Chapter 2), as

Figure 3–5

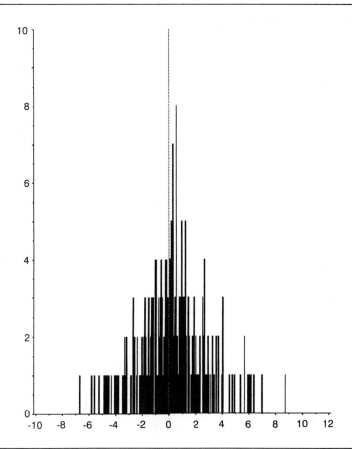

our data. We will translate these "raw" prices into a series of arbitrary symbols based on an unvarying rule. In this case, the rule is that we will examine two sequential prices and determine if the first price is larger than the second, in which case we will write a "1" or if it is smaller than the second, we will write a "2." Therefore, a "2" represents a price increase, while a "1" represents a price decrease. We will then examine price 2 and price 3, then price 3 and price 4, etc., and make this same determination and record the results, sequentially.

For example, the first ten "prices" from Table 2-1, Chapter 2 are shown below:

Table 3–4   Differential Spectrum S&P 500 Daily Delta-1

Bins	Observed	Expected	Observed-Expected	(Observed-Expected)^2	(Observed-Expected)^2/ Expected	Σ
.05	16	25	9	81	3.240	3.240
.1	14	24	10	100	4.167	7.407
.15	10	27	17	289	10.704	18.110
.2	13	18	5	25	1.389	19.499
.25	22	18	4	16	0.889	20.388
.3	18	25	7	49	1.96	22.348
.35	15	19	4	16	0.842	23.190
.4	15	9	4	16	1.778	24.968
.45	16	18	2	4	0.222	25.190
.5	25	15	10	100	6.667	31.857
.55	21	12	9	81	6.75	38.607
.6	16	12	4	16	1.333	39.940
.65	8	18	10	100	5.556	45.496
.7	10	25	15	225	9	54.496
.75	10	17	7	49	2.882	57.378
.8	13	12	1	1	.083	57.462
.85	17	14	3	9	0.643	58.104
.9	10	17	7	49	2.882	60.987
.95	21	18	3	9	.5	61.487
1.0	14	12	2	4	0.333	61.820
1.05	5	16	11	121	7.563	69.383
1.10	11	14	3	9	0.643	70.025
1.15	10	11	1	1	0.091	70.116
1.20	17	17	0	0	0	70.116
1.25	8	9	1	1	0.111	70.228
1.30	10	16	6	36	2.25	72.478
1.35	7	16	9	81	5.063	77.540
1.40	9	9	0	0	0	77.540
1.45	12	7	5	25	3.571	81.111
1.50	6	9	3	9	1	82.111
1.55	4	10	6	36	3.60	85.711
1.60	10	10	0	0	0	85.711
1.65	12	8	4	16	2.0	87.711
1.70	2	1	1	1	1	88.711
1.75	12	8	4	16	2	90.711
1.80	12	5	7	49	9.80	100.511
1.85	7	10	3	9	.90	101.41
1.90	5	5	0	0	0	101.41
1.95	12	7	5	25	3.571	104.983
2.0	3	8	5	25	3.125	108.108

Table 3–5   S&P 500 Index

Bins	Observed	Expected	Observed-Expected	(Observed-Expected)^2	(Observed-Expected)^2/ Expected	Σ
1	86	111	25	625	5.631	5.631
2	36	70	34	1156	16.51	22.145
3	27	38	11	121	3.184	25.329
4	10	27	17	289	10.704	36.033
5	15	13	2	4	0.308	36.341
6	6	11	5	25	2.273	38.613
7	6	6	0	0	0	38.613
8	4	3	1	1	0.333	38.947
9	0	2	2	4	2	40.946
10	2	2	0	0	0	40.946
11	2	1	1	1	1	41.946
12	1	3	2	4	1.333	43.280
13	0	3	3	9	3	46.280
14	0	1	1	1	1	47.280
15	0	0	0	0	0	47.280
16	0	1	1	1	1	48.280
17	0	1	1	1	1	49.280

```
9... 10... 4... 15... 6... 4... 3... 13... 12... 1... 3... 4... 15... 13... 1    and
 2    1   2    1   1   1   2   1    1   2   2   2   1    1
```

They represent the "decisions" as described above and these 14 "symbols" are the first 14 entries in Table 3-7 (column 1 and 3, respectively).

Now arrange this long sequential list of 1s and 2s into a series of transition matrices. This is not as complicated as it might sound. In the simplest case, the digram transition matrix allows you to specify how often a "1" is followed by a "1" or a "2" and how often a "2" is followed by a "1" or a "2."

We will construct the digram matrix using the data from Table 3-7. We will need a matrix with 4 cells, as shown in Table 3-8. The small arrow at the upper-left hand corner of the matrix means "followed by." For example, the first pair of symbols in the list above (and in Table 3-7) is a

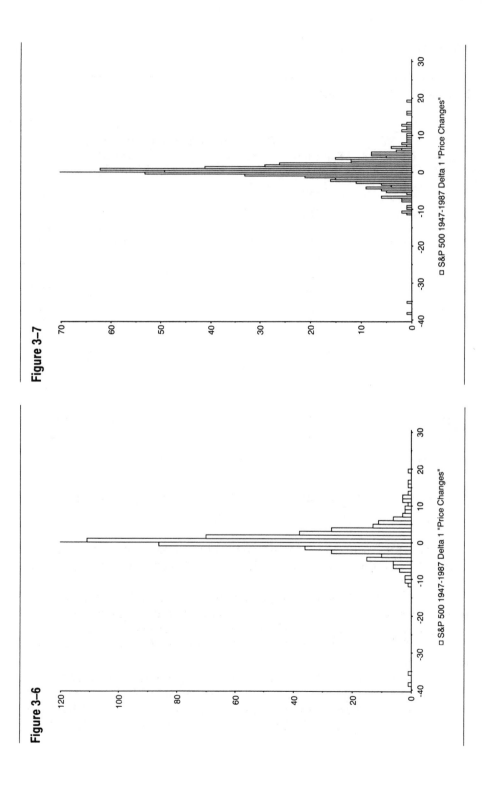

Figure 3–6

S&P 500 1947-1987 Delta 1 "Price Changes"

Figure 3–7

S&P 500 1947-1987 Delta 1 "Price Changes"

Table 3–6

Bin Width	Observed	Expected	Observed-Expected	(Observed-Expected)^2	(Observed-Expected)^2/ Expected	Σ
.5	49	53	4	16	0.327	0.327
1.0	62	33	29	841	13.564	13.891
1.5	41	21	20	400	9.756	23.647
2.0	29	15	14	196	6.759	30.406
2.5	26	16	10	100	3.846	34.252
3.0	12	11	1	1	0.083	34.335
3.5	12	6	6	36	3	37.335
4.0	15	4	11	121	8.067	45.402
4.5	5	9	4	16	3.20	48.602
5.0	8	6	2	4	5	49.102
5.5	8	5	3	9	1.125	50.227
6.0	3	1	2	4	1.333	51.560
6.5	2	0	2	4	2	53.560
7.0	4	6	2	4	2	55.560
7.5	1	2	1	1	1	56.560
8.0	2	2	0	0	0	56.560
8.5	1	0	1	1	1	57.560
9.0	1	0	1	1	1	58.560
9.5	1	1	0	0	0	58.560
10.0	1	1	0	0	0	58.560
10.5	1	0	1	1	1	59.560
11.0	0	2	2	—	—	59.560
11.5	2	1	1	1	.5	60.060
12.0	1	0	1	1	1	61.060
12.5	1	0	1	1	1	62.060
13.0	2	0	2	4	2	64.060
13.5	1	0	1	1	1	65.060
14.0	0	0				
14.5	0	0				

Table 3–7

	Artificial	Delta-1	± Digram	Digram	Trigram	Tetragram
1	9.000	•	•	•	•	•
2	10.000	1.000	2	•	•	•
3	4.000	−6.000	1	21.000	•	•
4	15.000	11.000	2	12.000	212.000	•
5	6.000	−9.000	1	21.000	121.000	2121.000
6	4.000	−2.000	1	11.000	211.000	1211.000
7	3.000	−1.000	1	11.000	111.000	2111.000
8	13.000	10.000	2	12.000	112.000	1112.000
9	12.000	−1.000	1	21.000	121.000	1121.000
10	1.000	−11.000	1	11.000	211.000	1211.000
11	3.000	2.000	2	12.000	112.000	2112.000
12	4.000	1.000	2	22.000	122.000	1122.000
13	15.000	11.000	2	22.000	222.000	1222.000
14	13.000	−2.000	1	21.000	221.000	2221.000
15	1.000	−12.000	1	11.000	211.000	2211.000
16	4.000	3.000	2	12.000	112.000	2112.000
17	8.000	4.000	2	22.000	122.000	1122.000
18	13.000	5.000	2	22.000	222.000	1222.000
19	4.000	−9.000	1	21.000	221.000	2221.000
20	2.000	−2.000	1	11.000	211.000	2211.000
21	12.000	10.000	2	12.000	112.000	2112.000
22	9.000	−3.000	1	21.000	121.000	1121.000
23	12.000	3.000	2	12.000	212.000	1212.000
24	1.000	−11.000	1	21.000	121.000	2121.000
25	4.000	3.000	2	12.000	212.000	1212.000
26	14.000	10.000	2	22.000	122.000	2122.000
27	1.000	−13.000	1	21.000	221.000	1221.000
28	15.000	14.000	2	12.000	212.000	2212.000
29	6.000	−9.000	1	21.000	121.000	2121.000
30	11.000	5.000	2	12.000	212.000	1212.000
31	12.000	1.000	2	22.000	122.000	2122.000
32	8.000	−4.000	1	21.000	221.000	1221.000
33	14.000	6.000	2	12.000	212.000	2212.000
34	11.000	−3.000	1	21.000	121.000	2121.000

Table continues

Table 3–7   Continued

	Artificial	Delta-1	± Digram	Digram	Trigram	Tetragram
35	2.000	–9.000	1	11.000	211.000	1211.000
36	15.000	13.000	2	12.000	112.000	2112.000
37	11.000	–4.000	1	21.000	121.000	1121.000
38	8.000	–3.000	1	11.000	211.000	1211.000
39	4.000	–4.000	1	11.000	111.000	2111.000
40	8.000	4.000	2	12.000	112.000	1112.000
41	15.000	7.000	2	22.000	122.000	1122.000
42	14.000	–1.000	1	21.000	221.000	1221.000
43	12.000	–2.000	1	11.000	211.000	2211.000
44	5.000	–7.000	1	11.000	111.000	2111.000
45	12.000	7.000	2	12.000	112.000	1112.000
46	10.000	–2.000	1	21.000	121.000	1121.000
47	9.000	–1.000	1	11.000	211.000	1211.000
48	15.000	6.000	2	12.000	112.000	2112.000
49	12.000	–3.000	1	21.000	121.000	1121.000
50	13.000	1.000	2	12.000	212.000	1212.000
51	2.000	–11.000	1	21.000	121.000	2121.000
52	6.000	4.000	2	12.000	212.000	1212.000
53	13.000	7.000	2	22.000	122.000	2122.000
54	9.000	–4.000	1	21.000	221.000	1221.000
55	5.000	–4.000	1	11.000	211.000	2211.000
56	15.000	10.000	2	12.000	112.000	2112.000
57	11.000	–4.000	1	21.000	121.000	1121.000
58	14.000	3.000	2	12.000	212.000	1212.000
59	11.000	–3.000	1	21.000	121.000	2121.000
60	1.000	–10.000	1	11.000	211.000	1211.000
61	7.000	6.000	2	12.000	112.000	2112.000
62	5.000	–2.000	1	21.000	121.000	1121.000
63	6.000	1.000	2	12.000	212.000	1212.000
64	14.000	8.000	2	22.000	122.000	2122.000
65	8.000	–6.000	1	21.000	221.000	1221.000
66	2.000	–6.000	1	11.000	211.000	2211.000
67	4.000	2.000	2	12.000	112.000	2112.000
68	5.000	1.000	2	22.000	122.000	1122.000

Table continues

Table 3–7   Continued

	Artificial	Delta-1	± Digram	Digram	Trigram	Tetragram
69	8.000	3.000	2	22.000	222.000	1222.000
70	13.000	5.000	2	22.000	222.000	2222.000
71	2.000	−11.000	1	21.000	221.000	2221.000
72	1.000	−1.000	1	11.000	211.000	2211.000
73	8.000	7.000	2	12.000	112.000	2112.000
74	12.000	4.000	2	22.000	122.000	1122.000
75	6.000	−6.000	1	21.000	221.000	1221.000
76	9.000	3.000	2	12.000	212.000	2212.000
77	15.000	6.000	2	22.000	122.000	2122.000
78	10.000	−5.000	1	21.000	221.000	1221.000
79	8.000	−2.000	1	11.000	211.000	2211.000
80	9.000	1.000	2	12.000	112.000	2112.000
81	3.000	−6.000	1	21.000	121.000	1121.000
82	2.000	−1.000	1	11.000	211.000	1211.000
83	9.000	7.000	2	12.000	112.000	2112.000
84	10.000	1.000	2	22.000	122.000	1122.000
85	15.000	5.000	2	22.000	222.000	1222.000
86	10.000	−5.000	1	21.000	221.000	2221.000
87	6.000	−4.000	1	11.000	211.000	2211.000
88	11.000	5.000	2	12.000	112.000	2112.000
89	2.000	−9.000	1	21.000	121.000	1121.000
90	1.000	−1.000	1	11.000	211.000	1211.000
91	12.000	11.000	2	12.000	112.000	2112.000
92	9.000	−3.000	1	21.000	121.000	1121.000
93	12.000	3.000	2	12.000	212.000	1212.000
94	1.000	−11.000	1	21.000	121.000	2121.000
95	8.000	7.000	2	12.000	212.000	1212.000
96	15.000	7.000	2	22.000	122.000	2122.000
97	2.000	−13.000	1	21.000	221.000	1221.000
98	8.000	6.000	2	12.000	212.000	2212.000
99	9.000	1.000	2	22.000	122.000	2122.000
100	15.000	6.000	2	22.000	222.000	1222.000
101	14.000	−1.000	1	21.000	221.000	2221.000
102	12.000	−2.000	1	11.000	211.000	2211.000

Table continues

Table 3–7   Continued

	Artificial	Delta-1	± Digram	Digram	Trigram	Tetragram
103	8.000	–4.000	1	11.000	111.000	2111.000
104	10.000	2.000	2	12.000	112.000	1112.000
105	2.000	–8.000	1	21.000	121.000	1121.000
106	13.000	11.000	2	12.000	212.000	1212.000
107	1.000	–12.000	1	21.000	121.000	2121.000
108	6.000	5.000	2	12.000	212.000	1212.000
109	2.000	–4.000	1	21.000	121.000	2121.000
110	9.000	7.000	2	12.000	212.000	1212.000
111	3.000	–6.000	1	21.000	121.000	2121.000
112	7.000	4.000	2	12.000	212.000	1212.000
113	1.000	–6.000	1	21.000	121.000	2121.000
114	4.000	3.000	2	12.000	212.000	1212.000
115	14.000	10.000	2	22.000	122.000	2122.000
116	8.000	–6.000	1	21.000	221.000	1221.000
117	9.000	1.000	2	12.000	212.000	2212.000
118	2.000	–7.000	1	21.000	121.000	2121.000
119	8.000	6.000	2	12.000	212.000	1212.000
120	12.000	4.000	2	22.000	122.000	2122.000
121	10.000	–2.000	1	21.000	221.000	1221.000
122	1.000	–9.000	1	11.000	211.000	2211.000
123	11.000	10.000	2	12.000	112.000	2112.000
124	14.000	3.000	2	22.000	122.000	1122.000
125	12.000	–2.000	1	21.000	221.000	1221.000
126	1.000	–11.000	1	11.000	211.000	2211.000
127	14.000	13.000	2	12.000	112.000	2112.000
128	4.000	–10.000	1	21.000	121.000	1121.000
129	11.000	7.000	2	12.000	212.000	1212.000
130	2.000	–9.000	1	21.000	121.000	2121.000
131	9.000	7.000	2	12.000	212.000	1212.000
132	8.000	–1.000	1	21.000	121.000	2121.000
133	13.000	5.000	2	12.000	212.000	1212.000
134	9.000	–4.000	1	21.000	121.000	2121.000
135	5.000	–4.000	1	11.000	211.000	1211.000
136	11.000	6.000	2	12.000	112.000	2112.000

Table continues

Table 3–7   Continued

	Artificial	Delta-1	± Digram	Digram	Trigram	Tetragram
137	12.000	1.000	2	22.000	122.000	1122.000
138	6.000	–6.000	1	21.000	221.000	1221.000
139	9.000	3.000	2	12.000	212.000	2212.000
140	5.000	–4.000	1	21.000	121.000	2121.000
141	11.000	6.000	2	12.000	212.000	1212.000
142	9.000	–2.000	1	21.000	121.000	2121.000
143	3.000	–6.000	1	11.000	211.000	1211.000
144	4.000	1.000	2	12.000	112.000	2112.000
145	12.000	8.000	2	22.000	122.000	1122.000
146	13.000	1.000	2	22.000	222.000	1222.000
147	6.000	–7.000	1	21.000	221.000	2221.000
148	5.000	–1.000	1	11.000	211.000	2211.000
149	15.000	10.000	2	12.000	112.000	2112.000
150	2.000	–13.000	1	21.000	121.000	1121.000
151	14.000	12.000	2	12.000	212.000	1212.000
152	1.000	–13.000	1	21.000	121.000	2121.000
153	6.000	5.000	2	12.000	212.000	1212.000
154	5.000	–1.000	1	21.000	121.000	2121.000
155	11.000	6.000	2	12.000	212.000	1212.000
156	5.000	–6.000	1	21.000	121.000	2121.000
157	4.000	–1.000	1	11.000	211.000	1211.000
158	8.000	4.000	2	12.000	112.000	2112.000
159	6.000	–2.000	1	21.000	121.000	1121.000
160	2.000	–4.000	1	11.000	211.000	1211.000
161	5.000	3.000	2	12.000	112.000	2112.000
162	9.000	4.000	2	22.000	122.000	1122.000
163	3.000	–6.000	1	21.000	221.000	1221.000
164	1.000	–2.000	1	11.000	211.000	2211.000
165	11.000	10.000	2	12.000	112.000	2112.000
166	6.000	–5.000	1	21.000	121.000	1121.000
167	11.000	5.000	2	12.000	212.000	1212.000
168	7.000	–4.000	1	21.000	121.000	2121.000
169	9.000	2.000	2	12.000	212.000	1212.000
170	3.000	–6.000	1	21.000	121.000	2121.000

Table continues

Table 3–7   Continued

	Artificial	Delta-1	± Digram	Digram	Trigram	Tetragram
171	15.000	12.000	2	12.000	212.000	1212.000
172	10.000	−5.000	1	21.000	121.000	2121.000
173	12.000	2.000	2	12.000	212.000	1212.000
174	3.000	−9.000	1	21.000	121.000	2121.000
175	7.000	4.000	2	12.000	212.000	1212.000
176	6.000	−1.000	1	21.000	121.000	2121.000
177	13.000	7.000	2	12.000	212.000	1212.000
178	3.000	−10.000	1	21.000	121.000	2121.000
179	1.000	−2.000	1	11.000	211.000	1211.000
180	6.000	5.000	2	12.000	112.000	2112.000
181	1.000	−5.000	1	21.000	121.000	1121.000
182	9.000	8.000	2	12.000	212.000	1212.000
183	7.000	−2.000	1	21.000	121.000	2121.000
184	1.000	−6.000	1	11.000	211.000	1211.000
185	6.000	5.000	2	12.000	112.000	2112.000
186	5.000	−1.000	1	21.000	121.000	1121.000
187	8.000	3.000	2	12.000	212.000	1212.000
188	12.000	4.000	2	22.000	122.000	2122.000
189	5.000	−7.000	1	21.000	221.000	1221.000
190	6.000	1.000	2	12.000	212.000	2212.000
191	8.000	2.000	2	22.000	122.000	2122.000
192	10.000	2.000	2	22.000	222.000	1222.000
193	14.000	4.000	2	22.000	222.000	2222.000
194	13.000	−1.000	1	21.000	221.000	2221.000
195	15.000	2.000	2	12.000	212.000	2212.000
196	10.000	−5.000	1	21.000	121.000	2121.000
197	11.000	1.000	2	12.000	212.000	1212.000
198	1.000	−10.000	1	21.000	121.000	2121.000
199	2.000	1.000	2	12.000	212.000	1212.000
200	6.000	4.000	2	22.000	122.000	2122.000

Table 3–8

↓	1							2						
1	4	5	8	13	18	33	36	1	3	7	12	20	22	25
	37	41	42	45	53	58	64	27	30	32	35	40	44	47
	70	77	80	85	88	100	101	49	52	55	57	60	63	69
	120	124	133	141	146	155	158	73	76	79	84	87	90	92
	162	177	182					95	99	103	105	107	109	111
								114	116	119	123	126	128	130
								132	136	138	140	145	148	150
								152	154	157	161	164	166	168
								170	172	174	176	179	181	184
								187	192	194	196			
2	2	6	9	14	19	21	23	10	11	15	16	24	29	39
	26	28	31	34	38	43	46	51	62	66	67	68	72	75
	48	50	54	56	59	61	65	82	83	94	97	98	113	118
	71	74	78	81	86	89	91	122	135	143	144	160	186	189
	93	96	102	104	106	108	110	190	191	198				
	112	115	117	121	125	127	129							
	131	134	137	139	142	147	149							
	151	153	156	159	163	165	167							
	169	171	173	175	178	180	183							
	185	188	193	195	197									

"2" followed by a "1," so we increase the frequency of "cell-2,1" (a 2 followed by a 1) in Table 3-8 from 0 to 1. For the purpose of illustration, the numbers in the "cells" in this table represent the number of the comparison. If you were using a computer to generate this matrix, the cells would contain the frequency of occurrence of each digram.

The next pair of symbols in the list above and in Table 3-7 is a "1" followed by a "2," so we increase the frequency of "cell—1,2" from 0 to 1 (represented by a "2" in Table 3-8). It is important to note that each pair of symbols represents the sequential relationships of three prices. For example, the pair of symbols 2,1 represents the sequential relationships between three prices: 9, 10, 4, where the 10 is the second price in the first comparison and the first price in the second comparison. The fact that each price is used twice has a significant impact on how these data are analyzed, as described below.

The next pair of symbols is a "2" followed by a "1," so we increase the frequency of "cell-2,1" from "1" to "2," represented by the "3" in this cell. The next pair of symbols is a "1" followed by a "1," so we increase the frequency of "cell-1,1" in Table 3-8 from "0" to "1" as indicated by the "4" in this cell. We continue this process until we reach the last pair of symbols "2" followed by a "2" (which represents the sequential relationships between prices 1,2,6).

Now compare the digram transition matrix that we just generated with one generated under the assumption of independence. If we do not allow ties to occur, then it has been demonstrated that the matrix that represents the independent case is relatively easy to construct and is independent of the underlying probability density function. But, if we allow ties to occur, then the digram matrix generated under the assumption of independence is dependent on the underlying probability density function and the calculations become rather complex and involved (see appendix to this chapter).

A tie is defined as a price that is followed by a price of the same magnitude. For example, the first price in the series used above is 10. Now, assume for the sake of argument that the second price is also 10. Therefore, we have a tie. We can resolve any ties that occur in some arbitrary manner (for example, when we encounter a tie, we can flip a coin and allow a head to represent a 1 and a tail a 2) and replace the tie with that value. If the number of ties in our time series is small compared to the total number of prices (less than 10%) and if we resolve each tie as described above, then the probability of a 1,2 or a 2,1 is 0.3333, while the probability of a 1,1 or a 2,2 is 0.1667. We convert these probabilities into frequencies by multiplying by the number of prices in our sample, which in this case is 198. Therefore, the frequency of a 1,2 or a 2,1 is 65.93, while the frequency of occurrence of a 1,1 or a 2,2 is 33.01.

We will compare these expected frequencies with the observed frequencies in Table 3-9, using Chi-square methodology. The running total in row 4, column 7 of the table is 0.362, which is not statistically significant. This indicates that the artificial prices are independent. **Generally, we would stop the analysis at this point.** However, for the purpose of illustration, we will not stop but we will generate the trigram transition matrix which allows us to specify how often a specific digram (1,1; 1,2; 2,1; 2,2) is followed by either a 1 or a 2. In this case, the matrix will have 8 cells, as shown in Table 3-10.

In Table 3–7, note that the digram 2,1 is followed by a 2, so we increase the frequency of "cell-2,1,2" from 0 to 1, as indicated by the 1 in this cell in Table 3-10. The next digram is 1,2 and it is followed by a 1, so we increase the frequency of "cell-1,2,1" from 0 to 1, as indicated for the purpose of illustration, as a 2 in this cell in the table. The next digram is 2,1, which is followed by a 1, so we increase the frequency of "cell-2,1,1" from 0 to 1, as indicated by the 3 in this cell in the table. The next digram is 1,1, which is followed by a 1, so we increase the frequency of "cell-1,1,1" from 0 to 1, as indicated by the 4 in this cell in the table. We continue this process until we reach the last group of symbols in Table 3-7. The first 25 trigrams are shown in Table 3-10.

We compare this transition matrix with the one generated under the assumption of independence. If we have not allowed ties to occur, as discussed above, then the probability of occurrence of the eight trigrams is as follows:

1,1,1 and 2,2,2	0.04167
2,2,1; 2,1,1; 1,2,2; and 1,1,2	0.12500
1,2,1 and 2,1,2	0.20833

We compare these two transition matrices using Chi-square methodology. The Chi-square calculations are shown in Table 3-11, where the running sum in row 8, column 7 is 4.102. **This value is not statistically significant, so under ordinary circumstances, we would stop.** But, for the purpose of illustration, we will use the artificial data to generate the tetragram transition matrix, which specifies the sequential relationships of four symbols (five sequential prices). This matrix contains 16 bins as shown in Table 3-12. In this case, the trigram 2,1,2 is followed by a 1, so we increase the frequency of "cell-2,1,2,1" from 0 to 1, as indicated by the 1 in Table 3-12.

Table 3–9

Digram	Observed	Expected	Observed-Expected	(Observed-Expected)^2	(Observed-Expected)^2/ Expected	Σ
11	31	33	−2	4	0.121	0.121
12	68	65.93	2.07	4.28	0.06	0.181
21	68	65.93	2.07	4.28	0.06	0.241
22	31	33	−2	4	0.121	0.362

Table 3–10

→	1					2			
11	4					5	8	13	18
12	2	6	14	19	21	9	23		
21	3	7	12	17		1	20	22	25
22	11	16	24			10	15		

The next trigram is 1,2,1 which is followed by a 1, so we increase the frequency of "cell-1,2,1,1" from 0 to 1, as indicated by the 2 in this cell. The trigram is 2,1,1 which is followed by a 1, so we increase the frequency of "cell-2,1,1,1" from 0 to 1, as indicated by the 3 in this cell. We continue this process until we reach the last symbol. The first 25 tetragrams are shown in Table 3-12. We then compare this transition matrix with one generated under the assumption of independence. The probability of occurrence of each tetragram under the assumption of independence is shown in Table 3-13. We merely multiply this probability times the total number of prices

Table 3–11

Trigram	Observed	Expected	Observed-Expected	(Observed-Expected)^2	(Observed-Expected)^2/ Expected	Σ
111	4	8.21	−4.21	17.72	2.158	2.158
112	27	24.62	2.38	5.66	0.230	2.388
121	46	41.05	4.95	24.50	0.597	2.985
122	22	24.62	−2.62	6.86	0.279	3.264
211	27	24.62	2.38	5.66	0.230	3.494
212	41	41.05	−0.05	0.0025	0.0001	3.4941
221	21	24.62	−3.62	13.10	0.532	4.026
222	9	8.21	0.79	0.624	0.076	4.102

Table 3–12

→	1			2		
111				4		
112	5	18		8	13	
121	2	6		19	21	
122	23			9	14	
211	3			7	12	17
212	1	20	25	22		
221	11	16		24		
222	10	15				

in our time series. We can compare these two matrices using Chi-square as shown in Table 3-14. This Chi-square is also not significant, thus indicating sequential relationships of our artificial price time series is independent. **So, we would stop our analysis at this point.** If the Chi-square had

Table 3–13

1111; 2222	0.00833
1112; 1222; 2111; 2221	0.03333
1121; 1211; 2122; 2212	0.07500
1122; 2211	0.0500
1212; 2121	0.13333
1221; 2112	0.09166

Table 3–14

Tetra-grams	Observed	Expected	Observed-Expected	(Observed-Expected)^2	(Observed-Expected)^2/ Expected	Σ
1111	0	1.633	−1.633	2.667	1.633	1.633
1112	4	6.533	−2.533	6.416	0.982	2.615
1121	17	14.700	2.30	5.29	0.360	2.975
1122	10	9.800	0.200	0.040	0.004	2.979
1211	14	14.700	−0.7	0.49	0.033	3.012
1212	32	26.133	5.867	34.422	1.317	4.329
1221	14	17.965	−3.965	15.721	0.875	5.204
1222	7	6.533	0.467	0.218	0.033	5.237
2111	4	6.533	−2.533	6.416	0.982	6.219
2112	23	17.965	5.035	25.351	1.411	7.630
2121	29	26.133	2.867	8.220	0.315	7.945
2122	12	14.700	−2.700	7.29	0.496	8.441
2211	13	9.800	3.200	10.24	1.045	9.486
2212	8	24.700	−6.700	44.89	3.054	12.54
2221	7	6.533	0.467	0.218	0.033	12.573
2222	2	1.633	0.367	0.134	0.082	12.655

been significant, then this would indicate that the time series did contain serial dependencies and we would continue this process with the penta-gram transition matrix, which would contain 32 cells, etc.

But, one of the unique features of the relative price change transition matrices is that they can be used to determine if a "temporal window" exists during which the prices or *price changes* are not independent. Further, this technique can be used to determine the duration of this *temporal window*. If we trade within the confines of this *window*, when prices are not independent, then we should be able to develop a reasoned trading strategy using techniques outlined in other chapters of this book or any other appropriate techniques that you have developed. If we trade outside the confines of this *window*, then we become involved in a Gambler's Paradox type situation, as described earlier, which means that in the long run, we will be depending on luck and ultimately we will probably lose.

In order to generate the lag-5 (pentagram) *temporal window*, we will pair the first symbol with the fifth, the second with the sixth, the third with the seventh, etc., as shown in Figure 3-8 and Table 3-15, column 2. We then use these pairs of symbols to create a lag-5 *temporal window* transition matrix. In this case a 2 is followed by a 1, so we increase the frequency of "cell 2,1" from 0 to 1 as indicated by the 1 in this cell in the figure. The next pair of symbols is a 1 followed by a 1, so we increase the frequency of "cell-1,1" from 0 to 1, as indicated by the 2 in that cell. We follow this procedure until we reach the last pair of symbols. We then compare the lag-5 *temporal window* transition matrix to the independent case, as indicated above, where the probability of a 1,1 or a 2,2 is 0.1667 and the probability of occurrence of 1,2 or 2,1 is 0.3333. The frequency of occurrence of the lag-5 digrams and the frequency of occurrence of these digrams under the assumption of independence are shown in columns 2 and 3, respectively, of Table 3-16, along with the Chi-square calculations. The running sum is 31.575, which is significant.

We can generate higher order *temporal windows* in the same manner. For example, to create the lag-10 *window*, pair the first and tenth symbol, the second and eleventh symbol, the third and twelfth symbol, etc., as shown in Table 3-15, column 3. In this case, the first lag-10 digram is a 2 followed by a 2, so we increase the frequency of "cell-2,2" from 0 to 1 as indicated by the 1 in this cell. The second pair of symbols is a 1 followed by a 2, so we increase the frequency of "cell-1,2" from 0 to 1, as indicated by the 2 in that cell. We can compare the lag-10 *temporal window* transition matrix with the matrix generated under the assumption of independence using the method described above and shown in Table 3-17, where the running sum is 13.337.

Figure 3–8

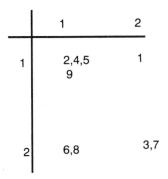

Relative Price Change—Real Data

We will use the Standard & Poor's 500 Stock Index closing prices for 1988 as our data set. The first eight prices are (see Table 2-5, column 1, Chapter 2 for the full data set):

255.94...258.63...258.89...261.07..2 43.40... 247.49...245.42... 245.81.   and
      2   2   2   1   2   1   2

They represent the decisions for converting these prices into arbitrary symbols as described above. A 2 represents a price increase, while a 1

Table 3–15

	+ − Symbols	Lag-5 Temporal Window	Lag-10 Temporal Window			+ − Symbols	Lag-5 Temporal Window	Lag-10 Temporal Window
1	•	•	•		35	1.000	21.000	21.000
2	2.000	•	•		36	2.000	12.000	12.000
3	1.000	•	•		37	1.000	21.000	21.000
4	2.000	•	•		38	1.000	11.000	11.000
5	1.000	•	•		39	1.000	11.000	21.000
6	1.000	21.000	•		40	2.000	22.000	22.000
7	1.000	11.000	•		41	2.000	12.000	12.000
8	2.000	22.000	•		42	1.000	11.000	21.000
9	1.000	11.000	•		43	1.000	11.000	11.000
10	1.000	11.000	•		44	1.000	21.000	11.000
11	2.000	12.000	22.000		45	2.000	22.000	22.000
12	2.000	22.000	12.000		46	1.000	11.000	11.000
13	2.000	12.000	22.000		47	1.000	11.000	11.000
14	1.000	11.000	11.000		48	2.000	12.000	12.000
15	1.000	21.000	11.000		49	1.000	21.000	21.000
16	2.000	22.000	12.000		50	2.000	12.000	22.000
17	2.000	22.000	22.000		51	1.000	11.000	11.000
18	2.000	12.000	12.000		52	2.000	22.000	12.000
19	1.000	11.000	11.000		53	2.000	12.000	12.000
20	1.000	21.000	21.000		54	1.000	21.000	21.000
21	2.000	22.000	22.000		55	1.000	11.000	11.000
22	1.000	21.000	21.000		56	2.000	22.000	12.000
23	2.000	12.000	12.000		57	1.000	21.000	21.000
24	1.000	11.000	11.000		58	2.000	12.000	12.000
25	2.000	22.000	22.000		59	1.000	11.000	21.000
26	2.000	12.000	22.000		60	1.000	21.000	11.000
27	1.000	21.000	21.000		61	2.000	12.000	22.000
28	2.000	12.000	12.000		62	1.000	21.000	21.000
29	1.000	21.000	11.000		63	2.000	12.000	12.000
30	2.000	22.000	22.000		64	2.000	12.000	12.000
31	2.000	12.000	12.000		65	1.000	21.000	21.000
32	1.000	21.000	21.000		66	1.000	11.000	11.000
33	2.000	12.000	12.000		67	2.000	22.000	22.000
34	1.000	21.000	21.000		68	2.000	22.000	12.000

Table continues

Table 3–15   Continued

	+ – Symbols	Lag-5 Temporal Window	Lag-10 Temporal Window		+ – Symbols	Lag-5 Temporal Window	Lag-10 Temporal Window
69	2.000	12.000	12.000	103	1.000	21.000	11.000
70	2.000	12.000	22.000	104	2.000	22.000	22.000
71	1.000	21.000	11.000	105	1.000	11.000	21.000
72	1.000	21.000	21.000	106	2.000	12.000	12.000
73	2.000	22.000	22.000	107	1.000	11.000	21.000
74	2.000	22.000	12.000	108	2.000	22.000	22.000
75	1.000	11.000	11.000	109	1.000	11.000	21.000
76	2.000	12.000	22.000	110	2.000	22.000	12.000
77	2.000	22.000	22.000	111	1.000	11.000	11.000
78	1.000	21.000	21.000	112	2.000	22.000	12.000
79	1.000	11.000	21.000	113	1.000	11.000	21.000
80	2.000	22.000	12.000	114	2.000	22.000	12.000
81	1.000	21.000	11.000	115	2.000	12.000	22.000
82	1.000	11.000	21.000	116	1.000	21.000	11.000
83	2.000	12.000	22.000	117	2.000	12.000	22.000
84	2.000	22.000	12.000	118	1.000	21.000	11.000
85	2.000	12.000	22.000	119	2.000	22.000	22.000
86	1.000	11.000	21.000	120	2.000	12.000	12.000
87	1.000	21.000	11.000	121	1.000	21.000	21.000
88	2.000	22.000	12.000	122	1.000	11.000	11.000
89	1.000	21.000	21.000	123	2.000	22.000	22.000
90	1.000	11.000	11.000	124	2.000	22.000	22.000
91	2.000	12.000	12.000	125	1.000	11.000	11.000
92	1.000	21.000	21.000	126	1.000	11.000	21.000
93	2.000	12.000	22.000	127	2.000	22.000	12.000
94	1.000	11.000	21.000	128	1.000	21.000	21.000
95	2.000	22.000	12.000	129	2.000	12.000	22.000
96	2.000	12.000	12.000	130	1.000	11.000	11.000
97	1.000	21.000	21.000	131	2.000	22.000	12.000
98	2.000	12.000	12.000	132	1.000	11.000	21.000
99	2.000	22.000	12.000	133	2.000	22.000	22.000
100	2.000	22.000	22.000	134	1.000	11.000	11.000
101	1.000	11.000	11.000	135	1.000	21.000	11.000
102	1.000	21.000	21.000	136	2.000	12.000	22.000

Table continues

Table 3–15   Continued

	+ – Symbols	Lag-5 Temporal Window	Lag-10 Temporal Window		+ – Symbols	Lag-5 Temporal Window	Lag-10 Temporal Window
137	2.000	22.000	12.000	169	2.000	22.000	12.000
138	1.000	11.000	21.000	170	1.000	11.000	21.000
139	2.000	12.000	12.000	171	2.000	22.000	22.000
140	1.000	21.000	21.000	172	1.000	11.000	11.000
141	2.000	22.000	12.000	173	2.000	22.000	12.000
142	1.000	11.000	21.000	174	1.000	11.000	21.000
143	1.000	21.000	11.000	175	2.000	22.000	12.000
144	2.000	12.000	12.000	176	1.000	11.000	21.000
145	2.000	22.000	22.000	177	2.000	22.000	12.000
146	2.000	12.000	22.000	178	1.000	11.000	21.000
147	1.000	11.000	11.000	179	1.000	21.000	11.000
148	1.000	21.000	21.000	180	2.000	12.000	22.000
149	2.000	22.000	12.000	181	1.000	21.000	11.000
150	1.000	21.000	21.000	182	2.000	12.000	22.000
151	2.000	12.000	12.000	183	1.000	11.000	11.000
152	1.000	11.000	11.000	184	1.000	21.000	21.000
153	2.000	22.000	22.000	185	2.000	12.000	12.000
154	1.000	11.000	21.000	186	1.000	21.000	21.000
155	2.000	22.000	22.000	187	2.000	12.000	12.000
156	1.000	11.000	11.000	188	2.000	12.000	12.000
157	1.000	21.000	11.000	189	1.000	21.000	21.000
158	2.000	12.000	22.000	190	2.000	12.000	12.000
159	1.000	21.000	11.000	191	2.000	22.000	22.000
160	1.000	11.000	21.000	192	2.000	22.000	12.000
161	2.000	12.000	12.000	193	2.000	12.000	12.000
162	2.000	22.000	22.000	194	1.000	21.000	21.000
163	1.000	11.000	11.000	195	2.000	22.000	12.000
164	1.000	11.000	21.000	196	1.000	21.000	21.000
165	2.000	22.000	12.000	197	2.000	22.000	22.000
166	1.000	21.000	11.000	198	1.000	11.000	11.000
167	2.000	12.000	22.000	199	2.000	22.000	22.000
168	1.000	11.000	11.000	200	2.000	12.000	22.000

Table 3–16

Lag-5 Temporal Window	Observed	Expected	Observed-Expected	(Observed-Expected)^2	(Observed-Expected)^2/ Expected	Σ
11	51	32.5065	−18.4935	342.0095	10.52126	31.57464
12	47	64.9935	17.9935	323.7660	4.981514	
21	46	64.9935	18.9935	360.7530	5.550601	
22	51	32.5065	−18.4935	342.0095	10.52126	

Table 3–17

Lag-10 Temporal Window	Observed	Expected	Observed-Expected	(Observed-Expected)^2	(Observed-Expected)^2/ Expected	Σ
11	43	31.673	−11.327	128.3009	4.050798	13.33711
12	53	63.327	10.327	106.6469	1.684067	
21	50	63.327	13.327	177.6089	2.804631	
22	44	31.673	−12.327	151.9549	4.797617	

represents a price decrease. The entire symbol set is shown in Table 3-18. We use these symbols to generate a digram transition matrix which has four cells. The first pair of symbols is a 2 followed by a 2, so we increase the frequency of "cell-2,2" from 0 to 1. The second pair of symbols is also a 2 followed by a 2, so we increase the frequency of "cell-2,2" from 1 to 2. The third pair of symbols is a 2 followed by a 1, so we increase the frequency of "cell-2,1" from 0 to 1. Next, a 1 is followed by a 2, so we increase the frequency of "cell-1,2" from 0 to 1. We follow this same procedure until we reach the last pair of symbols. The completed matrix is shown in Table 3-19, column 2. We compare this matrix to one generated under the assumption of independence, as described above. The probability of occurrence of the digram 1,1 and 2,2 is 0.1667 and the probability of occurrence of 1,2 or 2,1 is 0.3333. The frequency of occurrence of each digram under the assumption of independence is shown in Table 3-19, column 3.

Table 3–18

	S&P 500	S&P 500 Daily Delta-1	Symbols	Digrams	Trigrams
1	255.940	•	•	•	•
2	258.630	2.690	2	•	•
3	258.890	.260	2	22.000	•
4	261.070	2.180	2	22.000	222.000
5	243.400	−17.670	1	21.000	221.000
6	247.490	4.090	2	12.000	212.000
7	245.420	−2.070	1	21.000	121.000
8	245.810	.390	2	12.000	212.000
9	245.880	.070	2	22.000	122.000
10	252.050	6.170	2	22.000	222.000
11	251.880	−.170	1	21.000	221.000
12	249.320	−2.560	1	11.000	211.000
13	242.630	−6.690	1	11.000	111.000
14	243.140	.510	2	12.000	112.000
15	246.500	3.360	2	22.000	122.000
16	252.170	5.670	2	22.000	222.000
17	249.570	−2.600	1	21.000	221.000
18	249.380	−.190	1	11.000	211.000
19	252.290	2.910	2	12.000	112.000
20	257.070	4.780	2	22.000	122.000
21	255.040	−2.030	1	21.000	221.000
22	255.570	.530	2	12.000	212.000
23	252.210	−3.360	1	21.000	121.000
24	252.210	0	1	11.000	211.000
25	250.960	−1.250	1	11.000	111.000
26	249.100	−1.860	1	11.000	111.000
27	251.720	2.620	2	12.000	112.000
28	256.660	4.940	2	22.000	122.000
29	255.950	−.710	1	21.000	221.000
30	257.630	1.680	2	12.000	212.000
31	259.830	2.200	2	22.000	122.000
32	259.210	−.620	1	21.000	221.000
33	257.910	−1.300	1	11.000	211.000
34	261.610	3.700	2	12.000	112.000

Table continues

Table 3–18   Continued

	S&P 500	S&P 500 Daily Delta-1	Symbols	Digrams	Trigrams
35	265.640	4.030	2	22.000	122.000
36	265.020	−.620	1	21.000	221.000
37	264.430	−.590	1	11.000	211.000
38	261.580	−2.850	1	11.000	111.000
39	262.460	.880	2	12.000	112.000
40	267.820	5.360	2	22.000	122.000
41	267.220	−.600	1	21.000	221.000
42	267.980	.760	2	12.000	212.000
43	267.880	−.100	1	21.000	121.000
44	267.300	−.580	1	11.000	211.000
45	267.380	.080	2	12.000	112.000
46	269.430	2.050	2	22.000	122.000
47	269.060	−.370	1	21.000	221.000
48	263.840	−5.220	1	11.000	211.000
49	264.940	1.100	2	12.000	112.000
50	266.370	1.430	2	22.000	122.000
51	266.130	−.240	1	21.000	221.000
52	268.650	2.520	2	12.000	212.000
53	271.220	2.570	2	22.000	122.000
54	271.120	−.100	1	21.000	221.000
55	268.740	−2.380	1	11.000	211.000
56	268.840	.100	2	12.000	112.000
57	268.910	.070	2	22.000	122.000
58	263.350	−5.560	1	21.000	221.000
59	258.510	−4.840	1	11.000	211.000
60	258.060	−.450	1	11.000	111.000
61	260.070	2.010	2	12.000	112.000
62	258.070	−2.000	1	21.000	121.000
63	258.890	.820	2	12.000	212.000
64	260.140	1.250	2	22.000	122.000
65	258.510	−1.630	1	21.000	221.000
66	265.490	6.980	2	12.000	212.000
67	266.160	.670	2	22.000	122.000
68	269.430	3.270	2	22.000	222.000

Table continues

Table 3–18   Continued

	S&P 500	S&P 500 Daily Delta-1	Symbols	Digrams	Trigrams
69	270.160	.730	2	22.000	222.000
70	271.370	1.210	2	22.000	222.000
71	271.570	.200	2	22.000	222.000
72	259.750	−11.820	1	21.000	221.000
73	259.770	.020	2	12.000	212.000
74	259.210	−.560	1	21.000	121.000
75	257.920	−1.290	1	11.000	211.000
76	256.130	−1.790	1	11.000	111.000
77	256.420	.290	2	12.000	112.000
78	260.140	3.720	2	22.000	122.000
79	262.460	2.320	2	22.000	222.000
80	263.930	1.470	2	22.000	222.000
81	263.800	−.130	1	21.000	221.000
82	262.610	−1.190	1	11.000	211.000
83	261.330	−1.280	1	11.000	111.000
84	261.560	.230	2	12.000	112.000
85	263.000	1.440	2	22.000	122.000
86	260.320	−2.680	1	21.000	221.000
87	258.790	−1.530	1	11.000	211.000
88	257.480	−1.310	1	11.000	111.000
89	256.540	−.940	1	11.000	111.000
90	257.620	1.080	2	12.000	112.000
91	253.310	−4.310	1	21.000	121.000
92	253.850	.540	2	12.000	212.000
93	256.780	2.930	2	22.000	122.000
94	258.710	1.930	2	22.000	222.000
95	255.390	−3.320	1	21.000	221.000
96	251.350	−4.040	1	11.000	211.000
97	252.570	1.220	2	12.000	112.000
98	253.020	.450	2	22.000	122.000
99	250.830	−2.190	1	21.000	221.000
100	253.510	2.680	2	12.000	212.000
101	253.760	.250	2	22.000	122.000
102	254.630	.870	2	22.000	222.000

Table continues

Table 3–18   Continued

	S&P 500	S&P 500 Daily Delta-1	Symbols	Digrams	Trigrams
103	253.420	−1.210	1	21.000	221.000
104	262.160	8.740	2	12.000	212.000
105	266.690	4.530	2	22.000	122.000
106	265.330	−1.360	1	21.000	221.000
107	266.450	1.120	2	12.000	212.000
108	267.050	.600	2	22.000	122.000
109	265.170	−1.880	1	21.000	221.000
110	271.520	6.350	2	12.000	212.000
111	270.200	−1.320	1	21.000	121.000
112	271.260	1.060	2	12.000	212.000
113	271.430	.170	2	22.000	122.000
114	274.300	2.870	2	22.000	222.000
115	274.450	.150	2	22.000	222.000
116	269.770	−4.680	1	21.000	221.000
117	270.680	.910	2	12.000	212.000
118	268.940	−1.740	1	21.000	121.000
119	271.670	2.730	2	12.000	212.000
120	275.660	3.990	2	22.000	122.000
121	274.820	−.840	1	21.000	221.000
122	273.780	−1.040	1	11.000	211.000
123	269.060	−4.720	1	11.000	111.000
124	272.310	3.250	2	12.000	112.000
125	270.980	−1.330	1	21.000	121.000
126	273.500	2.520	2	12.000	212.000
127	271.780	−1.720	1	21.000	121.000
128	275.810	4.030	2	12.000	212.000
129	272.020	−3.790	1	21.000	121.000
130	271.780	−.240	1	11.000	211.000
131	270.020	−1.760	1	11.000	111.000
132	270.550	.530	2	12.000	112.000
133	267.850	−2.700	1	21.000	121.000
134	269.320	1.470	2	12.000	212.000
135	270.260	.940	2	22.000	122.000
136	272.050	1.790	2	22.000	222.000

Table continues

Table 3–18   Continued

	S&P 500	S&P 500 Daily Delta-1	Symbols	Digrams	Trigrams
137	270.510	−1.540	1	21.000	221.000
138	268.470	−2.040	1	11.000	211.000
139	270.000	1.530	2	12.000	112.000
140	266.660	−3.340	1	21.000	121.000
141	263.500	−3.160	1	11.000	211.000
142	264.680	1.180	2	12.000	112.000
143	265.190	.510	2	22.000	122.000
144	262.500	−2.690	1	21.000	221.000
145	266.020	3.520	2	12.000	212.000
146	272.020	6.000	2	22.000	122.000
147	272.210	.190	2	22.000	222.000
148	272.060	−.150	1	21.000	221.000
149	272.980	.920	2	12.000	212.000
150	271.930	−1.050	1	21.000	121.000
151	271.150	−.780	1	11.000	211.000
152	269.980	−1.170	1	11.000	111.000
153	266.490	−3.490	1	11.000	111.000
154	261.900	−4.590	1	11.000	111.000
155	262.750	.850	2	12.000	112.000
156	262.550	−.200	1	21.000	121.000
157	258.690	−3.860	1	11.000	211.000
158	260.560	1.870	2	12.000	112.000
159	260.770	.210	2	22.000	122.000
160	261.030	.260	2	22.000	222.000
161	260.240	−.790	1	21.000	221.000
162	256.980	−3.260	1	11.000	211.000
163	257.090	.110	2	12.000	112.000
164	261.130	4.040	2	22.000	122.000
165	259.180	−1.950	1	21.000	221.000
166	259.680	.500	2	12.000	212.000
167	262.330	2.650	2	22.000	122.000
168	262.510	.180	2	22.000	222.000
169	261.520	−.990	1	21.000	221.000
170	258.350	−3.170	1	11.000	211.000

Table continues

Table 3–18   Continued

	S&P 500	S&P 500 Daily Delta-1	Symbols	Digrams	Trigrams
171	264.480	6.130	2	12.000	112.000
172	265.590	1.110	2	22.000	122.000
173	265.870	.280	2	22.000	222.000
174	265.880	.010	2	22.000	222.000
175	266.840	.960	2	22.000	222.000
176	266.470	−.370	1	21.000	221.000
177	267.430	.960	2	12.000	212.000
178	269.310	1.880	2	22.000	122.000
179	268.130	−1.180	1	21.000	221.000
180	270.650	2.520	2	12.000	212.000
181	268.820	−1.830	1	21.000	121.000
182	269.730	.910	2	12.000	212.000
183	270.160	.430	2	22.000	122.000
184	269.180	−.980	1	21.000	221.000
185	269.760	.580	2	12.000	212.000
186	268.880	−.880	1	21.000	121.000
187	268.260	−.620	1	11.000	211.000
188	269.080	.820	2	12.000	112.000
189	272.590	3.510	2	22.000	122.000
190	271.910	−.680	1	21.000	221.000
191	271.380	−.530	1	11.000	211.000
192	270.620	−.760	1	11.000	111.000
193	271.860	1.240	2	12.000	112.000
194	272.390	.530	2	22.000	122.000
195	278.070	5.680	2	22.000	222.000
196	278.240	.170	2	22.000	222.000
197	277.930	−.310	1	21.000	221.000
198	273.980	−3.950	1	11.000	211.000
199	275.220	1.240	2	12.000	112.000
200	275.500	.280	2	22.000	122.000
201	276.410	.910	2	22.000	222.000
202	279.380	2.970	2	22.000	222.000
203	276.970	−2.410	1	21.000	221.000
204	282.880	5.910	2	12.000	212.000

Table continues

Table 3–18   Continued

	S&P 500	S&P 500 Daily Delta-1	Symbols	Digrams	Trigrams
205	283.660	.780	2	22.000	122.000
206	282.280	−1.380	1	21.000	221.000
207	282.380	.100	2	12.000	212.000
208	281.380	−1.000	1	21.000	121.000
209	277.280	−4.100	1	11.000	211.000
210	278.530	1.250	2	12.000	112.000
211	278.970	.440	2	22.000	122.000
212	279.060	.090	2	22.000	222.000
213	279.060	0	1	21.000	221.000
314	279.200	.140	2	12.000	212.000
215	276.310	−2.890	1	21.000	121.000
216	273.930	−2.380	1	11.000	211.000
217	275.150	1.220	2	12.000	112.000
218	273.330	−1.820	1	21.000	121.000
219	273.690	.360	2	12.000	212.000
220	267.920	−5.770	1	21.000	121.000
221	267.720	−.200	1	11.000	211.000
222	268.340	.620	2	12.000	112.000
223	263.820	−4.520	1	21.000	121.000
224	264.600	.780	2	12.000	212.000
225	266.470	1.870	2	22.000	122.000
226	266.220	−.250	1	21.000	221.000
227	267.210	.990	2	12.000	212.000
228	269.000	1.790	2	22.000	122.000
229	267.230	−1.770	1	21.000	221.000
230	268.640	1.410	2	12.000	212.000
231	270.910	2.270	2	22.000	122.000
232	273.700	2.790	2	22.000	222.000
233	272.490	−1.210	1	21.000	221.000
234	271.810	−.680	1	11.000	211.000
235	274.930	3.120	2	12.000	112.000
236	277.590	2.660	2	22.000	122.000
237	278.130	.540	2	22.000	222.000
238	276.590	−1.540	1	21.000	221.000

Table continues

Table 3–18   Continued

	S&P 500	S&P 500 Daily Delta-1	Symbols	Digrams	Trigrams
239	277.030	.440	2	12.000	212.000
240	276.520	−.510	1	21.000	121.000
241	276.310	−.210	1	11.000	211.000
242	275.310	−1.000	1	11.000	111.000
243	274.280	−1.030	1	11.000	111.000
244	276.290	2.010	2	12.000	112.000
245	278.910	2.620	2	22.000	122.000
246	277.470	−1.440	1	21.000	221.000
247	277.380	−.090	1	11.000	211.000
248	276.870	−.510	1	11.000	111.000
249	277.870	1.000	2	12.000	112.000
250	276.830	−1.040	1	21.000	121.000
251	277.080	.250	2	12.000	212.000
252	279.400	2.320	2	22.000	122.000
253	277.720	−1.680	1	21.000	221.000

Table 3–19   S&P 500 Daily Digram

Digrams	Observed	Expected	Observed-Expected	(Observed-Expected)^2	(Observed-Expected)^2/Expected	Σ
11	72	41.50	30.50	930.26	22.42	22.42
12	67	82.99	15.99	255.68	3.080	25.50
21	66	82.99	16.99	288.66	3.478	28.978
22	44	41.50	2.50	6.25	0.151	29.129

If the digram Chi-square is not significant, we would stop our analysis here and conclude that the Standard and Poor's prices are independent. On the other hand, the running sum of the Chi-square shown in Table 3-19, row 4, column 7 is 29.129 which is statistically significant and indicates that the Standard & Poor's time series is not independent. In this case, this means that the sequential relationships of two symbols (three prices) can be used to detect "real" patterns that can potentially be used to develop a workable trading strategy. It also means that it is appropriate to determine if there are higher order sequential relationships that could potentially be used to make trading decisions. Therefore, we will generate the trigram transition matrix.

The trigram matrix is generated in the manner described above. In this case, the first digram, "2,2" is followed by a "2," so we increase the frequency of "cell-2,2,2" from 0 to 1. The next digram is "2,2," which is followed by a "1," so we increase the frequency of "cell-2,2,1" from 0 to 1. The digram, "2,1" is followed by a "2," so we increase the frequency of "cell-2,1,2" from 0 to 1. We continue this process until we reach the last of the symbols. The completed trigram transition matrix, the matrix generated under the assumption of independence, and the Chi-square calculations are shown in Table 3-20. The running sum shown in row 8, column 7 of this table is 64.446, which is significant. This means that the Standard & Poor's 500 Stock Index time series contains serial dependencies involving at least three symbols (four prices).

At this point, we will increase the size of our time series so that we can generate higher order transition matrices. We will use the closing prices of Standard & Poor's 500 Stock Index for January 3, 1983 to September 15, 1988, which contains more than 1,400 individual prices. We will re-do the digram and trigram transition matrices to demonstrate that adding the additional data to our time series did not cause any changes in the overall statistical properties of the time series. The completed transition matrices, the matrices generated under the assumption of independence, and the Chi-square calculations are shown in Tables 3-21 and 3-22, respectively, where the running sums are 142.63 and 483.40, which are highly statistically significant. This means that the longer time series also has serial dependencies. It also means that it is appropriate to test for higher order dependencies.

We will generate the tetragram transition matrix in the same manner as described above and the completed transition matrix is shown in Table 3-23, column 2. We will find the frequency of occurrence of each tetragram under the assumption of independence, using the probabilities shown in Table 3-13 and multiplying by the number of prices in the time series. The frequency of occurrence of each tetragram is shown in Table 3-23, column 2, while the frequency of each tetragram under the assumption of independence is shown in column 3. The Chi-square calculations are also

Table 3–20   S&P 500 Daily Trigram

Tri-grams	Observed	Expected	Observed-Expected	(Observed-Expected)^2	(Observed-Expected)^2/Expected	Σ
111	29	10.29	18.71	350.06	34.02	34.02
112	43	30.875	12.125	147.02	4.762	38.78
121	36	51.458	15.458	238.95	4.644	43.423
122	29	30.875	1.875	3.516	0.114	43.536
211	42	30.875	11.125	123.77	4.009	47.544
212	24	51.458	27.458	753.94	14.65	62.196
221	29	30.875	1.875	3.516	0.1138	62.3100
222	15	10.29	4.71	22.18	1.156	64.446

Table 3–21   S&P 500 Daily Digram

Di-grams	Observed	Expected	Observed-Expected	(Observed-Expected)^2	(Observed-Expected)^2/Expected	Σ
11	272	239.38	32.61	1063.41	4.44	4.44
12	384	478.62	94.62	8952.94	18.706	23.146
21	385	478.62	93.62	8764.70	18.31	41.458
22	395	239.38	155.62	24217.58	101.168	142.626

shown in this table. The running sum is 1078.87, which is statistically significant, so we will generate the pentagram transition matrix.

The pentagram transition matrix is generated using the following two different methods: the standard tetragram transition matrix using the methods outlined in detail above and the "lag-5 (pentagram) *temporal window.*" The standard pentagram transition matrix is shown in Table 3-24, column 2, and the matrix generated under the assumption of indepen-

Table 3–22   S&P 500 Daily Trigram

Tri-grams	Observed	Expected	Observed-Expected	(Observed-Expected)^2	(Observed-Expected)^2/ Expected	Σ
111	110	59.796	50.204	2520.44	42.151	42.151
112	162	179.375	17.375	301.89	1.683	43.834
121	162	298.95	136.95	1875.30	62.737	106.57
122	222	179.375	42.625	1816.89	10.129	116.699
211	190	179.375	10.625	112890	0.629	117.328
212	195	298.95	103.95	10805.60	36.145	153.473
221	194	179.375	14.625	213.89	1.192	154.665
222	200	59.796	140.204	19657.16	328.737	483.404

Table 3–23   S&P 500 Daily Tetragram

Tetra-grams	Observed	Expected	Observed-Expected	(Observed-Expected)^2	(Observed-Expected)^2/ Expected	Σ
1111	42	11.945	30.055	903.30	75.62	75.62
1112	68	47.795	20.205	408.24	8.541	84.162
1211	68	107.55	39.55	1564.20	14.54	98.706
1212	94	191.195	97.195	9446.868	49.410	148.116
2111	75	47.795	27.205	740.112	15.485	163.601
2112	115	131.44	16.44	270.274	2.0562	165.657
2211	87	71.70	15.3	234.09	3.264	168.92
2212	107	107.55	.55	.3025	0.0028	168.923
1121	71	107.55	36.55	1335.90	12.421	181.134
1122	91	71.70	19.30	372.49	5.195	186.329
1221	119	131.44	12.44	154.75	1.177	187.506
1222	103	47.795	55.205	3047.59	63.764	251.270
2121	101	191.195	90.195	8135.138	42.549	293.82
2122	94	107.55	13.55	183.60	1.707	295.53
2221	93	47.795	45.205	2043.49	42.755	338.285
2222	106	11.945	94.055	8846.34	740.589	1078.87

Table 3–24   S&P 500 Daily Pentagram

Penta-grams	Observed	Expected	Observed-Expected	(Observed-Expected)^2	(Observed-Expected)^2/ Expected	Σ
11111	15	1.99	13.01	169.26	85.06	85.06
11112	27	9.95	17.05	290.70	29.22	114.27
12111	30	27.86	2.14	4.58	0.164	114.44
12112	38	79.60	41.60	1730.56	21.74	136.18
21111	26	9.95	16.05	257.60	25.89	162.07
21112	49	37.82	11.18	124.99	3.30	165.37
22111	44	19.90	24.10	580.81	29.19	194.56
22112	43	51.75	8.75	76.56	1.48	196.04
11211	30	37.82	7.82	61.15	1.62	197.66
11212	41	69.66	28.66	821.40	11.79	209.45
12211	62	51.75	10.25	105.06	2.03	211.48
12212	57	79.60	22.60	510.76	6.42	217.89
21211	45	69.66	24.66	608.12	8.73	226.62
21212	55	121.40	66.40	4408.96	36.32	262.94
22211	45	19.90	25.10	630.10	31.66	294.60
22212	48	27.86	20.14	405.62	14.56	309.16
11121	27	27.86	.86	.7396	0.027	309.18
11122	41	19.90	21.10	445.21	22.372	331.56
12121	45	121.40	76.40	5836.96	48.08	379.64
12122	49	69.66	20.66	426.83	6.13	385.76
21121	45	79.60	34.60	1197.16	15.03	400.80
21122	70	51.75	18.25	333.06	6.44	407.24
22121	57	69.66	12.66	160.28	2.30	409.54
22122	50	37.82	12.18	148.35	3.92	413.46
11221	38	51.75	13.75	189.06	3.65	417.12
11222	53	19.90	33.10	1095.61	55.06	472.17
12221	53	37.82	15.18	230.43	6.09	478.27
12222	50	9.95	40.05	1604.00	161.21	639.47
21221	46	79.60	33.60	1128.96	14.18	653.66
21222	48	27.86	20.14	405.62	14.56	668.21
22221	49	9.95	39.05	1524.90	153.26	821.47
22222	57	1.99	55.01	3026.10	1520.65	2342.12

dence is shown in column 3, while the Chi-square calculations are shown in the remainder of the table. The running sum is 2342.12 which is significant. This indicates that there are serial dependencies involving 5 symbols (6 prices). This matrix contains 32 cells, which means that the calculations are beginning to become a bit tedious.

The other method, the lag-5 (pentagram) *temporal window*, can be used to simplify the transition matrix and decrease the number of calculations. Briefly, we compare the first and fifth symbol, the second and sixth symbol, etc., as shown in Figure 3-8, using the artificial data. The lag-5 *temporal window* is shown in Table 3-25, column 2. The frequency of occurrence of each "lag-5" digram, assuming independence, is found by multiplying the number of prices by 0.1667 to find the frequency of occurrence of the digram 1,1 and 2,2, while we multiply by 0.3333 to find the frequency of the digrams 1,2 and 2,1. The results are shown in Table 3-25, column 3. The running sum in Table 3-25, column 7 is 207.88, which means that the underlying time series contains serial dependencies and it is appropriate to generate higher-order *temporal windows*. We will continue this process by generating the lag-10 *temporal window,* as well as lag-15, 20, 25, 30, 35, 40, 45, and 50 *windows* and the Chi-square running sums of each calculation are shown in Table 3-26. Each of these values is statistically significant. This means that the Standard and Poor's 500 Stock Index contains serial dependencies involving as many as 50 symbols (51 prices), as shown in Figure 3-9. This figure shows the plot of the closing prices of this time series and the insert shows a blow-up of a portion of this plot. The square indicates the limits of the *temporal window*. The right edge of the *window* is hatched to indicate that we should continue to test higher order *temporal windows* until we reach a nonsignificant Chi-square running sum. The last significant Chi-square represents the outer margin of the *temporal window*. For example, if the "lag-50 window" was significant, but the "lag-55 window" was not, we can conclude that the *window* is 50 symbols (51 prices) long.

It is important to realize that the *window* involves any group of 51 prices. For example, the *window* shown in Figure 3-9 could move to the right or left and the prices within the window would still contain serial dependencies. If we trade within the confines of this *window*, we should be able to use an appropriate pattern detection or statistical technique to develop a trading strategy and this strategy should work. If, on the other hand, we trade outside this window, the prices will be independent and will not contain serial dependencies. Therefore, any strategy that we develop will probably not work, especially in the long run.

Table 3–25

Lag-5 Window	Observed	Expected	Observed-Expected	(Observed-Expected)^2	(Observed-Expected)^2/ Expected	Σ
11	298	239	59	3481	14.57	14.57
12	358	478	−120	14400	30.13	44.69
21	360	478	−118	13924	29.13	73.82
22	418	239	179	32041	134.06	207.88

Table 3–26

Lag Value	Chi-square
10	157.012
15	257.516
20	198.391
25	224.033
30	226.404
35	197.402
40	215.805
45	227.632
50	223.168

Category Price Transition Matrix

It is possible that you might want to examine a time series in more detail than provided by the relative price transition matrix methodology. For example, you might want to determine if relatively large or small *price changes* deviate from independence. In this case, divide the time series into thirds, as shown in Figure 3-10, where the area to the left of the leftmost line represents the lowest 10% of the delta-1 *price changes*, the space between the two lines, the middle 80% of the *price changes*, and the area to the right of the rightmost line, the highest 10% of the *price changes*. In this

Figure 3-10

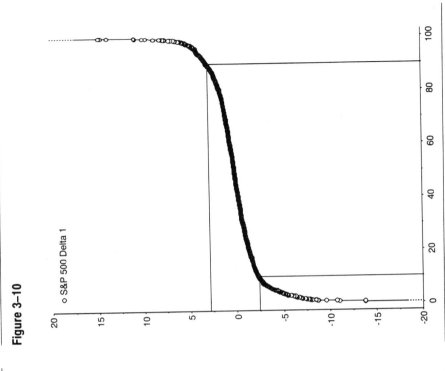

Figure 3-9

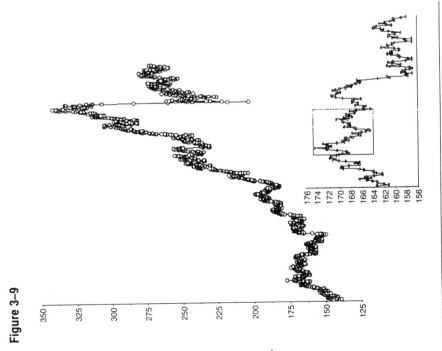

case, the *price changes* in the lowest 10% range from -80.83 to -2.327, the middle 80% from -2.31 to +3.02, and the highest 10% from +3.03 to +41.84. Then examine the *price change* time series (the first 25 *price changes* are shown in Table 3-27) and determine to which third each belongs.

For example, the first *price change* is +3.50, so it belongs in the highest third and we would encode this as a "3." The next *price change* is +0.42, so we would encode it as a "2." The next *price change* is +4.08, which we would encode as a "3." *Price changes* that fall in the lowest third would be encoded as a "1." Continue this process until you reach the last *price change*. Then generate the digram category price transition matrix, which specifies how often a 1 is followed by a 1, 2, or 3, etc. This matrix has nine cells, as indicated in Table 3-28. The total number of prices in this time series is 1,435. The probability of occurrence of a "1" is 0.0997, of a "2" is 0.80139, and a "3" is 0.09895. In contrast to the relative price matrix, determining the probability of occurrence of each digram follows rules developed within classical probability theory. We merely multiply the probability of occurrence of each component in the digram and then multiply the result by the total number of prices in the time series. For example, the digram 1,1 is:

$$(0.0997) * (0.0997) * (1,435) = 14.250$$

The probability of occurrence of the digram 1,2 is:

$$(0.0997) * (0.80139) * (1,435) = 114.65$$

Calculate the independence case of the other six digrams in the same manner. The 10%-90% category transition matrix is shown in Table 3-28, column 2, while the transition matrix under the assumption of independence is shown in column 3. The Chi-square is calculated as described above and the running total is 10.25, which is not statistically significant. This means that relatively large and small *price changes* do not diverge from independence.

We could divide our time series into four unequal quarters, where the first quarter contains *price changes* ranging from –80.83 to –0.48, the second quarter from –0.47 to +0.51, the third quarter from +0.52 to +2.1, and the fourth quarter from +2.2 to 41.84, which we would encode as a 1, 2, 3, and 4, respectively. In this case, the probability of occurrence of a "1" is 0.3463, a "2" is 0.2481, a "3" is 0.2502, and a "4" is 0.1554. The probability of occurrence of the digram 1,1 in this case is:

$$(0.3463) * (0.3463) * (1,435) = 172.09$$

Table 3–27

	S&P 500 Long	10%–90% Digram			S&P 500 Long	10%–90% Digram
1	•	•		14	1.450	2.000
2	3.500	3.000		15	−3.770	1.000
3	.410	2.000		16	−2.230	2.000
4	4.080	3.000		17	.590	2.000
5	.060	2.000		18	−.060	2.000
6	1.740	2.000		19	4.140	3.000
7	−.800	2.000		20	−.930	2.000
8	.060	2.000		21	1.880	2.000
9	.170	2.000		22	−3.960	1.000
10	0	2.000		23	.860	2.000
11	.400	2.000		24	.860	2.000
12	−.090	2.000		25	3.520	3.000
13	−2.120	2.000				

Table 3–28

10%–90% Digram	Observed	Expected	Observed-Expected	(Observed-Expected)^2	(Observed-Expected)^2/ Expected	Σ
11	24	14.26	9.74	94.87	3.95	3.95
12	101	114.66	−13.66	186.60	1.85	5.80
13	18	14.16	3.84	14.75	0.82	6.62
21	104	114.66	−10.66	113.64	1.09	7.71
22	941	921.62	19.38	375.58	0.40	8.11
23	105	113.85	−8.85	78.32	0.75	8.86
31	16	14.16	1.84	3.39	0.21	9.07
32	108	113.85	−5.85	34.22	0.32	9.39
33	18	14.06	3.94	15.52	0.86	10.25

and the probability of the digram 1,2 is:

$$(0.3463) * (0.2481) * (1,435) = 123.30.$$

The probability of occurrence of the other digrams, assuming independence, is calculated in the same manner. The completed quarters category transition matrix is shown in Table 3-29, column 2, while the independence case is shown in column 3. The Chi-square running total is 11.999, which is not statistically significant. This means that when the S&P 500 Stock Index is categorized in this manner, it is independent.

It is important to realize that if a time series categorized by one set of criteria is independent, that does not mean that if we categorized it by a different set of criteria, that the new categories would also be independent.

For example, we can divide the S&P 500 delta-1 *price changes* for 1983-1988 into approximately equal thirds. In this case, the lowest third would run from -80.83 to -0.53 and would be encoded as a "1" (0.3312), the middle third from -0.529 to +0.805 and be encoded as a "2," while the third would run from +0.806 to +41.84 and be encoded as a "3" (0.3389). The digram transition matrix is shown in Table 3-30, column 2, while the matrix generated under the assumption of independence is shown in column 3 of this table. The Chi-square running total is 3.106, which is not significant. This means that the S&P 500 delta-1 *price changes* for 1983-1988, when categorized as equal thirds, is independent. **Normally, we would stop at this point and recategorize our time series to test a different hypothesis.** But, for the purpose of illustration, we will use these categories to generate the trigram and tetragram transition matrices, as shown in Tables 3-31 and 3-32, respectively. The Chi-square sums are 20.658 and 66.332, which are not statistically significant. This confirms the idea that the S&P 500 delta-1 *price changes* are independent. Further, it suggests that if the digram transitions are independent, that higher order transitions will also be independent.

We can also use prices rather than *price changes* to generate our categories. Because prices often have significant trends, this would tend to bias the results, favoring a finding of divergence from independence. The closing prices for Comex Silver for 1988 are shown in Figure 3-11 and Table 3-33. We will compare the results for the prices and delta-1 *price changes* using the category price transition matrix. We will divide each time series into approximately equal thirds, where the range of prices in the lowest third are 1330 to 6130, the middle third are 6131-7730, and the highest third are 731 to 14490 while the *price change* ranges are -13160 to

Table 3–29

Quarters	Observed	Expected	Observed-Expected	(Observed-Expected)^2	(Observed-Expected)^2/Expected	Σ
11	159	172.09	13.09	171.36	0.9958	
12	119	123.29	4.29	18.41	0.1493	
13	143	124.33	−18.67	348.40	2.8021	
14	76	77.22	1.22	1.50	0.0194	
21	120	123.29	3.29	10.83	0.0878	
22	93	88.33	−4.67	21.81	0.2470	
23	93	89.08	−3.92	15.39	0.1728	
24	50	55.33	5.32	28.37	0.5127	
31	137	124.33	−12.67	160.41	1.2902	
32	92	89.07	−2.92	8.54	0.0959	
33	76	89.83	13.83	191.30	2.1295	
34	54	55.79	1.79	3.21	0.0577	
41	82	77.23	−4.78	22.80	0.2953	
42	52	55.33	3.330	11.06	0.2000	
43	47	55.79	8.79	77.34	1.3862	
44	42	34.65	−7.35	53.96	1.5572	11.9989

Table 3–30

Digram	Observed	Expected	Observed-Expected	(Observed-Expected)^2	(Observed-Expected)^2/Expected	Σ
11	145	157.6770	12.67707	160.7081	1.019223	
12	164	157.0106	−6.98933	48.85085	0.311130	
13	167	161.3185	−5.68148	32.27923	0.200096	
21	158	157.0106	−0.98933	0.978790	0.006233	
22	154	156.3470	2.347069	5.508734	0.035234	
23	162	160.6367	−1.36328	1.858534	0.011569	
31	174	161.3185	−12.6814	160.8199	0.996909	
32	156	160.6367	4.636719	21.49916	0.133837	
33	157	165.0440	8.044062	64.70694	0.392058	3.106293

Table 3–31

Tri-gram	Observed	Expected	Observed-Expected	(Observed-Expected)^2	(Observed-Expected)^2/Expected	Σ
111	40	52.23052	12.23052	149.5858	2.863954	
112	52	52.00978	0.009781	0.000095	0.000001	
113	53	53.43675	0.436759	0.190758	0.003569	
121	52	52.00978	0.009781	0.000095	0.000001	
122	53	51.78996	−1.21003	1.464180	0.028271	
123	59	53.21091	−5.78908	33.51352	0.629824	
131	55	53.43675	−1.56324	2.443722	0.045731	
132	50	53.21091	3.210913	10.30996	0.193756	
133	62	54.67084	−7.32915	53.71650	0.982543	
211	44	52.00978	8.009781	64.15660	1.233548	
212	66	51.78996	−14.2100	201.9250	3.898922	
213	48	53.21091	5.210913	27.15361	0.510301	
221	55	51.78996	−3.21003	10.30431	0.198963	
222	46	51.57108	5.571080	31.03694	0.601828	
223	53	52.98602	−0.01397	0.000195	0.000003	
231	60	53.21091	−6.78908	46.09169	0.866207	
232	57	52.98602	−4.01397	16.11202	0.304080	
233	45	54.43978	9.439784	89.10952	1.636845	
311	61	53.43675	−7.56324	57.20261	1.070473	
312	46	53.21091	7.210913	51.99726	0.977191	
313	66	54.67084	−11.3291	128.3497	2.347681	
321	51	53.21091	2.210913	4.888137	0.091863	
322	55	52.98602	−2.01397	4.056108	0.076550	
323	50	54.43978	4.439784	19.71168	0.362082	
331	59	54.67084	−4.32915	18.74157	0.342807	
332	48	54.43978	6.439784	41.47081	0.761774	
333	50	55.93343	5.933432	35.20562	0.629420	20.65820

-110, -109 to +90, and +91 to +8930, respectively. The digram transition matrices for prices and *price changes* are shown in Tables 3-34 and 3-35, respectively. The running sums are 453.9589 and 13.15399, respectively. This indicates that the prices, when categorized in this manner, are highly

Table 3–32

Quad-gram	Observed	Expected	Observed-Expected	(Observed-Expected)^2	(Observed-Expected)^2/Expected	Σ
1111	11	17.30136	6.301362	39.70717	2.295031	
1112	12	17.22824	5.228240	27.33449	1.586609	
1113	17	17.70092	0.700926	0.491297	0.027755	
1121	18	17.22824	−0.77175	0.595613	0.034571	
1122	14	17.15542	3.155426	9.956716	0.580382	
1123	20	17.62611	−2.37388	5.635329	0.319714	
1131	13	17.70092	4.700926	22.09870	1.248449	
1132	18	17.62611	−0.37388	0.139789	0.007930	
1133	22	18.10971	−3.89028	15.13429	0.835700	
1211	16	17.22824	1.228240	1.508573	0.087564	
1212	22	17.15542	−4.84457	23.46989	1.368073	
1213	14	17.62611	3.626114	13.14870	0.745978	
1221	19	17.15542	−1.84457	3.402451	0.198330	
1222	13	17.08292	4.082920	16.67023	0.975842	
1223	21	17.55161	−3.44838	11.89132	0.677505	
1231	20	17.62611	−2.37388	5.635329	0.319714	
1232	21	17.55161	−3.44838	11.89132	0.677505	
1233	18	18.03317	0.033178	0.001100	0.000061	
1311	15	17.70092	2.700926	7.295003	0.412125	
1312	14	17.62611	3.626114	13.14870	0.745978	
1313	26	18.10971	−7.89028	62.25655	3.437743	
1321	17	17.62611	0.626114	0.392019	0.022240	
1322	24	17.55161	−6.44838	41.58160	2.369103	
1323	9	18.03317	9.033178	81.59831	4.524899	
1331	23	18.10971	−4.89028	23.91486	1.320554	
1332	19	18.03317	−0.96682	0.934743	0.051834	
1333	20	18.52794	−1.47205	2.166932	0.116954	
2111	10	17.22824	7.228240	52.24745	3.032663	
2112	20	17.15542	−2.84457	8.091598	0.471664	
2113	14	17.62611	3.626114	13.14870	0.745978	
2121	20	17.15542	−2.84457	8.091598	0.471664	
2122	22	17.08292	−4.91707	24.17767	1.415312	
2123	24	17.55161	−6.44838	41.58160	2.369103	
2131	17	17.62611	0.6526114	0.392019	0.022240	

Table continues

Table 3–32   Continued

Quad-gram	Observed	Expected	Observed-Expected	(Observed-Expected)^2	(Observed-Expected)^2/Expected	Σ
2132	12	17.55161	5.551619	30.82048	1.755990	
2133	19	18.03317	−0.96682	0.934743	0.051834	
2211	12	17.15542	5.155426	26.57842	1.549272	
2212	21	17.08292	−3.91707	15.34351	0.898178	
2213	22	17.55161	−4.44838	19.78808	1.127422	
2221	15	17.08292	2.082920	4.338557	0.253970	
2222	16	17.01072	1.021556	1.021556	0.060053	
2223	15	17.47743	2.477439	6.137705	0.351178	
2231	20	17.55161	−2.44838	5.994565	0.341539	
2232	21	17.47743	−3.52256	12.40843	0.709968	
2233	12	17.95696	5.956962	35.48540	1.976136	
2311	23	17.62611	−5.37388	28.87864	1.638400	
2312	18	17.55161	−0.44838	0.201044	0.011454	
2313	19	18.03317	−0.96682	0.934743	0.051834	
2321	17	17.55161	0.551619	0.304284	0.017336	
2322	21	17.47743	−3.52256	12.40843	0.709968	
2323	19	17.95696	−1.04303	1.087926	0.060585	
2331	17	18.03317	1.033178	1.067457	0.059194	
2332	14	17.95696	3.956962	15.65755	0.971948	
2333	14	18.44964	4.449642	19.79932	1.073154	
3111	19	17.70092	−1.29907	1.687592	0.095339	
3112	20	17.62611	−2.37388	5.635329	0.319714	
3113	22	18.10971	−3.89028	15.13429	0.835700	
3121	14	17.62611	3.626114	13.14870	0.745978	
3122	17	17.55161	0.551619	0.304284	0.017336	
3123	15	18.03317	3.033178	9.200171	0.510180	
3131	25	18.10971	−6.89028	47.47599	2.621575	
3132	20	18.03317	−1.96682	3.868386	0.214514	
3133	21	18.52794	−2.47205	6.111032	0.329827	
3211	16	17.62611	1.626114	2.644249	0.150018	
3212	23	17.55161	−5.44838	29.68484	1.691288	
3213	12	18.03317	6.033178	36.39924	2.018459	
3221	21	17.55161	−3.44838	11.89132	0.677505	
3222	17	17.47743	0.477439	0.227948	0.013042	

Table continues

Table 3–32   Continued

Quad-gram	Observed	Expected	Observed-Expected	(Observed-Expected)^2	(Observed-Expected)^2/ Expected	Σ
3223	17	17.95696	0.956962	0.915777	0.050998	
3231	20	18.03317	–1.96682	3.868386	0.214514	
3232	15	17.95696	2.956962	8.743628	0.486921	
3233	15	18.44964	3.449642	11.90003	0.64500	
3311	23	18.10971	–4.89028	23.91486	1.320554	
3312	14	18.03317	4.033178	16.26652	0.902033	
3313	21	18.52794	–2.47205	6.111032	0.329827	
3321	17	18.03317	1.033178	1.067457	0.059194	
3322	10	17.95696	7.956962	63.31325	3.525833	
3323	21	18.44964	–2.55035	6.504321	0.352544	
3331	19	18.52794	–0.47205	0.222831	0.012026	
3332	15	18.44964	3.449642	11.90003	0.645000	
3333	16	18.95584	2.955840	8.736992	0.460912	66.33204

statistically significant. In other words, prices diverge from independence. This means that the price data contains serial dependencies. The *price changes*, on the other hand, are not statistically significant and are thus independent. The serial dependencies in the price data may be due to the significant trends that are clearly shown in Figure 3-11. Nevertheless, this information could be used to develop a trading strategy.

It is important to realize that you can have as many categories as you desire and you can define the categories in any way you like, as long as you use some nonvarying rule.

Markov Analysis—Category Price Transitions

A technique was developed by a Russian statistician, A. A. Markov, who worked around the turn of this century, which allows price category analysis to be carried one step further. Markov methodology allows you to specify the level at which the serial dependency exists. That is, an rth order

Table 3–33

	Delta-1 Digrams	Prices-Digrams	Comex Silver
1	•	•	8320.000
2	•	33.000	7830.000
3	12.000	33.000	7890.000
4	23.000	33.000	8280.000
5	33.000	33.000	8480.000
6	33.000	33.000	8610.000
7	31.000	33.000	8235.000
8	11.000	33.000	7795.000
9	11.000	32.000	7515.000
10	11.000	22.000	7020.000
11	12.000	22.000	7030.000
12	22.000	22.000	7065.000
13	22.000	22.000	7130.000
14	23.000	22.000	7520.000
15	32.000	22.000	7520.000
16	21.000	22.000	7260.000
17	11.000	22.000	7120.000
18	11.000	22.000	6865.000
19	11.000	22.000	6740.000
20	12.000	22.000	6695.000
21	21.000	22.000	6255.000
22	11.000	21.000	6030.000
23	12.000	11.000	5945.000
24	21.000	11.000	5160.000
25	12.000	11.000	5170.000
26	23.000	11.000	5940.000
27	33.000	12.000	6240.000
28	33.000	22.000	6400.000
29	33.000	22.000	7210.000
30	31.000	22.000	6560.000
31	13.000	22.000	6890.000
32	31.000	22.000	6410.000
33	13.000	22.000	7680.000
34	33.000	23.000	8060.000

Table continues

Table 3–33   Continued

	Delta-1 Digrams	Prices-Digrams	Comex Silver
35	33.000	33.000	8780.000
36	33.000	33.000	8990.000
37	32.000	33.000	9020.000
38	21.000	33.000	8890.000
39	11.000	33.000	8300.000
40	13.000	33.000	8975.000
41	33.000	33.000	9740.000
42	33.000	33.000	10340.000
43	31.000	33.000	10010.000
44	13.000	33.000	10565.000
45	31.000	33.000	9365.000
46	13.000	33.000	9880.000
47	31.000	33.000	9175.000
48	13.000	33.000	10260.000
49	33.000	33.000	10410.000
50	31.000	33.000	10290.000
51	13.000	33.000	10750.000
52	33.000	33.000	10900.000
53	33.000	33.000	11560.000
54	33.000	33.000	12440.000
55	33.000	33.000	12700.000
56	33.000	33.000	13570.000
57	33.000	33.000	14130.000
58	33.000	33.000	14300.000
59	33.000	33.000	14490.000
60	31.000	31.000	1330.000
61	13.000	13.000	10260.000
62	33.000	33.000	10730.000
63	31.000	33.000	10610.000
64	11.000	33.000	10400.000
65	13.000	33.000	10630.000
66	33.000	33.000	11050.000
67	33.000	33.000	11820.000
68	33.000	33.000	12110.000

Table continues

Table 3–33   Continued

	Delta-1 Digrams	Prices-Digrams	Comex Silver
69	31.000	33.000	11850.000
70	13.000	33.000	12400.000
71	33.000	33.000	13070.000
72	33.000	33.000	13200.000
73	33.000	33.000	13220.000
74	31.000	33.000	12040.000
75	11.000	33.000	11625.000
76	12.000	33.000	11570.000
77	23.000	33.000	12240.000
78	31.000	33.000	11620.000
79	13.000	33.000	11990.000
80	32.000	33.000	12060.000
81	23.000	33.000	12275.000
82	31.000	33.000	12160.000
83	11.000	33.000	11710.000
84	13.000	33.000	11850.000
85	33.000	33.000	12200.000
86	32.000	33.000	12190.000
87	22.000	33.000	12170.000
88	22.000	33.000	12230.000
89	21.000	33.000	11800.000
90	13.000	33.000	12060.000
91	31.000	33.000	11230.000
92	11.000	33.000	10425.000
93	12.000	33.000	10340.000
94	21.000	33.000	9560.000
95	11.000	33.000	8965.000
96	12.000	33.000	9010.000
97	21.000	33.000	8895.000
98	11.000	33.000	8520.000
99	12.000	33.000	8585.000
100	23.000	33.000	9585.000
101	31.000	33.000	9310.000
102	11.000	33.000	8540.000

Table continues

Table 3–33   Continued

	Delta-1 Digrams	Prices-Digrams	Comex Silver
103	13.000	33.000	8820.000
104	33.000	33.000	8950.000
105	31.000	33.000	8240.000
106	12.000	33.000	8200.000
107	22.000	33.000	8170.000
108	22.000	33.000	8250.000
109	23.000	33.000	8880.000
110	31.000	33.000	8725.000
111	13.000	33.000	9125.000
112	33.000	33.000	9670.000
113	31.000	33.000	9525.000
114	13.000	33.000	9950.000
115	31.000	33.000	9475.000
116	12.000	33.000	9460.000
117	23.000	33.000	9730.000
118	31.000	33.000	9125.000
119	12.000	33.000	9200.000
120	23.000	33.000	9310.000
121	31.000	33.000	9075.000
122	12.000	33.000	8990.000
123	21.000	33.000	8725.000
124	13.000	33.000	8990.000
125	33.000	33.000	9240.000
126	33.000	33.000	9445.000
127	31.000	33.000	9095.000
128	11.000	33.000	8475.000
129	13.000	33.000	8620.000
130	31.000	33.000	8380.000
131	11.000	32.000	7480.000
132	12.000	22.000	7480.000
133	21.000	22.000	7280.000
134	11.000	22.000	6900.000
135	13.000	22.000	7610.000
136	33.000	23.000	7790.000

Table continues

Table 3–33   Continued

	Delta-1 Digrams	Prices-Digrams	Comex Silver
137	32.000	33.000	7880.000
138	21.000	32.000	7630.000
139	11.000	22.000	7450.000
140	11.000	22.000	7070.000
141	13.000	22.000	7250.000
142	33.000	22.000	7470.000
143	32.000	22.000	7450.000
144	22.000	22.000	7355.000
145	22.000	22.000	7280.000
146	22.000	22.000	7255.000
147	22.000	22.000	7310.000
148	23.000	22.000	7480.000
149	33.000	22.000	7680.000
150	32.000	22.000	7600.000
151	21.000	22.000	7470.000
152	11.000	22.000	7025.000
153	12.000	22.000	6950.000
154	21.000	22.000	6735.000
155	11.000	22.000	6420.000
156	12.000	22.000	6360.000
157	21.000	21.000	6030.000
158	12.000	11.000	6110.000
159	23.000	12.000	6260.000
160	31.000	21.000	5970.000
161	13.000	12.000	6230.000
162	31.000	21.000	6080.000
163	13.000	12.000	6265.000
164	31.000	21.000	6040.000
165	11.000	11.000	5690.000
166	12.000	11.000	5705.000
167	22.000	11.000	5680.000
168	23.000	12.000	6315.000
169	33.000	22.000	6670.000
170	31.000	22.000	6425.000

Table continues

Table 3–33   Continued

	Delta-1 Digrams	Prices-Digrams	Comex Silver
171	13.000	22.000	6680.000
172	31.000	22.000	6435.000
173	11.000	22.000	6230.000
174	12.000	22.000	6205.000
175	23.000	22.000	6320.000
176	33.000	22.000	6510.000
177	31.000	21.000	6105.000
178	13.000	12.000	6210.000
179	32.000	22.000	6135.000
180	23.000	22.000	6230.000
181	32.000	22.000	6145.000
182	22.000	22.000	6140.000
183	21.000	21.000	5905.000
184	13.000	11.000	6055.000
185	32.000	11.000	6125.000
186	22.000	11.000	6115.000
187	22.000	12.000	6180.000
188	22.000	21.000	6120.000
189	23.000	12.000	6385.000
190	31.000	22.000	6200.000
191	12.000	22.000	6255.000
192	21.000	21.000	6090.000
193	12.000	11.000	6045.000
194	22.000	11.000	6000.000
195	23.000	11.000	6095.000
196	33.000	12.000	6320.000
197	32.000	22.000	6215.000
198	22.000	22.000	6140.000
199	22.000	22.000	6155.000
200	22.000	22.000	6145.000
201	21.000	21.000	6000.000
202	13.000	11.000	6125.000
203	33.000	12.000	6225.000
204	32.000	22.000	6170.000

Table continues

Table 3–33   Continued

	Delta-1 Digrams	Prices-Digrams	Comex Silver
205	21.000	21.000	6030.000
206	11.000	11.000	5865.000
207	12.000	11.000	5890.000
208	22.000	11.000	5880.000
209	22.000	11.000	5805.000
210	23.000	11.000	6115.000
211	32.000	11.000	6115.000
212	22.000	12.000	6190.000
213	21.000	21.000	6080.000
214	11.000	11.000	5880.000
215	12.000	11.000	5885.000
216	22.000	11.000	5880.000
217	21.000	11.000	5605.000
218	12.000	11.000	5600.000
219	22.000	11.000	5675.000
220	22.000	11.000	5760.000
221	21.000	11.000	5600.000
222	11.000	11.000	5140.000
223	13.000	11.000	5465.000
224	31.000	11.000	5240.000
225	11.000	11.000	5130.000
226	12.000	11.000	5125.000
227	23.000	11.000	5225.000
228	31.000	11.000	5060.000
229	13.000	11.000	5160.000
230	32.000	11.000	5250.000
231	22.000	11.000	5170.000
232	23.000	11.000	5275.000
233	31.000	11.000	5110.000
234	12.000	11.000	5010.000
235	22.000	11.000	5060.000
236	22.000	11.000	5060.000
237	22.000	11.000	5075.000
238	22.000	11.000	5020.000

Table continues

Table 3–33   Continued

	Delta-1 Digrams	Prices-Digrams	Comex Silver
239	23.000	11.000	5220.000
240	32.000	11.000	5265.000
241	22.000	11.000	5295.000
242	21.000	11.000	5175.000
243	12.000	11.000	5155.000
244	23.000	11.000	5470.000
245	33.000	11.000	5760.000
246	33.000	11.000	5940.000
247	31.000	11.000	5665.000
248	12.000	11.000	5715.000
249	22.000	11.000	5665.000
250	21.000	11.000	5545.000
251	13.000	11.000	5680.000
252	32.000	11.000	5645.000
253	23.000	11.000	5755.000
254	32.000	11.000	5795.000
255	21.000	11.000	5350.000
256	11.000	11.000	5240.000
257	13.000	11.000	5390.000
258	32.000	11.000	5385.000
259	22.000	11.000	5360.000
260	22.000	11.000	5280.000
261	23.000	11.000	5435.000
262	32.000	11.000	5445.000
263	23.000	11.000	5570.000
264	32.000	11.000	5505.000
265	22.000	11.000	5515.000
266	22.000	11.000	5540.000
267	22.000	11.000	5435.000
268	22.000	11.000	5440.000
269	22.000	11.000	5470.000
270	23.000	11.000	5585.000
271	32.000	11.000	5550.000
272	22.000	11.000	5510.000

Table continues

Table 3–33 Continued

	Delta-1 Digrams	Prices-Digrams	Comex Silver
273	23.000	11.000	5895.000
274	33.000	12.000	6325.000
275	33.000	22.000	6875.000
276	33.000	22.000	7175.000
277	33.000	23.000	9410.000
278	31.000	33.000	8080.000
279	13.000	33.000	8360.000
280	33.000	33.000	9090.000
281	31.000	33.000	8290.000
282	11.000	32.000	7610.000
283	13.000	23.000	7840.000
284	31.000	32.000	7700.000
285	11.000	22.000	7300.000
286	11.000	22.000	6890.000
287	13.000	22.000	7375.000
288	33.000	22.000	7640.000
289	32.000	22.000	7535.000
290	23.000	22.000	7680.000
291	33.000	23.000	8255.000
292	31.000	33.000	8030.000
293	11.000	32.000	7505.000
294	12.000	22.000	7550.000
295	21.000	22.000	7385.000
296	13.000	22.000	7720.000
297	32.000	22.000	7680.000
298	21.000	22.000	7515.000
299	13.000	22.000	7620.000
300	31.000	22.000	7500.000
301	13.000	23.000	7790.000
302	32.000	33.000	7840.000
303	21.000	32.000	7500.000
304	11.000	22.000	6950.000
305	11.000	22.000	6420.000
306	13.000	22.000	6675.000

Table continues

Table 3–33   Continued

	Delta-1 Digrams	Prices-Digrams	Comex Silver
307	31.000	22.000	6505.000
308	13.000	22.000	6960.000
309	31.000	22.000	6600.000
310	13.000	22.000	6860.000
311	32.000	22.000	6840.000
312	22.000	22.000	6740.000
313	22.000	22.000	6695.000
314	23.000	22.000	6930.000
315	31.000	22.000	6795.000
316	12.000	22.000	6705.000
317	21.000	22.000	6500.000
318	11.000	22.000	6290.000
319	12.000	22.000	6335.000
320	22.000	22.000	6340.000
321	21.000	22.000	6190.000
322	13.000	22.000	6430.000
323	31.000	22.000	6175.000
324	13.000	22.000	6315.000
325	33.000	22.000	6635.000
326	32.000	22.000	6710.000
327	21.000	22.000	6440.000
328	12.000	22.000	6480.000
329	22.000	22.000	6420.000
330	22.000	22.000	6450.000
331	22.000	22.000	6350.000
332	23.000	22.000	6540.000
333	33.000	22.000	6635.000

Markov process means that the probability of occurrence of a specific price depends on the immediately preceding "r" prices.

The first step in this analysis is to define a number of "states" you will allow your time series to have, as previously described. It is important to realize that you can define these "states" in any way that you like,

Figure 3–11

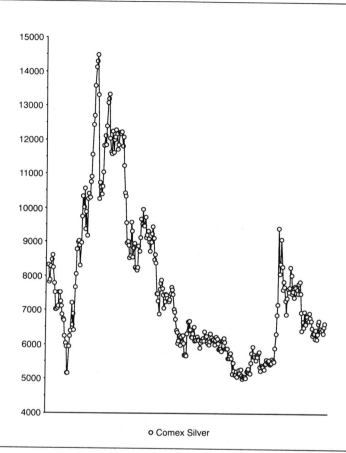

o Comex Silver

as long as they are all inclusive. We will use the delta-1 *price changes* (closing prices) of the Standard & Poor's 500 stock index for 1983-1988, divided into approximately equal thirds, as described earlier. The test for a zero-order Markov process is essentially the same as the ordinary test for independence previously described (see Table 3-30). We will use the Chi-square goodness of fit tests to determine if the Markov model is significant or not. In the case of the zero-order Markov process, the degrees of freedom are $(C-1)^2$, where C is the number "states"; that is, 3. Therefore, the degrees of freedom are $(3-1)^2 = (2)^2 = 4$. If the value we obtain is statistically significant, then it means that the process (that is, the prices or *price changes*) is not independent and we should test it against an order-1 Markov model. The running sum shown in Table 3-30 is 3.106, which is

Table 3–34

Digram	Observed	Expected	Observed-Expected	(Observed-Expected)^2	(Observed-Expected)^2/Expected	Σ
11	81	26.61398	−54.3860	2957.838	111.1385	
12	12	34.54187	22.54187	508.1359	14.71072	
13	1	32.84330	31.84330	1013.996	30.87375	
21	12	34.54187	22.54187	508.1359	14.71072	
22	104	44.83135	−59.1686	3500.928	78.09107	
23	6	42.62681	36.62681	1341.523	31.47135	
31	1	32.84330	31.84330	1013.996	30.87375	
32	7	42.62681	35.62681	1269.269	29.77632	
33	108	40.53067	−67.4693	4552.109	112.3126	453.9589

Table 3–35

Digram	Observed	Expected	Observed-Expected	(Observed-Expected)^2	(Observed-Expected)^2/Expected	Σ
11	36	35.89532	−0.10467	0.010957	0.000305	
12	32	34.24830	2.248305	5.054879	0.147595	
13	41	38.85907	−2.14092	4.583564	0.117953	
21	29	34.24830	5.248305	27.54471	0.804265	
22	46	32.67686	−13.3231	177.5059	5.432161	
23	29	37.07607	8.076071	65.22292	1.759165	
31	43	38.85907	−4.14092	17.14726	0.441268	
32	26	37.07607	11.07607	122.6793	3.308855	
33	49	42.06753	−6.93246	48.05907	1.142426	13.15399

not statistically significant. **Normally, we would stop the analysis at this point, but for the purpose of illustration, we will use these data for testing the higher order Markov models.**

The order-1 Markov model is calculated as follows:

$$\chi^2 = \sum_{ijk} \frac{(O_{ijk} - E_{ijk})^2}{E_{ijk}}$$

where O_{ijk} is the observed number of occurrences of each trigram "ijk." E_{ijk} is the expected number of occurrences of each trigram "ijk," which is defined and calculated as follows:

$$E_{ijk} = N_3 \frac{(O_{.jk})\ (O_{ij.})}{(O_{.j.})\ (N_3)}$$

where N_3 is the total number of trigrams.

The other quantities $O_{.jk}$, $O_{ij.}$, and $O_{.j.}$ are what statisticians call standard "dot" notation. Basically, what it means in the case of $O_{.jk}$ is that the trigram will begin with any "symbol" (that is, 1, 2, or 3), but it will end with a specific digram, jk. Similarly, $O_{ij.}$ means that the trigram will begin with a specific digram "ij," but it will end with any symbol. Finally, $O_{.j.}$ means that the trigram will begin and end with any symbol, but it will have a specific symbol "j" in the middle.

This process will be easier to understand if you refer to Tables 3-36 and 3-37. For example, if you want to calculate the expected probability of the trigram 111, proceed as follows. To obtain the value for $O_{.jk}$, in other words, a trigram that begins with any symbol but ends with the digram 11, sum up the frequency of all of the (al)s; that is, the frequency of 111, 211, and 311, which is 40, 44, and 61, respectively. Thus, the value of $O_{.jk}$ for the trigram 111 is 145. To obtain the value for $O_{.j.}$, sum over all of the trigrams with a "1" in the middle of the trigram; that is, 111, 112, 113, 211, 212, 213, 311, 312, and 313. The value of $O_{.j.}$ is 40 + 52 + 53 + 44 + 66 + 48 + 61 + 46 + 66 = 476. To obtain Oij., sum over all of the "A"s; that is, 111, 112, and 113, which is 40, 52, 53. Thus, Oij. is 145.

Thus, the frequency of O_{111} is 40. And the value of E_{111} is calculated as follows: 1437 (145/476) (145/1437) or 1437 x 0.3046 x 0.1009 = 44.1702. Therefore, the value of the 111 cell in the Chi-square test is (40 - 44.1702)^2/44.1702 = 0.3937. Continue this process for each of the 27 trigrams.

The frequency of O_{333} is 50. The value of $O_{.jk}$ is 62 + 45 + 50 = 157. The value of $O_{ij.}$ is 59 + 48 + 50 = 157. And the value of $O_{.j.}$ is 55 + 50 + 62 + 60 + 57 + 45 + 59 + 48 + 50 = 486. So the value of E_{333} is 1437 x 157/486 x 157/1437 = 1437 x 0.3231 x 0.1093 = 50.718. The value of the 333 cell in the Chi-square test is (50 - 50.718)^2/50.718 which equals 0.0102.

This model is based on the first order Markov process assumption that the conditional probability of k given ij equals the conditional proba-

Table 3–36   Trigram Worksheet

111	40	a1_____	1_____	a_____
112	52	a2_____	1_____	a_____
113	53	a3_____	1_____	a_____
121	52	b1_____	2_____	d_____
122	53	b2_____	2_____	d_____
123	59	b3_____	2_____	d_____
131	55	c1_____	3_____	g_____
132	50	c2_____	3_____	g_____
133	62	c3_____	3_____	g_____
211	44	a1_____	1_____	b_____
212	66	a2_____	1_____	b_____
213	48	a3_____	1_____	b_____
221	55	b1_____	2_____	e_____
222	46	b2_____	2_____	e_____
223	53	b3_____	2_____	e_____
231	60	c1_____	3_____	h_____
232	57	c2_____	3_____	h_____
233	45	c3_____	3_____	h_____
311	61	a1_____	1_____	c_____
312	46	a2_____	1_____	c_____
313	66	a3_____	1_____	c_____
321	51	b1_____	2_____	f_____
322	55	b2_____	2_____	f_____
323	50	b3_____	2_____	f_____
331	59	c1_____	3_____	i_____
332	48	c2_____	3_____	i_____
333	50	c3_____	3_____	i_____

Table 3–37   Tetragram Worksheet

Code	Label		#	Letter	Code	Label		#	Letter	Code	Label		#	Letter
1111	a1	___	1	a	1112	a2	___	1	a	1113	a3	___	1	a
1121	b1	___	2	j	1122	b2	___	2	j	1123	b3	___	2	j
1131	c1	___	3	s	1132	c2	___	3	s	1133	c3	___	3	s
1211	a4	___	4	b	1212	a5	___	4	b	1213	a6	___	4	b
1221	b4	___	5	k	1222	b5	___	5	k	1223	b6	___	5	k
1231	c4	___	6	t	1232	c5	___	6	t	1233	c6	___	6	t
1311	a7	___	7	c	1312	a8	___	7	c	1313	a9	___	7	c
1321	b7	___	8	l	1322	b8	___	8	l	1323	b9	___	8	l
1331	c7	___	9	u	1332	c8	___	9	u	1333	c9	___	9	u
2111	a1	___	1	d	2112	a2	___	1	d	2113	a3	___	1	d
2121	b1	___	2	m	2122	b2	___	2	m	2123	b3	___	2	m
2131	c1	___	3	v	2132	c2	___	3	v	2133	c3	___	3	v
2211	a4	___	4	e	2212	a5	___	4	e	2213	a6	___	4	e
2221	b4	___	5	n	2222	b5	___	5	n	2223	b6	___	5	n

Worksheet continues

Table 3–37 Continued

2232	c4	___	6	___	w	___	2232	c5	___	6	___	w	___
2311	a7	___	7	___	f	___	2312	a8	___	7	___	f	___
2321	b7	___	8	___	o	___	2322	b8	___	8	___	o	___
2331	c7	___	9	___	x	___	2332	c8	___	9	___	x	___
3111	a1	___	1	___	g	___	3112	a2	___	1	___	g	___
3121	b1	___	2	___	p	___	3122	b2	___	2	___	p	___
3131	c1	___	3	___	y	___	3132	c2	___	3	___	y	___
3211	a4	___	4	___	h	___	3212	a5	___	4	___	h	___
3221	b4	___	5	___	q	___	3222	b5	___	5	___	q	___
3231	c4	___	6	___	z	___	3232	c5	___	6	___	z	___
3311	a7	___	7	___	i	___	3312	a8	___	7	___	i	___
3321	b7	___	8	___	r	___	3322	b8	___	8	___	r	___
3331	c7	___	9	___	aa	___	3332	c8	___	9	___	aa	___

2233	c6	___	6	___	w	___
2313	a9	___	7	___	f	___
2323	b9	___	8	___	o	___
2333	c9	___	9	___	x	___
3113	a3	___	1	___	g	___
3123	b3	___	2	___	p	___
3133	c3	___	3	___	y	___
3213	a6	___	4	___	h	___
3223	b6	___	5	___	q	___
3233	c6	___	6	___	z	___
3313	a9	___	7	___	i	___
3323	b9	___	8	___	r	___
3333	c9	___	9	___	aa	___

Table 3-38 Continued

2232	c4	20	___	6	___	w	___	2232	c5	21	___	6	___	w	___	2233	c6	12	___	6	___	w	___

2232 c4 20 ___ 6 ___ w ___   2232 c5 21 ___ 6 ___ w ___   2233 c6 12 ___ 6 ___ w ___
2311 a7 23 ___ 7 ___ f ___   2312 a8 18 ___ 7 ___ f ___   2313 a9 19 ___ 7 ___ f ___
2321 b7 17 ___ 8 ___ o ___   2322 b8 21 ___ 8 ___ o ___   2323 b9 19 ___ 8 ___ o ___
2331 c7 17 ___ 9 ___ x ___   2332 c8 14 ___ 9 ___ x ___   2333 c9 14 ___ 9 ___ x ___
3111 a1 19 ___ 1 ___ g ___   3112 a2 20 ___ 1 ___ g ___   3113 a3 22 ___ 1 ___ g ___
3121 b1 14 ___ 2 ___ p ___   3122 b2 17 ___ 2 ___ p ___   3123 b3 15 ___ 2 ___ p ___
3131 c1 25 ___ 3 ___ y ___   3132 c2 20 ___ 3 ___ y ___   3133 c3 21 ___ 3 ___ y ___
3211 a4 16 ___ 4 ___ h ___   3212 a5 23 ___ 4 ___ h ___   3213 a6 12 ___ 4 ___ h ___
3221 b4 21 ___ 5 ___ q ___   3222 b5 17 ___ 5 ___ q ___   3223 b6 17 ___ 5 ___ q ___
3231 c4 20 ___ 6 ___ z ___   3232 c5 15 ___ 6 ___ z ___   3233 c6 15 ___ 6 ___ z ___
3311 a7 23 ___ 7 ___ i ___   3312 a8 14 ___ 7 ___ i ___   3313 a9 21 ___ 7 ___ i ___
3321 b7 17 ___ 8 ___ r ___   3322 b8 10 ___ 8 ___ r ___   3323 b9 21 ___ 8 ___ r ___
3331 c7 19 ___ 9 ___ aa ___   3332 c8 15 ___ 9 ___ aa ___   3333 c9 16 ___ 9 ___ aa ___

Table 3–39   Tetragram Chi-square Worksheet

nijk.	n.jk.	n.jkl
A_____	1 _____	a1_____
B_____	2 _____	a2_____
C_____	3 _____	a3_____
D_____	4 _____	a4_____
E_____	5 _____	a5_____
F_____	6 _____	a6_____
G_____	7 _____	a7_____
H_____	8 _____	a8_____
I_____	9 _____	a9_____
J_____		b1_____
K_____		b2_____
L_____		b3_____
M_____		b4_____
N_____		b5_____
O_____		b6_____
P_____		b7_____
Q_____		b8_____
R_____		b9_____
S_____		c1_____
T_____		c2_____
U_____		c3_____
V_____		c4_____
W_____		c5_____
X_____		c6_____
Y_____		c7_____
Z_____		c8_____
AA_____		c9_____

What Does it All Mean?

If you use one of the techniques in this chapter and discover that your time series is independent, what does that mean? It means that if you examine the time series and attempt to find "patterns" that you can use to develop a trading strategy, any patterns you detect may be spurious and you will be involved in a Gambler's Paradox type situation. Meaningless patterns? That seems like a contradiction in terms. But, consider the example that we talked about at the beginning of this chapter, flipping a *fair* coin. If you flip a *fair* coin 1,000 times or 10,000 times, you would find that you would have several occurrences of 3, 4, 5, maybe even 20 or 25 heads or tails occur in a row. Or, you could have a group of alternating heads and tails (H, T, H, T, H, T) and these patterns might be repeated several times. But, if you are dealing with an independent process (and flipping a *fair* coin is a classic example of an independent process), then these apparent patterns occur purely by chance. If you are dealing with an independent time series, then any patterns you happen to detect are probably spurious. If you are using these spurious patterns to make trading decisions, in the long run you will lose, because you are depending on luck rather than reason to make your trading decisions.

On the other hand, if you find that your time series is not independent, then you should be able to determine the duration of the "temporal window" during which the time series shows serial dependencies. If you work within the confines of this temporal window, then you can use a variety of pattern detection techniques to detect patterns. Traditional probability theory indicates that the patterns that we detect are probably not spurious and we can use them to make reasoned trading decisions.

Chapter 3 Appendix

If we have the following time series of prices (a) and relative price changes (b):

```
a) 3   4   2   2   5   8   4   4   9   3
b)  2   1   0   2   2   1   0   2   1
```

where a 1=a price decrease, a 2=a price increase, and a 0=a "tie"; that is, no change in price. As indicated in the above, if there are relatively few "ties" and if we resolve the "ties" in some arbitrary manner (such as flipping a fair coin and allowing a head to represent a price increase (a 2) and a tail to represent a price decrease (a 1), then there are only 4 digrams

1,1; 1,2; 2,1; and 2,2. The probability of occurrence of these digrams, assuming independence, is 0.3333 for the digrams 1,2 or a 2,1 and 0.1667 for the digrams 1,1 and 2,2. These probabilities of occurrence are not determined by the underlying probability density function of the prices or *price changes.*

On the other hand, if we allow "ties" to occur, then there are nine digrams—1,1; 1,0; 1,2; 0,1; 0,0; 0,2; 2,1; 2,0; 2,2—and their probability of occurrence is determined by the underlying probability density function of prices or *price changes.* Calculating these probabilities of occurrence is a relatively complex and time-consuming task. Consider two simple sets of prices, that each consist of ten prices. In the first case, price 1 and price 2 each occur four times, while price 3 occurs two times (see price frequency histogram 1), while in the second case, price 1 occurs three times, price 2, four times, and price 3, two times (see price frequency histogram 2) in Table 3-40.

The digram 2,2 can occur in one way, a 1 followed by a 2 followed by a 3. The probability of occurrence of this digram in the first time series is 0.4 x 0.4 x 0.2 = 0.032. The probability of occurrence of this digram in the second time series is 0.3 x 0.4 x 0.2 = 0.030. The probability of occurrence of the other eight digrams is shown in Table 3-40. Note that the probability of occurrence of the individual digrams in the two time series is different.

As the number of bins in the price or *price change* frequency histograms increases, so does the level of computational effort. For example, the summation formula for the digram 2,1 has the following form:

$$P_{2,1} = \sum_{i=1}^{n-1} P(i) * \sum_{j+1}^{n} P(j) * \sum_{1}^{j-1} P(k).$$

If 100 bins are included in the frequency histogram, then this formula would have to be executed 1,000,000 times to determine the probability of occurrence of this particular digram. The remaining summation formulas for the other eight digrams are equally complex and would require equal computational effort.

Therefore, it is probably best to eliminate ties and use the distribution free methods described above.

Table 3-40

		Price Frequency Histogram		Price Frequency Histogram	
		Frequency		Frequency	
		p(1) = 0.4; p(2) = 0.4; p(3) = 0.2*		p(1) = 0.3; p(2) = 0.5; p(3) = 0.2*	
Digram Pattern	Possible Price Arrangements	Digram Probabilities		Digram Probabilities	
1,1	3.2.1	p(3).p(2).p(1) = 0.032 = p(+1, +1) = 0.032		p(3).p(2).p(1) = 0.030 = p(+1, +1) = 0.030	
1,2	2.1.2 2.1.3 3.1.2 3.1.3 3.2.3	p(2).p(1).p(2) = 0.064 + p(2).p(1).p(3) = 0.032 + p(3).p(1).p(2) = 0.032 + p(3).p(1).p(3) = 0.016 + p(3).p(2).p(3) = 0.016 = 0.160		p(2).p(1).p(2) = 0.075 + p(2).p(1).p(3) = 0.030 + p(3).p(1).p(2) = 0.030 + p(3).p(1).p(3) = 0.020 + p(3).p(2).p(3) = 0.020 = 0.167	
2,1	1.2.1 1.3.1 1.3.2 2.3.1 2.3.2	p(1).p(2).p(1) = 0.064 + p(1).p(3).p(1) = 0.032 + p(1).p(3).p(2) = 0.032 + p(2).p(3).p(1) = 0.032 + p(2).p(3).p(2) = 0.032 = .192		p(1).p(2).p(1) = 0.045 + p(1).p(3).p(1) = 0.018 + p(1).p(3).p(2) = 0.030 + p(2).p(3).p(1) = 0.030 + p(2).p(3).p(2) = 0.050 = .173	

Table continues

Table 3-40   Continued

Digram Pattern	Possible Price Arrangements	Digram Probabilities	Digram Probabilities
0,1	2.2.1 3.3.1 3.3.2	p(2)·p(2)·p(1) = 0.064 + p(3)·p(3)·p(1) = 0.016 + p(3)·p(3)·p(2) = 0.016 = 0.096	p(2)·p(2)·p(1) = 0.075 + p(3)·p(3)·p(1) = 0.012 + p(3)·p(3)·p(2) = 0.020 = 0.107
0,2	1.1.2 1.1.3 2.2.3	p(1)·p(1)·p(2) = 0.064 + p(1)·p(1)·p(3) = 0.032 + p(2)·p(2)·p(3) = 0.032 = 0.128	p(1)·p(1)·p(2) = 0.045 + p(1)·p(1)·p(3) = 0.018 + p(2)·p(2)·p(3) = 0.050 = 0.113
0,0	1.1.1 2.2.2 3.3.3	p(1)·p(1)·p(1) = 0.064 + p(2)·p(2)·p(2) = 0.064 + p(3)·p(3)·p(3) = 0.008 = 0.136	p(1)·p(1)·p(1) = 0.027 + p(2)·p(2)·p(2) = 0.125 + p(3)·p(3)·p(3) = 0.008 = 0.160
1,0	2.1.1 3.1.1 3.2.2	p(2)·p(1)·p(1) = 0.064 + p(3)·p(1)·p(1) = 0.032 + p(3)·p(2)·p(2) = 0.032 = 0.128	p(2)·p(1)·p(1) = 0.045 + p(3)·p(1)·p(1) = 0.018 + p(3)·p(2)·p(2) = 0.050 = 0.113
2,0	1.2.2 1.3.3 2.3.3	p(1)·p(2)·p(2) = 0.064 + p(1)·p(3)·p(3) = 0.016 + p(2)·p(3)·p(3) = 0.016 = 0.096	p(1)·p(2)·p(2) = 0.075 + p(1)·p(3)·p(3) = 0.012 + p(2)·p(3)·p(3) = 0.020 = 0.107
2,2	1.2.3	p(1)·p(2)·p(3) = 0.032 = 0.032	p(1)·p(2)·p(3) = 0.030 = 0.030

*The value of a bin in the probability density function is determined as follows: f(t) = f(1) + f(2) + f(3), and p(1) = f(1)/f(t); p(2) = f(2)/f(t); p(3) = f(3)/f(t). In this example, the value of f(t) is 10 in each case, but the value of p(1), p(2), and p(3) is determined by the value of the respective bin in the individual histogram.

Randomness   4

Randomness may, on the surface, be somewhat more familiar as a concept than stationarity or independence. A random event is one whose outcome is determined by chance. For example, consider flipping a fair coin. Probability theorists (and common sense) tell us that a head or a tail are equally likely to occur. But, if we actually flip a real coin 10, 100, or even several hundred times, it is relatively unlikely that we would get an even number of heads and tails. This is one of the places where probability theorists hedge a little bit and bring up the "law of large numbers." This "law" states that if we flip a coin often enough (thousands of times), eventually the distribution of heads and tails would more and more closely approach a 50-50 distribution.

Although that may seem relatively straightforward, it becomes somewhat more complex and confusing if we use a "larger" system, such as our small urn filled with colored balls described in Chapters 2 and 3. If we assume that all of the balls are exactly the same except for color, then each ball is equally likely to be chosen, so the selection process is random. But, it is important to realize that if we are noting the color of the ball, then the probability of choosing a ball of a given color is determined by the probability distribution of the balls (100 white, 50 blue, 50 red, and 25 black). If we draw out one ball at a time, note its color, return it to the urn, and shake the urn, we would expect about half of the balls would be white and the remaining half would be about equally divided between blue and red balls, with a few black balls. This is an important point. As the size of the sample increases, we would expect to get a better and better "picture" of the relative distribution of balls in the population (all of the balls in the urn).

Basic Procedures

We will use the data from Table 2-1, Chapter 2 as our data. In order to test for randomness, we will divide the time series into parts by some arbitrary and unvarying rule. For example, we can divide this time series into halves and place the even prices in one frequency histogram and the odd prices in a second frequency histogram. If we are going to do this with paper and pencil, we would create two histograms. In the case of our artificial data, the "prices" run from 1 to 15, so each histogram should have 15 bins on the horizontal axis, labeled "bin-1," "bin-2," ..., "bin-15." The vertical axis would be labeled frequency.

The first artificial price is a "9," so we would write a "1" over "bin-9" in the first histogram. The second number is a "10," so we would write "2" over "bin-10" in the second histogram. The third "price" is a "4," so we would write a "3" over "bin-4" in the first histogram. We would continue this process until we reach the last "price." The summary statistics for the odd and even histograms are shown in Table 4-1. The placement of the first 15 "prices," as well as the completed histograms, are shown in Figures 4-1 and 4-2 for the odd and even "prices," respectively. The frequency histograms are converted into probability density functions (by dividing the frequency of occurrence of each "price" by the total number of "prices" in each histogram, which in this case is 100), as shown in Table 4-2, column 4. The two probability density functions are converted into two cumulative probability density functions by summing the probabilities for each bin, as shown in column 5 of Tables 4-2 for the odd and even histograms, respectively. The two cumulative probability density functions are also in Figure 4-3. If you examine this figure, note that these two cumulative probability density functions are similar. Although we could do a formal test, such as the quantal Chi-square test described in Chapter 2 or 3, it is not really necessary in this case. Our conclusion is confirmed by the insert in this figure. Since the cumulative probability density functions are essentially identical, then the underlying time series is random. If the two cumulative probability density functions are not identical, then the underlying time series is not random.

It is important to note that we can divide our time series into as many parts as we like, as long as we follow some unvarying rule. For example, we could divide the artificial prices into thirds and place the first "price" into the first histogram, the second into the second histogram, the third into the third histogram, the fourth into the first histogram, etc. The three histograms are shown in Figures 4-4, 4-5, and 4-6, for the first-, second-, and third-third, respectively. We can use any two of these histograms as

Table 4–1

x_1 : Artificial Data Evens

Mean	Std. Dev.	Std. Error	Variance	Coef. Var.	Count
8.15	4.317	.432	18.634	52.966	100

Minimum	Maximum	Range	Sum	Sum of Sqr.	# Missing
1	15	14	815	8487	1

# < 10th %	10th %	25th %	50th %	75th %	90th %
6	2	4	8	12	14

# > 90th %	Mode	Geo. Mean	Har. Mean	Kurtosis	Skewness
7	12	6.573	4.633	−1.197	−.094

x_2 : Artificial Data Odds

Mean	Std. Dev.	Std. Error	Variance	Coef. Var.	Count
7.68	4.467	.447	19.957	58.169	100

Minimum	Maximum	Range	Sum	Sum of Sqr.	# Missing
1	15	14	768	7874	1

# < 10th %	10th %	25th %	50th %	75th %	90th %
0	1	4	8	11	14

# > 90th %	Mode	Geo. Mean	Har. Mean	Kurtosis	Skewness
7	1	5.872	3.811	−1.185	.018

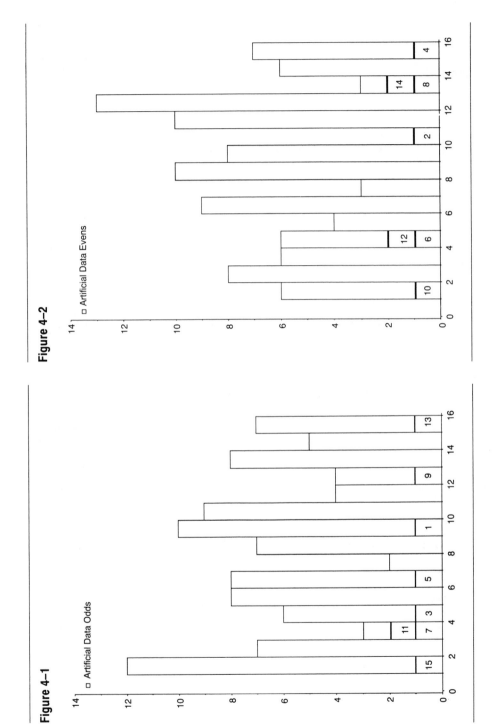

Figure 4–1

□ Artificial Data Odds

Figure 4–2

□ Artificial Data Evens

Table 4–2

Artificial Data Odds

From (≥)	To (<)	Count	%	%
0	1	0	0%	0%
1	2	12	12%	12%
2	3	7	7%	19%
3	4	3	3%	22%
4	5	6	6%	28%
5	6	8	8%	36%
6	7	8	8%	44%
7	8	2	2%	46%
8	9	7	7%	53%
9	10	10	10%	63%
10	11	9	9%	72%
11	12	4	4%	76%
12	13	4	4%	80%
13	14	8	8%	88%
14	15	5	5%	93%
15	16	7	7%	100%

Artificial Data Evens

From (≥)	To (<)	Count	%	%
0	1	0	0%	0%
1	2	6	6%	6%
2	3	8	8%	14%
3	4	6	6%	20%
4	5	6	6%	26%
5	6	4	4%	30%
6	7	9	9%	39%
7	8	3	3%	42%
8	9	10	10%	52%
9	10	8	8%	60%
10	11	1	1%	61%
11	12	10	10%	71%
12	13	13	13%	84%
13	14	3	3%	87%
14	15	6	6%	93%
15	16	7	7%	100%

Figure 4–3

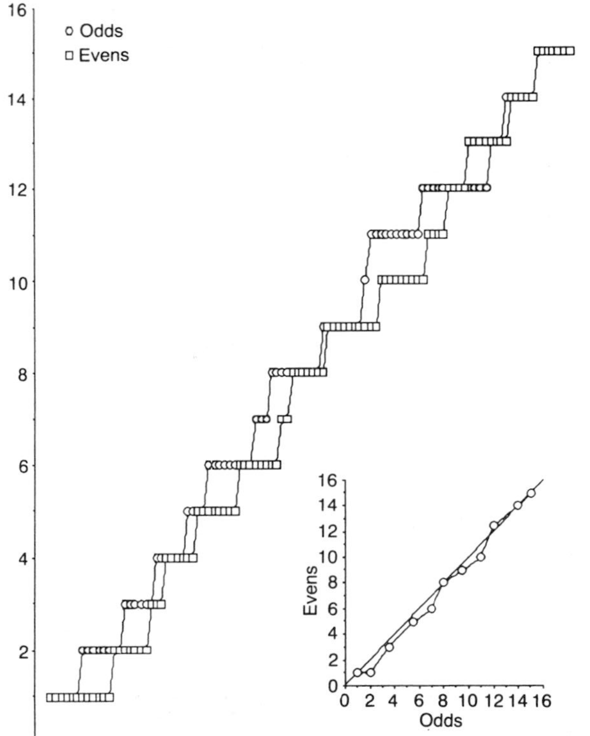

Figure 4–4

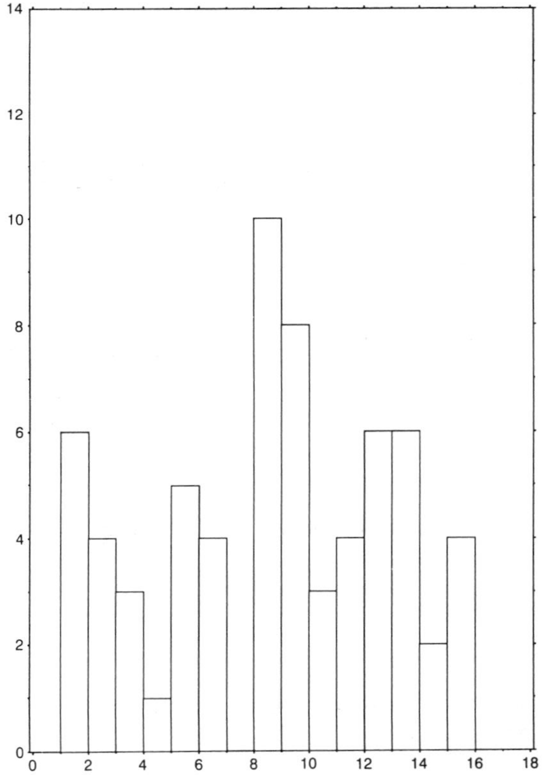

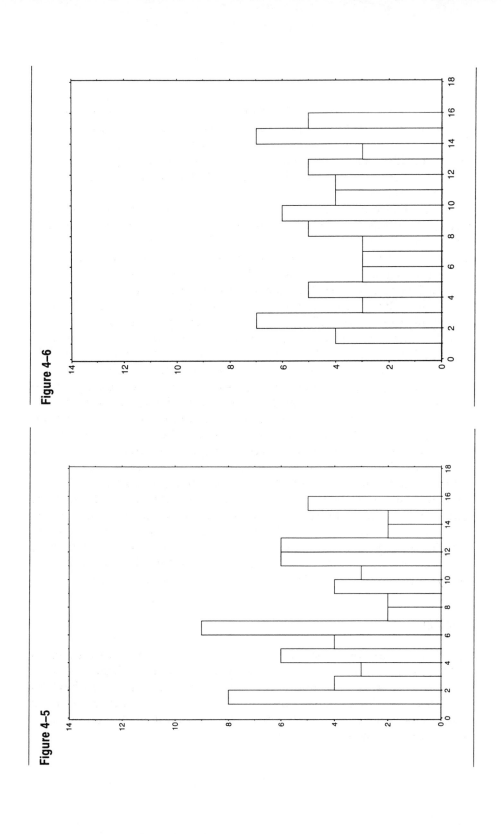

Figure 4–5

Figure 4–6

the basis for our comparison. In this example, we will use all three histograms and convert them to probability density functions and cumulative probability density functions, as previously described. The three cumulative probability density functions are shown in Figure 4-7 (1st third, triangles; 2nd third, squares; 3rd third, circles). The summary statistics are shown in Table 4-3.

We can also use *price changes* rather than prices as our data set. In this case, subtract the first price from the second, the second from the third, etc., to create our delta-1 *price change* data. The summary statistics for the delta-1 *price changes* are shown in Table 4-4. For example, the first price is a 9 and the second is a 10, so the first delta-1 *price change* data point is +1, the third price is a 4, so the second data point is a –6. We would then divide the delta-1 *price change* time series into two or more parts by some unvarying rule, as described earlier. If we are going to use paper and pencil, we need to create a frequency histogram with 30 bins on the horizontal axis labeled "bin –15," "bin -14," ... "bin 0," and "bin +1," "bin +2," ...., "bin +15." We then need to read our data into these histograms.

For example, the first *price change* is a 1, so increase the frequency of "bin +1" from 0 to 1, as indicated by the 1 immediately over this bin. The second *price change* is a –6, so increase the frequency of "bin-6" from 0 to 1, as indicated by the small "2" above this bin. The first five *price changes* are indicated by the small numbers over the appropriate bins in these histograms. Continue this process until the last *price change* is reached and the histograms should resemble those shown in Figures 4-8 and 4-9. Then convert these two frequency histograms into probability density functions and cumulative probability density functions as previously described. The cumulative probability density functions are shown in Figure 4-10. If you examine this figure, note that the two cumulative probability density functions are essentially identical, so the delta-1 artificial *price changes* are probably random. This is confirmed by the insert to this figure.

Real Data

The daily closing prices for the Standard and Poor's 500 Stock Index for 1988 are shown in Figure 4-11. We will use these data to determine if this time series is random or not. It is important to note that if you have too few prices in your frequency histograms and/or if you make the size of the bins too large or too small, you will decrease the likelihood of detecting randomness when it actually exists.

Figure 4–7

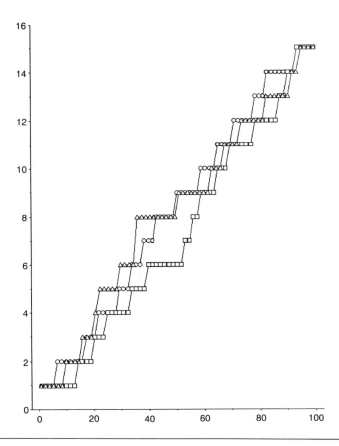

Divide this time series into two halves, placing the odd prices into the first histogram and the even prices into the second. The summary statistics for the odd and even prices are shown in Table 4-5. We could use a bin size of $0.10, where all of the prices from $0.00 to $0.10 would go into the first bin, the prices from $0.11 to $0.20 in the second, etc. These histograms are shown in Figures 4-12 and 4-13. This size bin seems too small, so we will use a bin size of $1.00. All of the prices from $0.01 to $1.00 will go in the first bin, the prices from $1.01 to $2.00 in the second bin, etc. The two frequency histograms are shown in Figures 4-14 and 4-15. We can convert these two frequency histograms into probability den-

Table 4–3

Mean	Std. Dev.	Std. Error	Variance	Coef. Var.	Count
8.224	4.525	.553	20.479	55.028	67

Minimum	Maximum	Range	Sum	Sum of Sqr.	# Missing
1	15	14	551	5883	0

# < 10th %	10th %	25th %	50th %	75th %	90th %
4	2	4	9	12	14

> 90th %
5

Mean	Std. Dev.	Std. Error	Variance	Coef. Var.	Count
7.254	4.507	.551	20.313	62.134	67

Minimum	Maximum	Range	Sum	Sum of Sqr.	# Missing
0	15	15	486	4866	0

# < 10th %	10th %	25th %	50th %	75th %	90th %
1	1	4	6	11	13.8

> 90th %
7

Mean	Std. Dev.	Std. Error	Variance	Coef. Var.	Count
8.182	4.22	.52	17.813	51.584	66

Minimum	Maximum	Range	Sum	Sum of Sqr.	# Missing
1	15	14	540	5576	1

# < 10th %	10th %	25th %	50th %	75th %	90th %
6	2	5	8.5	12	13

> 90th %
6

Table 4–4

x_1 : Random-Evens

Mean	Std. Dev.	Std. Error	Variance	Coef. Var.	Count
.444	6.464	.65	41.78	1454.343	99

Minimum	Maximum	Range	Sum	Sum of Sqr.	# Missing
−13	13	26	44	4114	2

# < 10th %	10th %	25th %	50th %	75th %	90th %
6	−9	−4	1	6	9.2

> 90th %
10

x_2 : Random-Odds

Mean	Std. Dev.	Std. Error	Variance	Coef. Var.	Count
−.47	6.104	.61	37.262	−1298.774	100

Minimum	Maximum	Range	Sum	Sum of Sqr.	# Missing
−13	14	27	−47	3711	1

# < 10th %	10th %	25th %	50th %	75th %	90th %
10	−9.5	−5	−1	4	7

> 90th %
9

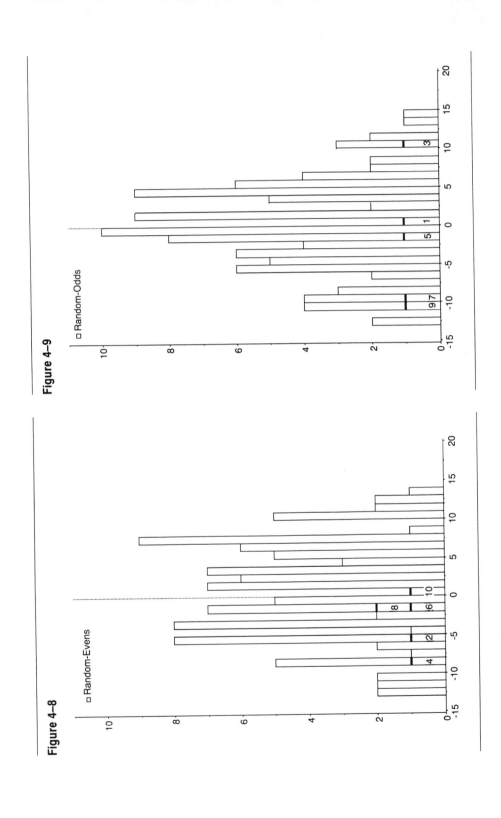

Figure 4–8

Figure 4–9

Figure 4–10

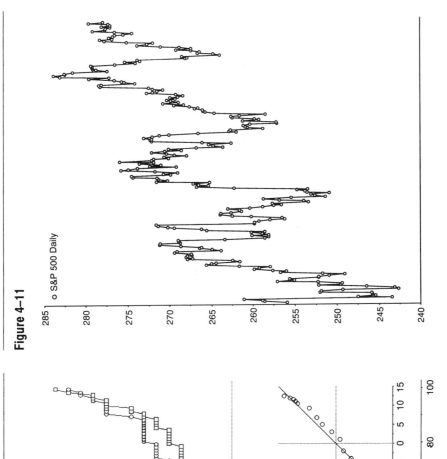

o Random-Evens
□ Random-Odds

Figure 4–11

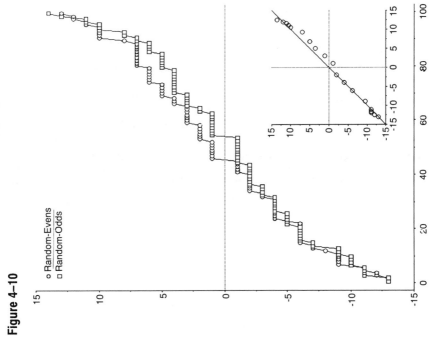

o S&P 500 Daily

Table 4–5

x_1 : S&P 500-Odd

Mean	Std. Dev.	Std. Error	Variance	Coef. Var.	Count
265.719	8.902	.79	79.241	3.35	127

Minimum	Maximum	Range	Sum	Sum of Sqr.	# Missing
242.63	283.66	41.03	33746.31	8977019.361	0

# < 10th %	10th %	25th %	50th %	75th %	90th %
13	252.718	258.962	267.21	271.753	277.07

> 90th %
13

x_2 : S&P 500-Even

Mean	Std. Dev.	Std. Error	Variance	Coef. Var.	Count
266.066	8.534	.76	72.829	3.207	126

Minimum	Maximum	Range	Sum	Sum of Sqr.	# Missing
243.14	282.88	39.74	33524.36	8928807.699	1

# < 10th %	10th %	25th %	50th %	75th %	90th %
13	253.928	260.14	267.56	272.02	276.806

> 90th %
13

Figure 4–12

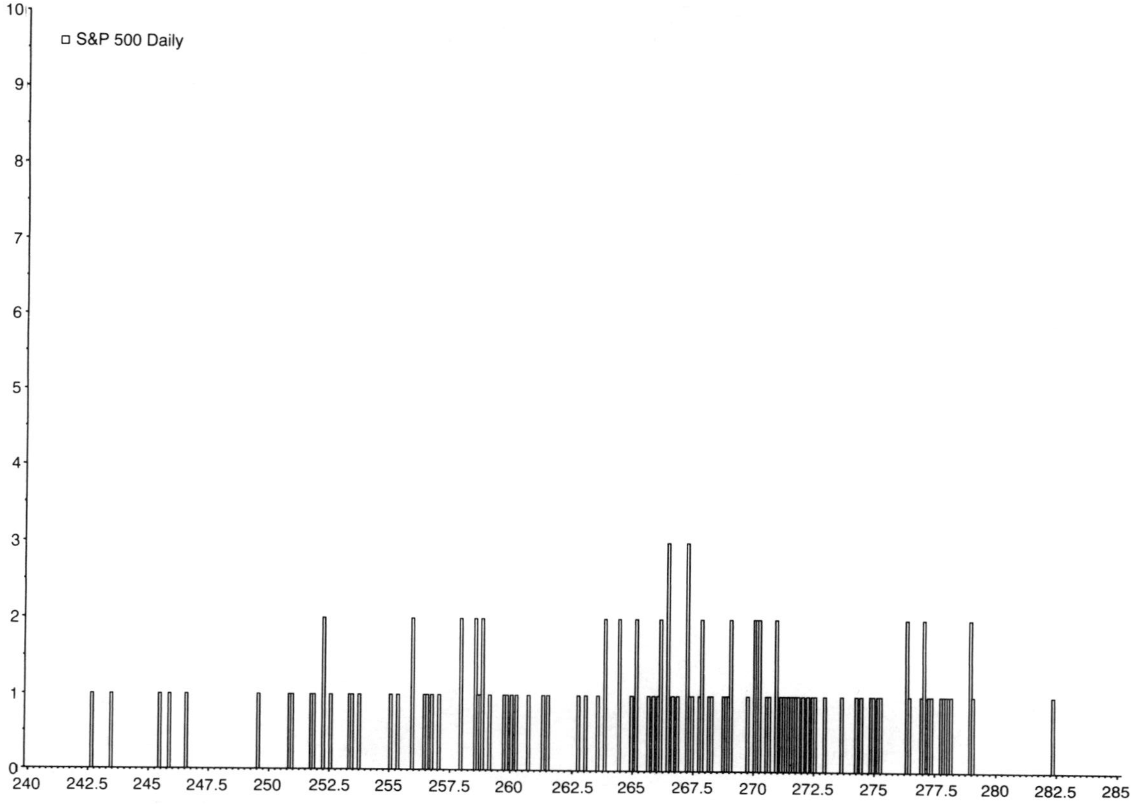

□ S&P 500 Daily

Figure 4–13

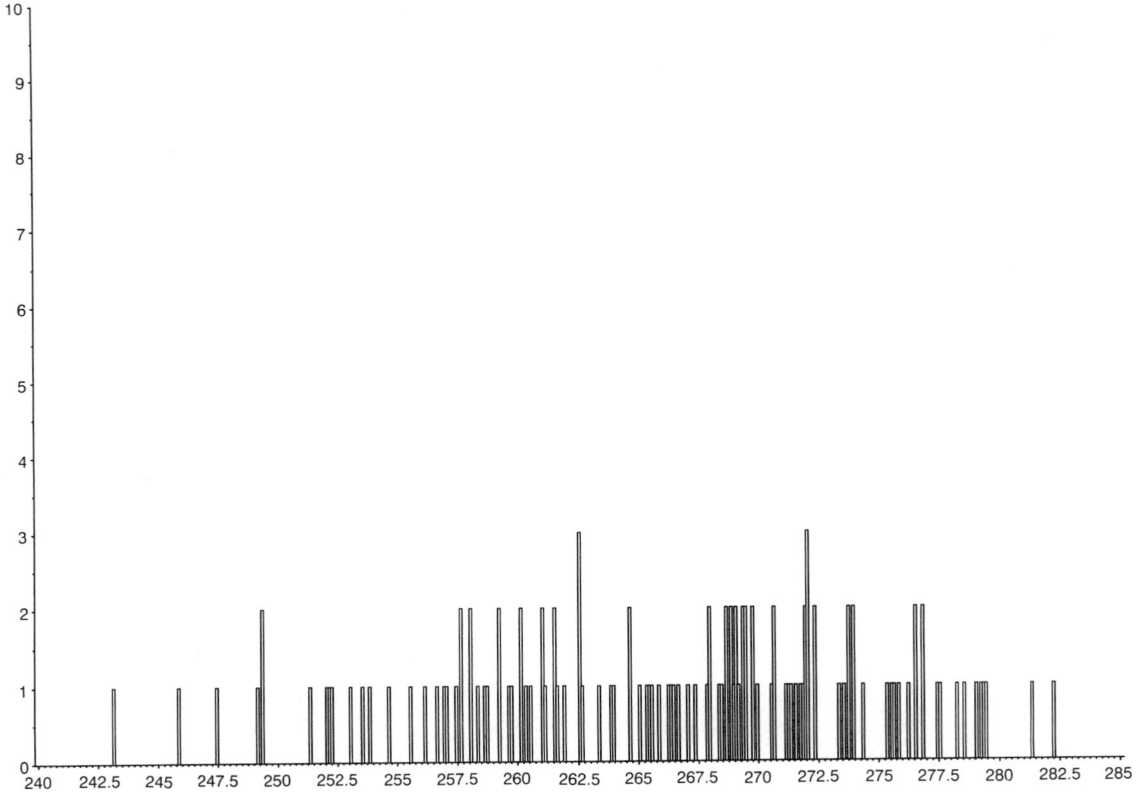

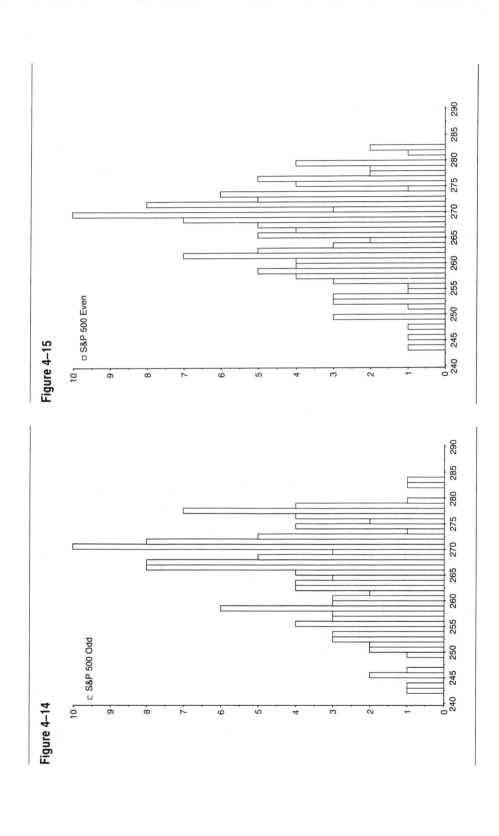

Figure 4–14

Figure 4–15

sity functions and cumulative probability density functions as previously described. The two cumulative probability density functions are shown in Figure 4-16. If we examine this figure, it is clear that the two distributions are essentially identical and this is confirmed by the insert.

We can also use the delta-1 *price changes* as our data. In order to do this, subtract the first price from the second, the second from the third, the third from the fourth, etc. We will then use the *price change* time series as our data, placing the first delta-1 *price change* into the first histogram, the second delta-1 *price change* into the second, as previously described. The completed frequency histograms for the even and odd delta-1 *price changes* are shown in Figures 4-17 and 4-18. The summary statistics for the delta-1 *price changes* are shown in Table 4-6. The two cumulative probability density functions for the odd and even delta-1 *price changes* are shown in Figure 4-19. Examining this figure, we will find that these two cumulative probability density functions are very similar and therefore the S&P 500 delta-1 *price changes* are probably random.

It is possible that the S&P 500 for 1988 appears random because we have a relatively small sample of prices or *price changes*. So, we can increase the number of prices by using the closing prices of Standard & Poor's 500 Stock Index from January 3, 1983 to September 15, 1988. This sample contains more than 1,400 individual prices. The summary statistics are shown in Table 4-7. The frequency histogram for the even and odd prices are shown in Figures 4-20 and 4-21, respectively. The two cumulative probability density functions are shown in Figure 4-22. If you examine this figure, you will note that these two cumulative probability density functions are identical and this is confirmed by the insert. This indicates that the longer time series is also random. In fact, if you examine these cumulative probability density functions displayed in this figure and the ones displayed in Figure 4-19, you will note that the cumulative probability density functions in Figure 4-22 are more similar than those in Figure 4-19, which are based on fewer prices.

It is possible that the S&P 500 time series appears random because it is an index rather than the price or *price change* of an individual stock. Therefore, we will determine if the closing prices (1988) of the common stocks of General Motors, Sears, and IBM are random or not. The summary statistics for the odd and even prices for these common stocks are shown in Tables 4-8 to 4-10, respectively. The cumulative probability density functions for the odd and even prices for these stocks are shown in Figures 4-23 to 4-25. If you examine these figures and their inserts, you will conclude that the closing prices of each of these stocks is random.

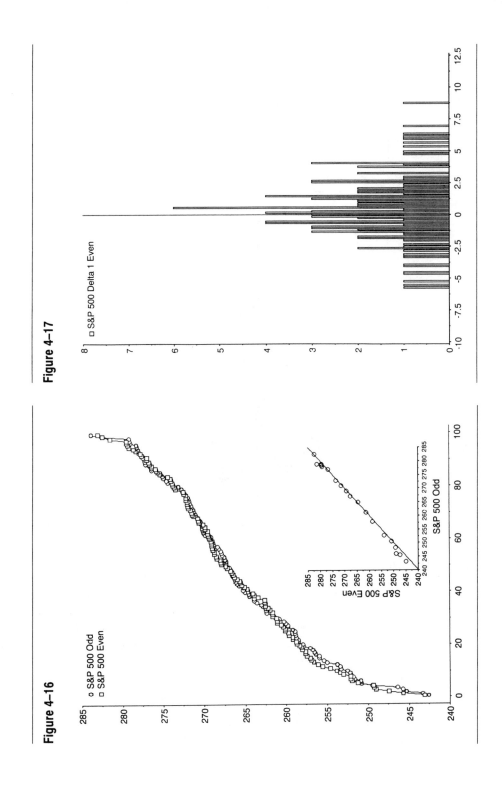

Figure 4-16

Figure 4-17

Figure 4–18

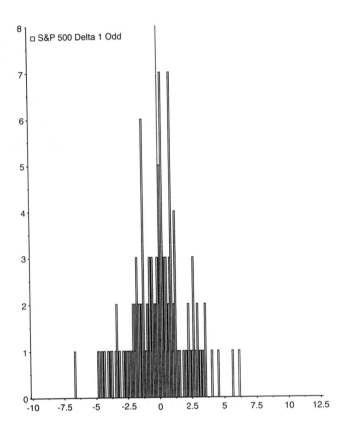

What Does it All Mean?

As indicated in the beginning of this chapter, randomness may seem like a more familiar concept than independence or stationarity. It is clear that the outcome of the flip of a fair coin is a random event. It is clear that if we draw colored balls from our ball-filled urn, the choice of an individual ball is a random event (assuming they are all identical except for color). It should also be clear that if we draw out a sample of 50 balls, one at a time, noting its color, replacing it, and shaking the urn before selecting the next ball, that the relative number of each color ball will follow the underlying distribution of balls in the urn. In other words, it is relatively unlikely that we would choose 50 black balls. It is far more likely that we would find

Table 4-6

x_1 : S&P 500 Daily Delta-1 Odds

Mean	Std. Dev.	Std. Error	Variance	Coef. Var.	Count
.443	2.853	.254	8.14	644.585	126

Minimum	Maximum	Range	Sum	Sum of Sqr.	# Missing
–11.82	8.74	20.56	55.77	1042.176	1

# < 10th %	10th %	25th %	50th %	75th %	90th %
13	–2.689	–1.04	.335	1.93	4.026

> 90th %
13

x_2 : S&P 500 Daily Delta-1 Evens

Mean	Std. Dev.	Std. Error	Variance	Coef. Var.	Count
–.258	2.653	.237	7.04	–1026.493	125

Minimum	Maximum	Range	Sum	Sum of Sqr.	# Missing
–17.67	6.13	23.8	–32.31	881.298	2

# < 10th %	10th %	25th %	50th %	75th %	90th %
12	–3.16	–1.323	.07	.96	2.62

> 90th %
12

Figure 4–19

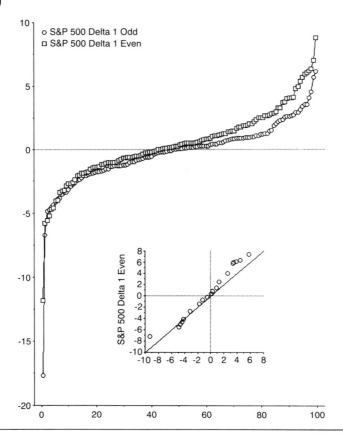

five or six black balls in any sample of 50 balls (25 black balls in the urn/225 balls x 50 balls in our sample). Finally, it is likely that each stock or commodity has its own unique probability distribution of prices or *price changes*.

If you examine the past history of the prices or *price changes* of a stock or commodity, you should be able to determine the approximate shape of this distribution. Because of the trends that are present in the prices of most stocks and commodities, it is probably best to deal with *price changes* rather than prices. The summary statistics for the delta-1 *price changes* for the closing prices of Standard & Poor's 500 Stock Index from January 3, 1983 to September 15, 1988 are shown in Table 4-11. If you examine this table, you will note that the delta-1 *price changes* vary from -80.83 to

Table 4–7

x_1 : S&P 500 Daily Even

Mean	Std. Dev.	Std. Error	Variance	Coef. Var.	Count
214.966	51.271	1.913	2628.716	23.851	718

Minimum	Maximum	Range	Sum	Sum of Sqr.	# Missing
142.57	340.54	197.97	154345.67	3.506E7	0

# < 10th %	10th %	25th %	50th %	75th %	90th %
72	158.483	168.12	196.38	254.82	288.653

> 90th %
72

x_2 : S&P 500 Daily Odd

Mean	Std. Dev.	Std. Error	Variance	Coef. Var.	Count
214.877	51.292	1.914	2630.822	23.87	718

Minimum	Maximum	Range	Sum	Sum of Sqr.	# Missing
139.12	338.63	199.51	154281.45	3.504E7	0

# < 10th %	10th %	25th %	50th %	75th %	90th %
72	158.735	168.08	195.89	254.85	287.565

> 90th %
72

Figure 4–20

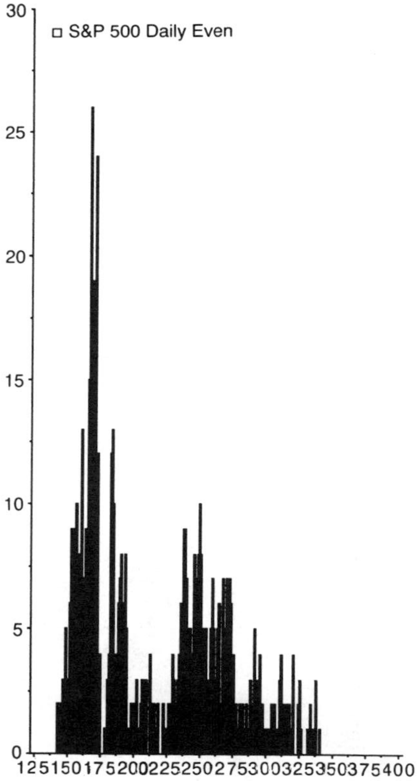

Figure 4–21

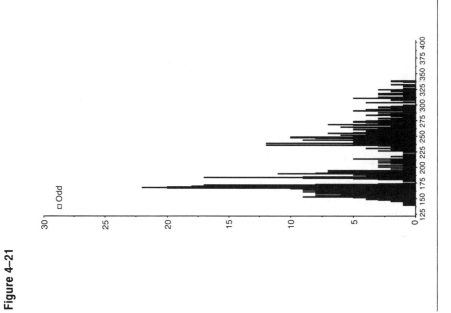

Figure 4–22

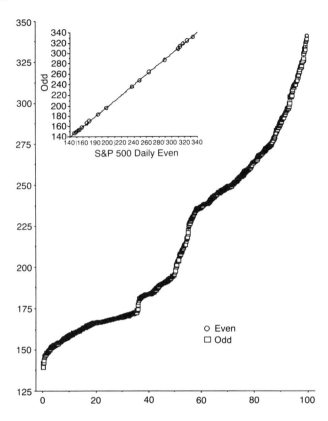

+41.84, but 90% of the *price changes* fall between -2.329 to +3.03. The delta-1 *price changes* are shown in Figure 4-26. It is important to note that the distribution of delta-2 *price changes* (price 3 - price 1, price 4 - price 2, etc.) may have a different shaped distribution, as would delta-n *price changes*. For example, the delta-10 *price changes* are shown in Figure 4-27 and the summary statistics are shown in Table 4-12. We can determine if the delta-10 *price changes* are random using the methods described earlier. The cumulative probability density functions for the odd and even delta-10 *price changes* are shown in Figure 4-28 and the summary statistics are shown in Table 4-13. If you examine this figure, you will note that these two cumulative probability density functions are essentially identical, as confirmed

Table 4–8

x_1 : GM Odd

Mean	Std. Dev.	Std. Error	Variance	Coef. Var.	Count
76.992	7.346	.588	53.959	9.541	156

Minimum	Maximum	Range	Sum	Sum of Sqr.	# Missing
61.03	93.07	32.04	12010.79	933101.312	0

# < 10th %	10th %	25th %	50th %	75th %	90th %
16	67.237	72.055	76.065	83.035	86.058

> 90th %
16

x_2 : GM Even

Mean	Std. Dev.	Std. Error	Variance	Coef. Var.	Count
77.128	7.249	.582	52.549	9.399	155

Minimum	Maximum	Range	Sum	Sum of Sqr.	# Missing
60.04	93.03	32.99	11954.81	930140.833	1

# < 10th %	10th %	25th %	50th %	75th %	90th %
15	68.05	72.07	76.06	83.05	87

> 90th %
15

Table 4–9

x_1 : Sears Odd

Mean	Std. Dev.	Std. Error	Variance	Coef. Var.	Count
36.746	2.602	.231	6.773	7.082	127

Minimum	Maximum	Range	Sum	Sum of Sqr.	# Missing
32.02	44.05	12.03	4666.7	172334.354	0

# < 10th %	10th %	25th %	50th %	75th %	90th %
13	34.024	35.04	36.03	38.06	40.07

> 90th %
14

x_2 : Sears Even

Mean	Std. Dev.	Std. Error	Variance	Coef. Var.	Count
36.773	2.631	.234	6.922	7.154	126

Minimum	Maximum	Range	Sum	Sum of Sqr.	# Missing
33.03	46	12.97	4633.46	171253.746	1

# < 10th %	10th %	25th %	50th %	75th %	90th %
13	34.031	35.03	36.035	38.07	40.06

> 90th %
12

Table 4–10

x_1 : IBM Daily 1988

Mean	Std. Dev.	Std. Error	Variance	Coef. Var.	Count
116.051	5.251	.466	27.574	4.525	127

Minimum	Maximum	Range	Sum	Sum of Sqr.	# Missing
105.07	127	21.93	14738.54	1713903.898	0

# < 10th %	10th %	25th %	50th %	75th %	90th %
13	110.002	112.305	115.04	120.06	123.814

> 90th %
13

x_2 : IBM Daily Lag-1

Mean	Std. Dev.	Std. Error	Variance	Coef. Var.	Count
116.146	5.386	.48	29.004	4.637	126

Minimum	Maximum	Range	Sum	Sum of Sqr.	# Missing
105.01	129.02	24.01	14634.38	1703348.397	1

# < 10th %	10th %	25th %	50th %	75th %	90th %
13	110.002	112.06	115.04	120.06	124.018

> 90th %
13

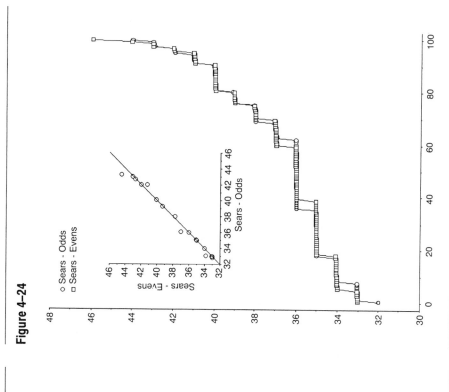

Figure 4–23

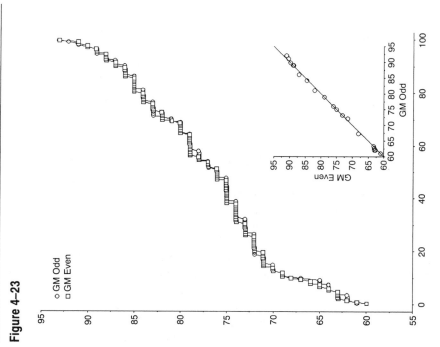

Figure 4–24

Figure 4–25

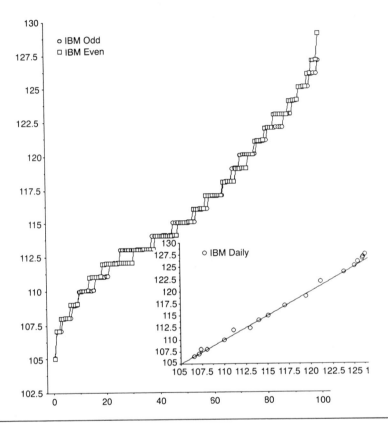

by the insert. This means that the delta-10 *price changes* are probably random.

It is not clear if randomness or divergence from it is a characteristic of individual prices or *price changes* or if there is evidence of *higher order* randomness. In other words, do sequential pairs of prices display randomness or divergence from it? In this case, we would add price 1 and price 2 to form *2sum1*, price 3 and 4 to form *2sum2*, price 5 and 6 to form *2sum3*, etc. We would continue to sum pairs of prices until we reached the last price. It is important to note that the starting point of your analysis is critical. For example, if you use the sum of price 1 and price 2 as your starting point, you will get one curve, but if you use the sum of price 2 and price 3 as your starting point, you would get a different curve. There-

Table 4–11

x_1 : Difference of S&P 500 Daily

Mean	Std. Dev.	Std. Error	Variance	Coef. Var.	Count
.092	3.631	.096	13.187	3931.769	1436

Minimum	Maximum	Range	Sum	Sum of Sqr.	# Missing
−80.83	41.84	122.67	132.63	18935.794	1

# < 10th %	10th %	25th %	50th %	75th %	90th %
144	−2.329	−.955	.135	1.27	3.03

> 90th %
143

Table 4–12

x_1 : S&P 500 Delta-10

Mean	Std. Dev.	Std. Error	Variance	Coef. Var.	Count
.767	9.685	.256	93.794	1262.694	1428

Minimum	Maximum	Range	Sum	Sum of Sqr.	# Missing
−129.12	57.59	186.71	1095.26	134683.749	9

# < 10th %	10th %	25th %	50th %	75th %	90th %
143	−6.254	−2.555	1.055	4.865	9.22

> 90th %
143

Figure 4–27

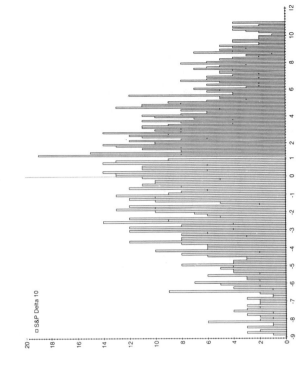

S&P Delta 10

Figure 4–26

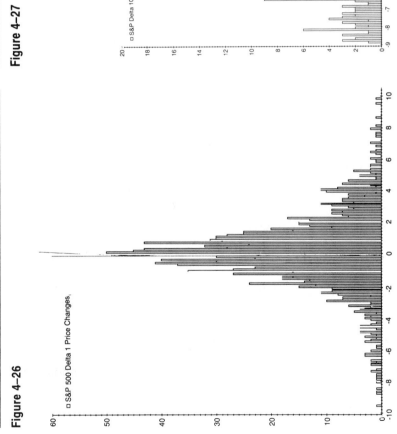

S&P 500 Delta 1 Price Changes,

Figure 4–28

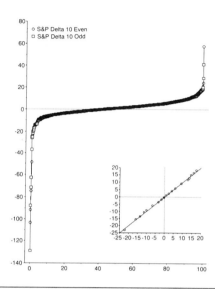

fore, to test all possibilities you would start your analysis with price 1 and figure your sums and then do a separate analysis starting with price 2. You would then treat these *2sums* as if they were individual prices. You would place the *2sum1* (price 1 + price 2) in the first histogram, *2sum2* (price 3 + price 4) in the second histogram, *2sum3* (price 5 + price 6) in the first histogram, as previously described. The summary statistics for the odd and even *2sums* are shown in Table 4-14 and the two cumulative probability density functions for the odd and even *2sums* are shown in Figure 4-29. If you examine this figure, it is clear that the *2sums* are also generated by a random process.

You can also look at higher order *sums*. For example, you can add price 1 + price 2 + price 3 + price 4 + price 5 + price 6 and call the sum, *6sum1* and add price 7 + price 8 + ...+ price 12 and call the sum, *6sum2*. You can treat these *6sums* like the *2sums* above. The summary statistics for the odd and even *6sums* are shown in Table 4-15 and the two cumulative probability density functions are shown in Figure 4-30. It is clear if you examine this figure that the *6sums* are also random.

If the prices or *price changes* of your index, stock, or commodity are random, then it is expected that all of the potential *price changes* would be equally likely to occur within the constraints of their individual frequency distributions. This is analogous to the impact of the relative distribution of

Table 4–13

x_1 : S&P 500 Delta-10 Even

Mean	Std. Dev.	Std. Error	Variance	Coef. Var.	Count
.772	9.676	.362	93.63	1253.764	714

Minimum	Maximum	Range	Sum	Sum of Sqr.	# Missing
–103.49	57.59	161.08	551.05	67183.813	9

# < 10th %	10th %	25th %	50th %	75th %	90th %
71	–6.753	–2.39	1.03	4.89	9.309

> 90th %
71

x_2 : Odd

Mean	Std. Dev.	Std. Error	Variance	Coef. Var.	Count
.762	9.7	.363	94.089	1272.624	714

Minimum	Maximum	Range	Sum	Sum of Sqr.	# Missing
–129.12	41.28	170.4	544.21	67499.936	9

# < 10th %	10th %	25th %	50th %	75th %	90th %
71	–5.982	–2.75	1.1	4.81	9.131

> 90th %
71

Table 4–14

x_1 : S&P 500 Price 1 + 2 Odd

Mean	Std. Dev.	Std. Error	Variance	Coef. Var.	Count
430.007	102.597	5.422	10526.19	23.859	358

Minimum	Maximum	Range	Sum	Sum of Sqr.	# Missing
284.55	675.33	390.78	153942.6	6.995E7	0

# < 10th %	10th %	25th %	50th %	75th %	90th %
36	317.201	336.42	393.165	508.93	577.078

> 90th %
36

x_2 : Even

Mean	Std. Dev.	Std. Error	Variance	Coef. Var.	Count
492.311	102.61	5.423	10528.735	23.901	358

Minimum	Maximum	Range	Sum	Sum of Sqr.	# Missing
281.74	678.76	397.02	153693.5	6.974E7	0

# < 10th %	10th %	25th %	50th %	75th %	90th %
36	317.751	336.04	389.84	506.33	580.153

> 90th %
36

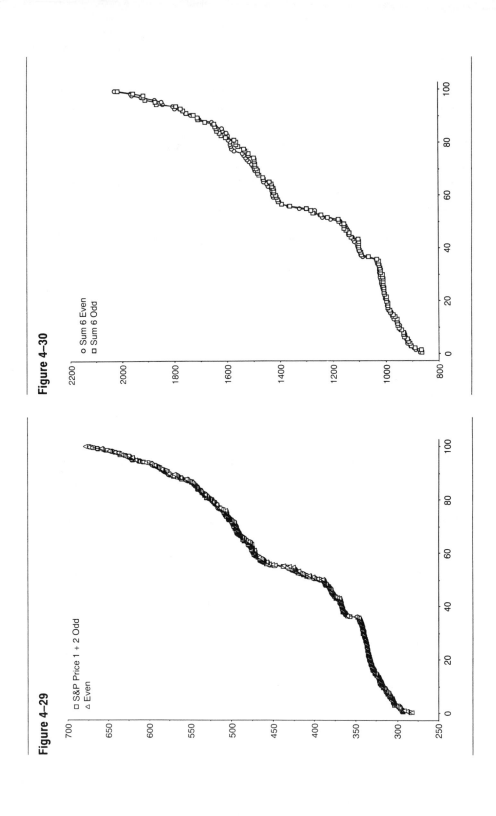

Figure 4–29

□ S&P Price 1 + 2 Odd
△ Even

Figure 4–30

○ Sum 6 Even
□ Sum 6 Odd

Table 4–15

x_1 : 3 – Price 1+2+3+4+5+6 Odd

Mean	Std. Dev.	Std. Error	Variance	Coef. Var.	Count
1290.302	308.127	28.246	94942.456	23.88	119

Minimum	Maximum	Range	Sum	Sum of Sqr.	# Missing
873.47	2026.98	1153.51	153545.92	2.093E8	955

# < 10th %	10th %	25th %	50th %	75th %	90th %
12	949.438	1013.297	1172.9	1532.115	1724.608

> 90th %
12

x_2 : Second Half Even

Mean	Std. Dev.	Std. Error	Variance	Coef. Var.	Count
1285.01	307.916	28.227	94812.366	23.962	119

Minimum	Maximum	Range	Sum	Sum of Sqr.	# Missing
865.78	2014.57	1148.79	152916.24	2.077E8	955

# < 10th %	10th %	25th %	50th %	75th %	90th %
12	954.488	1008.475	1176	1511.943	1718.146

> 90th %
12

white and blue balls in our small ball-filled urn. However, as demonstrated in Chapter 3, there are often significant divergences from independence in our prices or *price changes*. Therefore, and **this is an important point**, these prices or *price changes* do not behave in the same manner as the small balls in our ball-filled urn. The current price or *price change* has been impacted by a number of previous prices or *price changes* that have occurred (the precise number depends on the size of the *temporal window* that we detected when we found divergences from independence). The current price or *price change* will also have an impact on future prices or *price changes*.

Therefore, it seems likely that once a particular price or *price change* has been determined, this determination limits the size of the frequency histogram of potential future prices or *price changes*. Within the constraints of this new frequency histogram, the selection of a new price or *price change* is probably determined at random. The types of constraints placed on the frequency histogram of prices by the selection of a specific price is not clear at this point and requires further work.

Serial and Autocorrelation **5**

Background

Do the past history of prices or *price changes* of a stock or commodity contain useful information—information that can be used to develop a profitable trading strategy? Most statisticians and probability theorists would agree that if the prices or *price changes* are independent, that is, if the price at time t_i has no impact on the price at time t_{i+n}, then it would be difficult (or impossible) to use the past history of prices to develop a realistic trading strategy. (See Chapter 3.) On the other hand, if prices or *price changes* contain serial dependencies, then the past history of prices or *price changes* can potentially be used to develop a reasoned and profitable trading strategy. Two of the classical methods for detecting serial dependencies are serial and autocorrelation. These two classical methods are relatively powerful, but they can each show only one relatively specialized form of serial dependencies. If some other form of dependency is present, these techniques might and probably would miss it completely. Furthermore, there are some potentially serious technical problems associated with using certain forms of autocorrelation on price or *price change* data, as described in this chapter.

Basic Technique—Serial Correlation

The data from Chapter 2, Table 2-1 will be used to construct a lag-1 serial correlogram; that is, we will determine the correlation between a price and the next succeeding price. We will need a histogram with 15 cells on the horizontal axis and 15 on the vertical axis. The first pair of prices are 9,10, so we move up the vertical axis until we reach the 9th cell and then move along the horizontal axis at this level until we reach the 10th cell, and we increase the count in "cell-9,10" from 0 to 1. For the purposes of illustration, this is represented by the small "1" in Figure 5-1. The next pair of prices is 10,4, so we move up the vertical axis until we reach the 10th cell and then move along the horizontal axis at this level until we reach the 4th cell, and we increase the count in this "cell-10,4" from 0 to 1 (represented by the small 2 in Figure 5-1).

The next pair of prices are 4,15, so we move up the vertical axis until we reach the 4th cell and across to the 15th cell and increase the count in "cell 4,15" from 0 to 1, which is represented by the small 3 in Figure 5-1. We continue this process with each pair of prices until we reach the last pair. The completed histogram should resemble the one shown in Figure 5-2. The lag-2 histogram should be constructed in the same manner, but in this case, we would use the first price and the third price, the second and fourth, the third and fifth, etc. A lag-3 histogram would compare the first and fourth, the second and fifth, the third and sixth prices, etc.

We can then visually examine each serial correlogram and/or calculate a serial correlation coefficient. The formula used to calculate the serial correlation coefficient is as follows:

$$r = \frac{\Sigma(x - \bar{x})(y - \bar{y})}{\Sigma(x - \bar{x})^2 \, \Sigma(y - \bar{y})^2}$$

The serial correlation coefficient can vary from +1 to 0 to -1. A perfect positive correlation (+1) means that when the first price in a pair was high the second was also high, or when the first price was low the second was also low. A perfect negative correlation (-1) means that when the first price was high the second was low, or when the first price was low the second was high. Perfect correlation rarely, if ever, occurs in real life. Therefore, it is important to have some method for determining if the serial correlation coefficient obtained is significantly different from 0. Some authors recommend the formula below:

$$t = \frac{r}{(1 - r^2)} \sqrt{n - 2}$$

where r is the serial correlation coefficient as determined above and n is the number of prices in the time series.

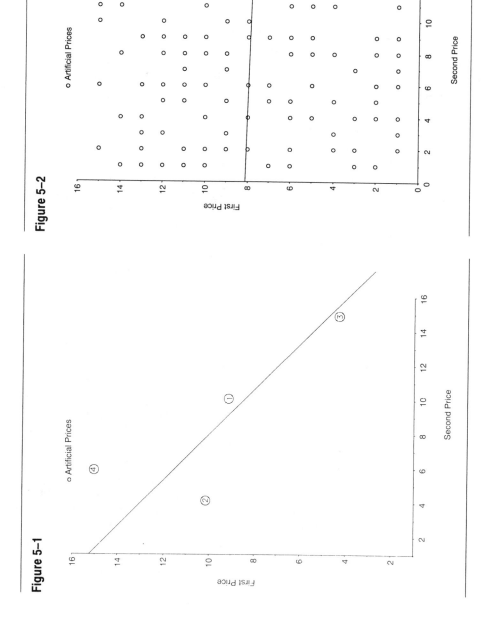

Figure 5-1

Figure 5-2

If it is less than 1.96, the serial correlation coefficient is not significantly different from 0. If larger than 1.96, it is significantly different.

Serial Correlogram—Real Data

The closing prices of Sears stock for 1988 are shown in Table 5-1 and in Figure 5-3. The serial correlogram and the serial correlation coefficient for the closing prices for Sears for 1988 for the lag-1 serial correlogram are shown in Figure 5-4. The correlograms and correlation coefficients for the lag-2, lag-5, lag-10, lag-15, and lag-20 correlograms are shown in Figures 5-5 through 5-9, respectively. In these figures, note that the correlation coefficients for lag-1 and lag-2 are relatively high, but that the correlation coefficients drop rapidly as we increase the lag.

This same pattern of decreasing correlation coefficients with increasing lag values is also seen in the lag-1, lag-2, lag-3, lag-4, lag-5, lag-10, lag-20, lag-30, lag-40, and lag-50 correlograms for the average monthly prices for the Standard and Poor's 500 Stock Index for 1947 to 1987, as shown in Figures 5-10 through 5-19, respectively. The size of the correlation coefficient drops somewhat more slowly with increasing lag than the Sears stock. This is probably due to the fact that the Standard & Poor's Index is an index number rather than an actual series of prices.

Basic Technique—Autocorrelation

There are at least three ways to construct an autocorrelogram. Theoretically, each method should disclose some aspect of *sequentialness*, *periodicity*, and/or *rhythmicity* that is present in a sequential list of prices or *price changes* that might be hidden or masked by background *noise*, such as random fluctuations or short- or long-term trends. The first two methods described are based on the assumption that the prices or *price changes* are generated by a *discrete* process. That means that the price *jumps* from one price to another in units of fixed size, such as units of a penny or a dime. In this latter case, for example, a price could be $2.00 or $2.10, but not $2.085, etc. The third method is based on the assumption that the prices are generated by a *continuous* process. In this case, the prices do not *jump* from one price to another. For example, the price might be $2.00, then $2.01, then $2.012, then $2.014. Unfortunately, there are some problems with using autocorrelation on this sort of data, especially the first two *discrete* methods. These problems are relatively subtle and difficult to see

Table 5–1

	Sears 1988		Sears 1988		Sears 1988		Sears 1988
1	35.03	33	36.00	65	35.07	97	33.07
2	34.07	34	37.00	66	37.01	98	33.04
3	35.01	35	36.07	67	37.00	99	33.07
4	35.00	36	36.00	68	36.06	100	34.01
5	32.02	37	36.02	69	36.04	101	34.02
6	33.05	38	35.07	70	36.04	102	34.04
7	33.04	39	36.01	71	36.03	103	33.04
8	33.05	40	37.06	72	34.00	104	34.06
9	33.04	41	38.02	73	34.07	105	35.04
10	34.03	42	39.06	74	34.03	106	35.01
11	34.04	43	38.06	75	34.06	107	35.05
12	34.00	44	38.04	76	34.06	108	35.05
13	33.05	45	38.03	77	35.00	109	35.04
14	33.03	46	38.07	78	35.04	110	36.01
15	33.04	47	38.06	79	36.00	111	35.04
16	34.04	48	38.01	80	36.01	112	35.05
17	33.07	49	37.07	81	36.02	113	35.06
18	33.07	50	38.00	82	35.07	114	36.00
19	33.03	51	37.06	83	35.07	115	36.05
20	34.01	52	37.07	84	36.01	116	35.04
21	34.04	53	38.01	85	36.01	117	36.01
22	34.05	54	38.01	86	35.06	118	36.03
23	34.04	55	38.02	87	35.02	119	36.06
24	34.04	56	38.06	88	35.00	120	37.03
25	34.02	57	38.01	89	34.06	121	37.02
26	34.01	58	37.02	90	35.04	122	37.02
27	34.05	59	36.00	91	34.06	123	36.03
28	35.03	60	35.07	92	34.07	124	36.05
29	35.04	61	36.02	93	34.05	125	36.04
30	35.05	62	35.05	94	34.06	126	36.07
31	36.00	63	35.06	95	34.02	127	36.05
32	36.05	64	35.03	96	33.04	128	37.01

Table continues

Table 5–1   Continued

	Sears 1988		Sears 1988		Sears 1988		Sears 1988
129	36.03	161	35.07	193	39.16	225	40.00
130	36.03	162	35.01	194	39.04	226	39.07
131	36.03	163	35.00	195	40.04	227	39.07
132	36.07	164	35.02	196	40.03	228	40.00
133	36.03	165	35.01	197	40.00	229	39.04
134	36.03	166	35.02	198	40.02	230	39.07
135	36.02	167	35.04	199	42.03	231	39.07
136	36.06	168	35.05	200	41.00	232	39.07
137	36.06	169	35.04	201	40.01	233	39.04
138	36.02	170	35.00	202	40.02	234	39.02
139	36.02	171	35.06	203	40.00	235	39.04
140	35.07	172	36.04	204	40.03	236	40.02
141	35.07	173	36.01	205	42.05	237	40.04
142	35.07	174	36.00	206	42.05	238	40.02
143	35.05	175	36.06	207	43.06	239	40.03
144	35.01	176	36.06	208	44.06	240	40.02
145	36.00	177	36.02	209	43.02	241	40.06
146	34.06	178	36.05	210	43.05	242	40.02
147	36.04	179	36.04	211	41.06	243	40.01
148	36.05	180	36.06	212	41.06	244	40.01
149	36.03	181	37.00	213	43.00	245	40.05
150	36.01	182	37.00	214	46.00	246	41.00
151	36.02	183	37.03	215	44.05	247	41.06
152	36.03	184	37.03	216	43.06	248	41.04
153	36.02	185	37.06	217	42.01	249	41.06
154	35.05	186	37.06	218	42.03	250	41.04
155	36.00	187	37.06	219	41.06	251	41.00
156	36.00	188	37.03	220	40.06	252	40.06
157	35.04	189	38.02	221	40.07	253	40.07
158	35.04	190	38.01	222	41.05		
159	35.07	191	38.04	223	40.00		
160	36.00	192	37.05	224	40.03		

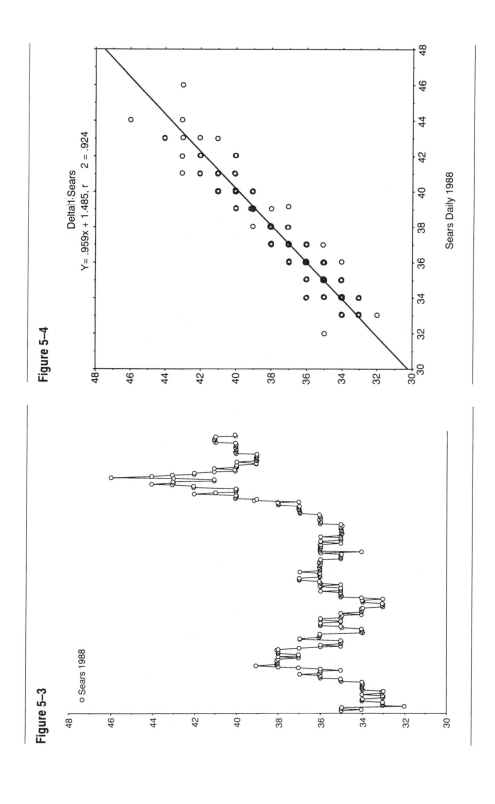

Figure 5-3

Figure 5-4

Delta1:Sears
Y= .959x + 1.485, r   2 = .924

o Sears 1988

Sears Daily 1988

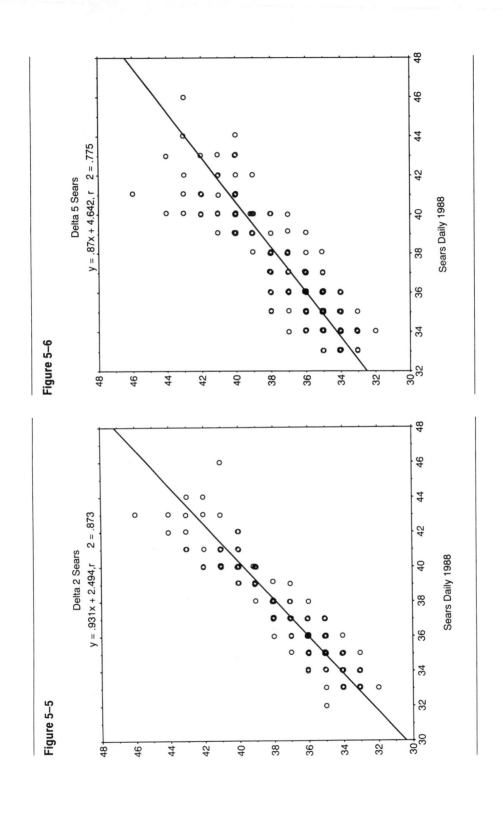

Figure 5-5

Delta 2 Sears

$y = .931x + 2.494$, $r^2 = .873$

Sears Daily 1988

Figure 5-6

Delta 5 Sears

$y = .87x + 4.642$, $r^2 = .775$

Sears Daily 1988

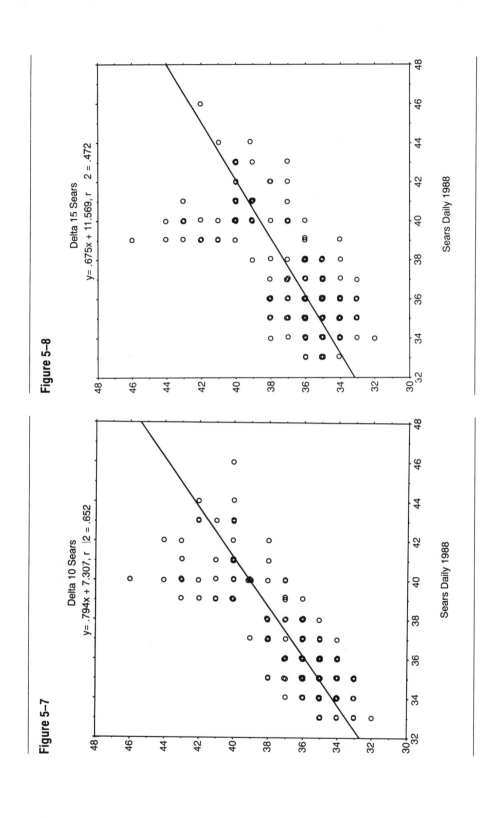

Figure 5-7

Figure 5-8

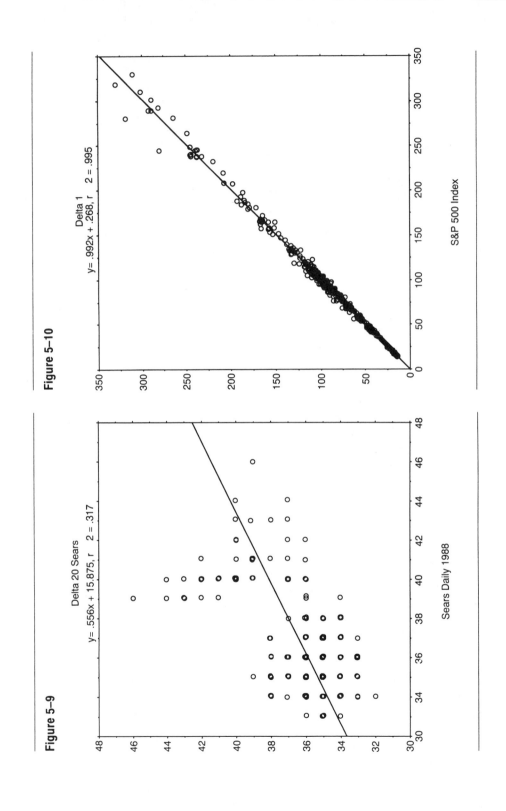

Figure 5–9

Delta 20 Sears
y= .556x + 15.875, r 2 = .317

Sears Daily 1988

Figure 5–10

Delta 1
y= .992x + .268, r 2 = .995

S&P 500 Index

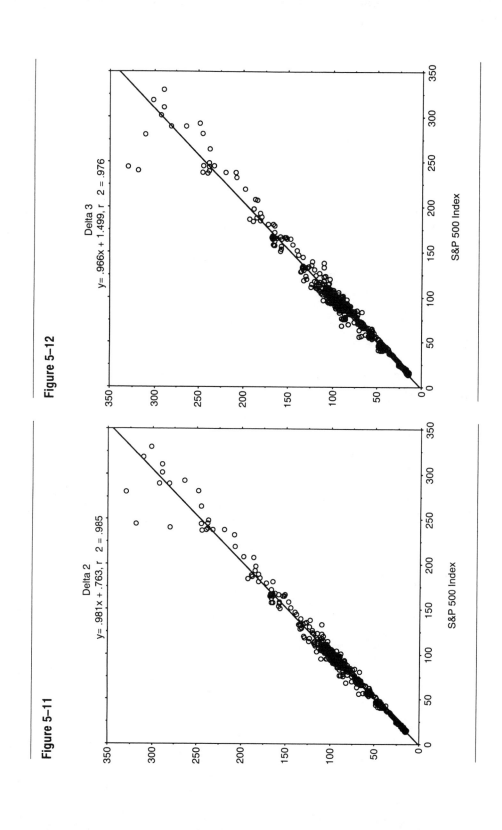

Figure 5-11

Delta 2
y= .981x + .763, r 2 = .985

S&P 500 Index

Figure 5-12

Delta 3
y= .966x + 1.499, r 2 = .976

S&P 500 Index

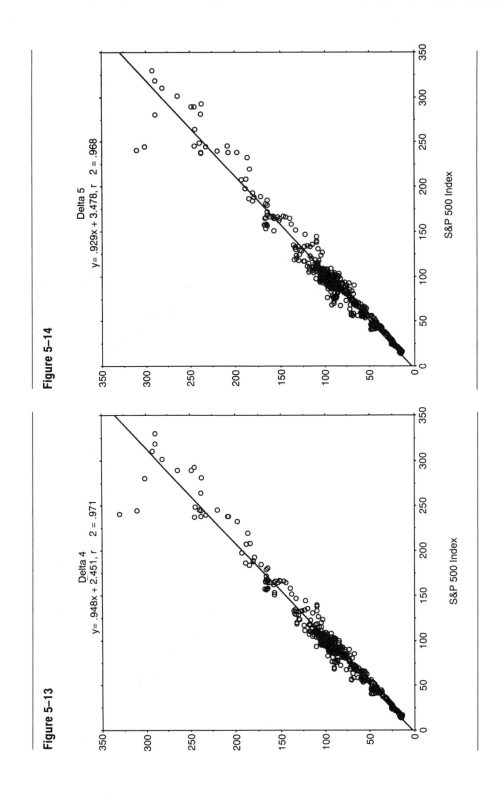

Figure 5–13

Delta 4
y= .948x + 2.451, r 2 =.971

S&P 500 Index

Figure 5–14

Delta 5
y= .929x + 3.478, r 2 = .968

S&P 500 Index

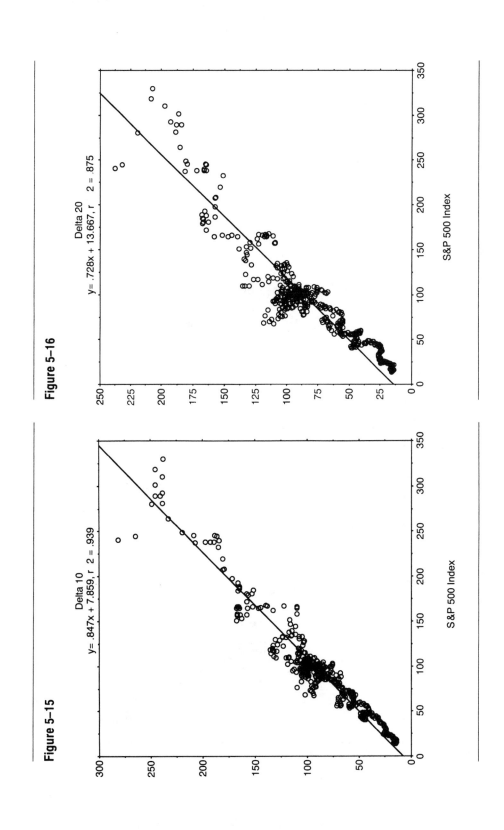

Figure 5–15

Delta 10
y= .847x + 7.859, r 2 = .939

S&P 500 Index

Figure 5–16

Delta 20
y= .728x + 13.667, r 2 = .875

S&P 500 Index

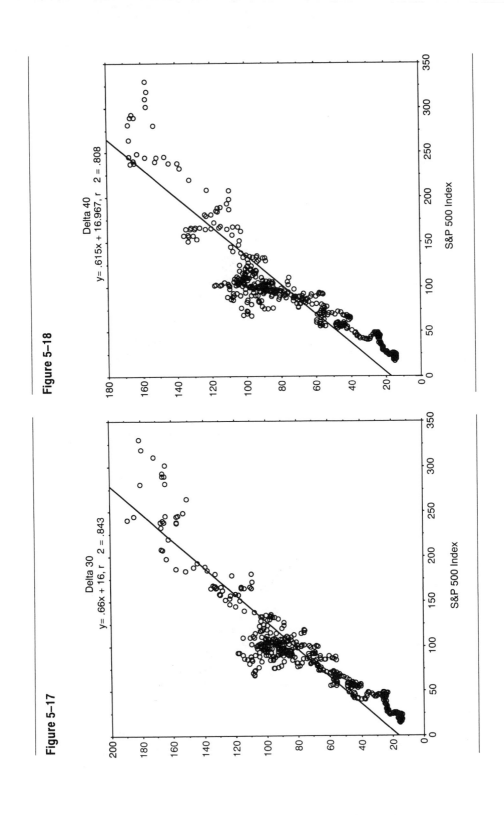

Figure 5-17

Delta 30
y= .66x + 16, r   2 = .843

S&P 500 Index

Figure 5-18

Delta 40
y= .615x + 16.967, r   2 = .808

S&P 500 Index

Figure 5–19

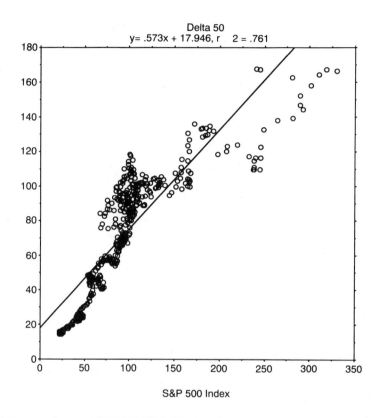

Delta 50
y= .573x + 17.946, r   2 = .761

S&P 500 Index

if we use *real* data, so we will use *idealized* data to show the problems. These data are shown in Table 5-2.

The first of the *discrete* autocorrelograms (autocorrelogram 1) is relatively easy to construct. The first step is to plot the first-order frequency histogram of prices onto a histogram with 30 bins labeled 1 to 30 on the horizontal axis, where the vertical axis would be labeled frequency. The first idealized price in Table 5-2 is 6, so increase the frequency of "bin-6" from 0 to 1. The next price is 10, so increase the frequency of "bin-10" from 0 to 1. We continue this process until we reach the last idealized price, which is 6, so we increase the frequency of "bin 6" from 14 to 15. Note this bin contains 15 counts; that is, price 1, 3, 4, 8, 11, 16, 21, 24, 28, 32, 34, 39, 42, 46, and 50, as shown in Table 5-3 and Figure 5-20.

Table 5–2

	Idealized Data		Idealized Data		Idealized Data		Idealized Data
1	6.0	14	5.0	27	1.0	40	8.0
2	10.0	15	1.0	28	6.0	41	2.0
3	6.0	16	6.0	29	5.0	42	6.0
4	6.0	17	3.0	30	3.0	43	2.0
5	2.0	18	1.0	31	2.0	44	3.0
6	1.0	19	2.0	32	6.0	45	5.0
7	1.0	20	4.0	33	10.0	46	6.0
8	6.0	21	6.0	34	6.0	47	7.0
9	9.0	22	8.0	35	1.0	48	2.0
10	1.0	23	2.0	36	2.0	49	1.0
11	6.0	24	6.0	37	4.0	50	6.0
12	3.0	25	7.0	38	3.0		
13	1.0	26	2.0	39	6.0		

On the same histogram, plot a series of higher-order frequency histograms. For example, for the second-order histogram, we sum sequential pairs of prices (6+10 = 16, 10+6 = 16, 6+6 = 12, 6+2 = 8, 2+1 = 3, etc.). Normally, we would plot these numbers; that is, the sums 16, 16, 12, 8, 3, etc., into the histogram that we just constructed. Since this is rather difficult to illustrate, we will show the higher-order histogram plots separately in Figure 5-21 (upper-left panel). We then construct a third-order histogram by summing three adjacent prices (6+10+6 = 22, 10+6+6 = 22, 6+6+2 = 14, 6+2+1 = 9, etc.) and plot the "sums" into the same histogram (see Figure 5-21, middle-left panel). Continue this process of constructing higher-order histograms and plotting the resulting "sums" into the same histogram. The plots for the 3rd- to 6th-order histogram are also shown in Figure 5-21. These histograms and the first-order histogram shown in Figure 5-20 are replotted into the same histogram and the resulting autocorrelogram should resemble the histogram shown in Figure 5-22.

The second discrete autocorrelogram (autocorrelogram 2) is a bit more difficult to construct. In this case, plot the prices on a line, as shown in Figure 5-23, where the space between the tick marks on the line is

Table 5-3

	1	2	3	4	5	6	7	8	9	10	11	12	13	14	15	16
1	6	5	12	20	14	1	25	22	9	2	•	•	•	•	•	•
2	7	19	17	37	29	3	47	40	•	33	•	•	•	•	•	•
3	10	23	30	•	45	4	•	•	•	•	•	•	•	•	•	•
4	13	26	38	•	•	8	•	•	•	•	•	•	•	•	•	•
5	15	31	44	•	•	11	•	•	•	•	•	•	•	•	•	•
6	18	36	•	•	•	16	•	•	•	•	•	•	•	•	•	•
7	27	41	•	•	•	21	•	•	•	•	•	•	•	•	•	•
8	35	43	•	•	•	24	•	•	•	•	•	•	•	•	•	•
9	49	48	•	•	•	28	•	•	•	•	•	•	•	•	•	•
10	•	•	•	•	•	32	•	•	•	•	•	•	•	•	•	•
11	•	•	•	•	•	34	•	•	•	•	•	•	•	•	•	•
12	•	•	•	•	•	39	•	•	•	•	•	•	•	•	•	•
13	•	•	•	•	•	42	•	•	•	•	•	•	•	•	•	•
14	•	•	•	•	•	46	•	•	•	•	•	•	•	•	•	•
15	•	•	•	•	•	50	•	•	•	•	•	•	•	•	•	•

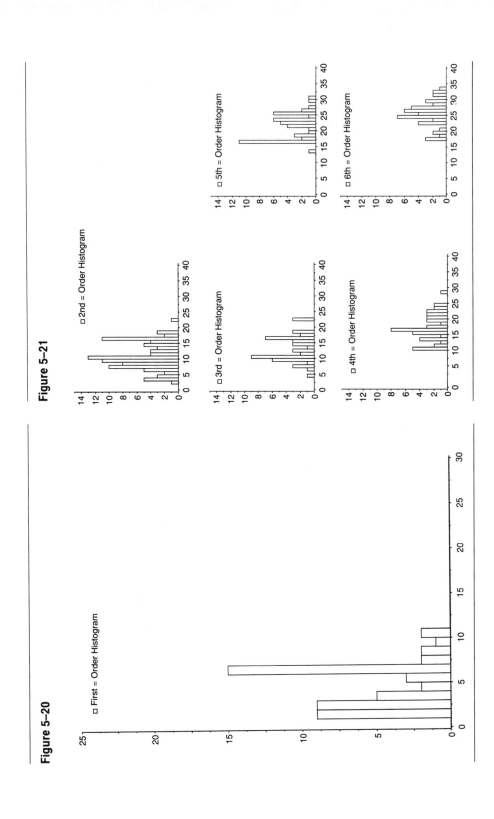

Figure 5–20

Figure 5–21

Figure 5–22

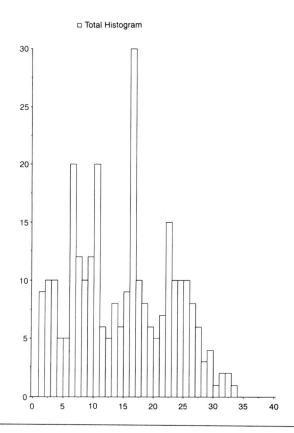

□ Total Histogram

proportional to the price. Then construct a histogram, with a series of bins 1, 2, 3, 4, 5, ..., n on the horizontal axis. Now, line up the origin of the "price line" (the left-most tick mark) we have just constructed with the left-most bin of the histogram and increase the frequency of each bin that is over a hatch mark in our price line, as shown in Figure 5-23.

For example, the first hatch mark falls below "bin-6," so increase the frequency in "bin-6" from 0 to 1 (indicated by the small circle in the bin). The next nine hatch marks occur under bins 16, 22, 28, 30, 31, 32, 38, 47, etc., so increase the frequency in each of these bins from 0 to 1, indicated by the small circles. Continue this until you reach the last price. Then, move the entire price line to the left one "price," thus eliminating price 6, and increase the frequency of any bin above a hatch mark on our price

Figure 5–23

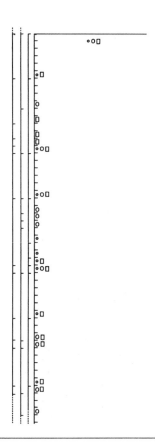

line. The first 10 hatch marks occur under bins 10, 16, 22, 24, 25, 26, 32, 41, 42, 48, and 51. So, we would increase the frequency in bins 10, 24, 25, 26, 41, 42, 48, and 51 from 0 to 1 and bins 16, 22, and 32 from 1 to 2, all indicated by the small oval in these bins. We would continue this process of moving the price line to the left by one price and entering the prices into the histogram until we reach the last price on the price line. The first three passes through our idealized data are shown in Figure 5-23.

The third method for generating an autocorrelogram (the one based on the assumption that the prices were generated by a "continuous" process) is a bit tedious to do by hand. We would normally use a computer, but to be sure that we understand the process, we will generate the first 10 points in this autocorrelogram using paper and pencil. The first 50 artifi-

Table 5–4

	Artificial	Lag-0	Lag-3			Artificial	Lag-0	Lag-3
1	9.000	81.000	•		26	14.000	196.000	14.000
2	10.000	100.000	•		27	1.000	1.000	4.000
3	4.000	16.000	36.000		28	15.000	225.000	210.000
4	15.000	225.000	150.000		29	6.000	36.000	6.000
5	6.000	36.000	24.000		30	11.000	121.000	165.000
6	4.000	16.000	60.000		31	12.000	144.000	72.000
7	3.000	9.000	18.000		32	8.000	64.000	88.000
8	13.000	169.000	52.000		33	14.000	196.000	168.000
9	12.000	144.000	36.000		34	11.000	121.000	88.000
10	1.000	1.000	13.000		35	2.000	4.000	28.000
11	3.000	9.000	36.000		36	15.000	225.000	165.000
12	4.000	16.000	4.000		37	11.000	121.000	22.000
13	15.000	225.000	45.000		38	8.000	64.000	120.000
14	13.000	169.000	52.000		39	4.000	16.000	44.000
15	1.000	1.000	15.000		40	8.000	64.000	64.000
16	4.000	16.000	52.000		41	15.000	225.000	60.000
17	8.000	64.000	8.000		42	14.000	196.000	112.000
18	13.000	169.000	52.000		43	12.000	144.000	180.000
19	4.000	16.000	32.000		44	5.000	25.000	70.000
20	2.000	4.000	26.000		45	12.000	144.000	144.000
21	12.000	144.000	48.000		46	10.000	100.000	50.000
22	9.000	81.000	18.000		47	9.000	81.000	108.000
23	12.000	144.000	144.000		48	15.000	225.000	150.000
24	1.000	1.000	9.000		49	12.000	144.000	108.000
25	4.000	16.000	48.000		50	13.000	169.000	195.000

cial prices from Chapter 2, Table 2-1 are shown in Table 5-4. The first step is to plot these prices in the usual manner, as shown in Figure 5-24 with circles. We will call this plot "a." Make an exact copy of this plot on tracing paper and call this copy plot "b." Now line up the two plots and multiply each price by itself, as shown in column 2 of Table 5-4, and then sum the results. So, the first point of the autocorrelogram would be the sum of 81 (9 x 9), 100 (10 x 10), ... , which yields 16361, the first point in the

Figure 5–24

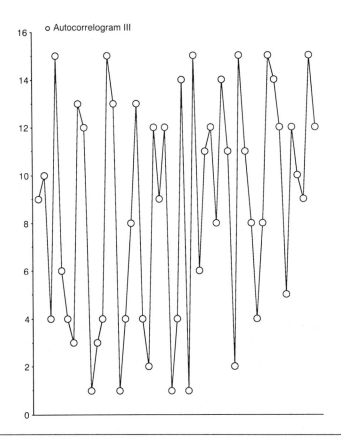

autocorrelogram (note that we used all of the prices in Chapter 2, Table 2-1 to make the calculations, rather than just the first 50 shown in Table 5-4). Then, move plot "b" one price to the right, so that the first 9 on plot "b" lines up with first 10 on plot "a" and multiply each of the prices in plot "a" by the price next to it in plot "b." Next, move plot "b" one more price to the right, so that the first 9 in plot "b" lines up with the 4 in plot "a," as shown in Figure 5-25, with "x"s. Multiply these values together (9 x 4 = 36; 10 x 15 = 150; etc.) and sum the results, which yields 12245. We continue this process of moving plot "b" one price to the right and multiplying the pairs of prices together and then summing. The first 10 points in the autocorrelogram are shown in Figure 5-26.

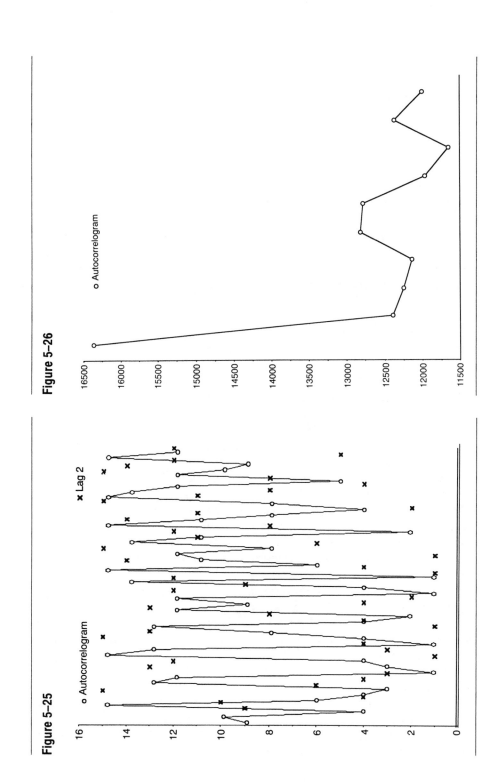

Figure 5-25

Figure 5-26

What Does it All Mean?

Serial Correlation

The decrease in the size of the correlation coefficient with increasing lag is not unique to Sears or the Standard & Poor's Index. It is a common finding with most stocks and other investment media. In fact, this finding is frequently used to argue that studying the past history of prices does not provide useful information. It is also used to argue that the prices of a stock or other investment media represent a random walk; that is, the prices are random and independent. There are several problems with this argument. First and most important, serial correlation provides a measure of only one, relatively restrictive type of dependency. As indicated in other chapters in this book, there are other measures of dependency (see Chapters 3 or 8) and these measures do suggest that there are significant serial dependencies in price or *price change* data. Second, there are some significant problems with using serial correlation on price data. For instance, if the prices contain a mixture of high, high and low, low, with high, low and low, high prices, the correlation coefficient will tend toward 0. This tendency will also occur if there is too much *jitter*.

For example, let us say that there are ten "10"s in a model time series (prices, *price changes*). Further, let us say that the following pattern of prices occur at some specific lag: 10,15 10,15 10,15 10,8 10,9 10,9 10,11 10,11 10,12 10,13. Clearly, at this lag, the high price is followed by a high price. But this *jitter* in the prices (the second price varied from 8 to 15) would tend to decrease the size of the correlation coefficient and thus our ability to detect this pattern of a high price followed by a high price. The more of this *jitter* that is present, the lower the correlation coefficient will be. Second, a trend in the prices will tend to distort the correlogram and decrease the size of the correlation coefficient. The effect of a trend can be minimized by detrending the data.

Another major disadvantage is that you need to make multiple passes through your data and each pass allows you to collect one serial correlogram and one serial correlation coefficient. With each pass, you generate a relatively large matrix. For example, the Standard & Poor's serial correlograms (Figures 5-8 through 5-13) each contain 122,500 cells (350 x 350). If the range (the difference between the largest and smallest price) of prices was larger, you would need even more cells. In any case, the vast majority of these cells contain counts of "0" or "1." However, you could increase the size of the cells. For example, the cells in Figure 5-8 each represent 1 dollar. You could increase the size of each cell to 5 dollars, so the first cell would collect prices from 1 to 5 dollars, the second, 6 to 10, etc. In this case, in Figure 5-8, you would have 4,900 cells (70 x 70). Unfortunately, this would tend to decrease the sensitivity of the technique.

Further, these correlograms and correlation coefficients provide information about the sequential relationships between just two prices. For example, in the lag-1 correlogram, it indicates the relationship between price 1 and price 2, price 2 and price 3, price 3 and price 4, etc. If you wanted to determine the sequential relationship between three prices, you would need a three-dimensional matrix with over 42 million cells (350 x 350 x 350). Matrices of this size would probably exceed the memory capacity available on a small computer.

Once you have done these manipulations, whether you do a two-dimensional matrix to see the relationships between two prices or a three-dimensional matrix to see the sequential relationship between three prices, you are still confronted with a large matrix in which the majority of the cells contain either a 0 or a 1. Therefore, it would be relatively difficult to see how the pattern of serial dependencies developed. If you cannot see this pattern, it is difficult to see how this information can be used to develop a workable trading strategy.

Autocorrelation

There are some significant problems in interpreting what the discrete autocorrelograms mean. First, and potentially most important, the individual peaks in the autocorrelogram and the interrelationship between the peaks are partly due to an artifact called the *partitioning effect*. For example, a peak of 10 can be summed from 2^{10-1} or 512 different prices: (10), (9,1), (1,9), (8,2),..,(6,3,1),....,(6,2,1,1), (2,1,1,6), ..., (5,2,1,1,1), ..., (1,1,1,1,1,1,1,1,1,1). If you examine Figure 5-22, "bin-10," you will note that six 10's occurred, but this bin also contains counts based on *sums* of three individual prices (1,6,3; 6,3,1; 1,6,3; 6,3,1; 7,2,1; 5,3,2; 2,6,2; 2,3,5; and 7,2,1), as well as the *sums* of four individual prices (6,2,1,1; 2,1,1,6; 3,1,5,1; 3,1,2,4; and 1,2,4,3). Second, the sequentialness, periodicity, or rhythmicity of the prices are not indicated by the height of the individual *peaks* in the autocorrelogram (number of counts in the individual cells) or by the interrelationships of the peaks in the autocorrelogram. Third, there is no generally accepted method for generating an autocorrelogram correlation coefficient, a statistical method for comparing autocorrelograms, or for determining if an autocorrelogram represents a *real* relationship. Finally, the two discrete methods for generating the autocorrelograms are probably not analogous.

It is generally agreed that the *continuous* autocorrelogram works with continuous data. But it is not clear if the prices or *price changes* of most stocks and commodities actually are continuous. If they *jump* from state to state by some fixed value, such as pennies, dimes, dollars, etc., then they are clearly not continuous. We tend to analyze daily closing prices (or daily high or low prices, etc.) or weekly averages, weekly highs or lows, etc., and it is unlikely that the prices or *price changes* are continuous in this time frame.

Unfortunately, it is not clear just how *robust* the autocorrelogram function is, if one of its basic assumptions are violated. If it is relatively sensitive to *violations* of this sort, then the autocorrelograms generated from noncontinuous or discrete data may be suspect. If this is the case, then functions that are generated from the autocorrelogram are also potentially suspect. This would include Fourier transforms and the power spectras.

Even if the autocorrelogram function is relatively robust with respect to these types of violations, it is still relatively difficult to know how to evaluate a specific autocorrelogram. There is no generally accepted method for calculating an autocorrelogram correlation coefficient, comparing autocorrelograms, or determining if a specific autocorrelogram is significantly different from 0.

Runs/Persistence

6

Background

If you examine a plot of the prices (opening, closing, high, low, etc.) of a stock or commodity, such as the one shown in Figure 6-1 (the closing prices of Security Pacific Corporation), you will note that the price tends to increase for one or more days, then decrease for one or more days. Even when there is a general trend upward or downward, prices tend to oscillate upward and downward around the trend. Do these short-term changes in price occur by chance alone or is there some deterministic process at work?

Statisticians have provided some simple, but relatively powerful techniques for determining if the number of *clusters*, such as a short series of price increases and decreases, occurs by chance or not. Statisticians call these clusters *runs*. Unfortunately, while most statisticians agree that the tests that are about to be described are very useful, they cannot seem to agree if they are tests of randomness and divergence from it or independence and divergence from it. As shown in Chapters 3 and 4 of this book, these terms and the concepts that they represent cannot be used interchangeably. Randomness and independence represent very different characteristics of a time series. The majority of statisticians seem to believe that *runs* tests are tests of divergence from randomness.

Figure 6–1

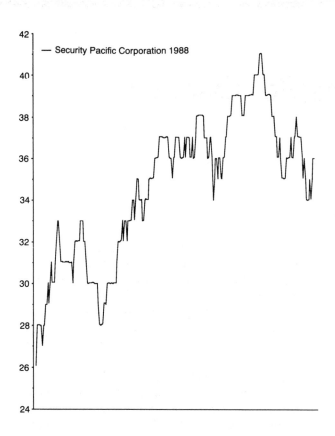

Basic Technique

If you examine Table 6-1 (artificial prices from Chapter 2, Table 2-1), you will find a sequential list of *price changes* (column 2). We will examine each *price change* in this column and determine if it represents a price increase (a positive value) which we will encode as a "2" or a price decrease (a negative value) which we will encode as a "1." The first 15 *price changes* from this table are shown below with their coded values:

Table 6–1

	Artificial Data	Artificial Delta-1	Increase/ Decrease	Median
1	9.000	•	•	2
2	10.000	1.000	2	2
3	4.000	−6.000	1	1
4	15.000	11.000	2	2
5	6.000	−9.000	1	1
6	4.000	−2.000	1	1
7	3.000	−1.000	1	1
8	13.000	10.000	2	2
9	12.000	−1.000	1	2
10	1.000	−11.000	1	1
11	3.000	2.000	2	1
12	4.000	1.000	2	1
13	15.000	11.000	2	2
14	13.000	−2.000	1	2
15	1.000	−12.000	1	1
16	4.000	3.000	2	1
17	8.000	4.000	2	1
18	13.000	5.000	2	2
19	4.000	−9.000	1	1
20	2.000	−2.000	1	1
21	12.000	10.000	2	2
22	9.000	−3.000	1	2
23	12.000	3.000	2	2
24	1.000	−11.000	1	1
25	4.000	3.000	2	1
26	14.000	10.000	2	2
27	1.000	−13.000	1	1
28	15.000	14.000	2	2
29	6.000	−9.000	1	1
30	11.000	5.000	2	2
31	12.000	1.000	2	2
32	8.000	−4.000	1	1
33	14.000	6.000	2	2
34	11.000	−3.000	1	2

Table continues

Table 6–1   Continued

	Artificial Data	Artificial Delta-1	Increase/ Decrease	Median
35	2.000	−9.000	1	1
36	15.000	13.000	2	2
37	11.000	−4.000	1	2
38	8.000	−3.000	1	1
39	4.000	−4.000	1	1
40	8.000	4.000	2	1
41	15.000	7.000	2	2
42	14.000	−1.000	1	2
43	12.000	−2.000	1	2
44	5.000	−7.000	1	1
45	12.000	7.000	2	2
46	10.000	−2.000	1	2
47	9.000	−1.000	1	2
48	15.000	6.000	2	2
49	12.000	−3.000	1	2
50	13.000	1.000	2	2
51	2.000	−11.000	1	1
52	6.000	4.000	2	1
53	13.000	7.000	2	2
54	9.000	−4.000	1	2
55	5.000	−4.000	1	1
56	15.000	10.000	2	2
57	11.000	−4.000	1	2
58	14.000	3.000	2	2
59	11.000	−3.000	1	2
60	1.000	−10.000	1	1
61	7.000	6.000	2	1
62	5.000	−2.000	1	1
63	6.000	1.000	2	1
64	14.000	8.000	2	2
65	8.000	−6.000	1	1
66	2.000	−6.000	1	1
67	4.000	2.000	2	1
68	5.000	1.000	2	1

Table continues

Table 6–1   Continued

	Artificial Data	Artificial Delta-1	Increase/ Decrease	Median
69	8.000	3.000	2	1
70	13.000	5.000	2	2
71	2.000	−11.000	1	1
72	1.000	−1.000	1	1
73	8.000	7.000	2	1
74	12.000	4.000	2	2
75	6.000	−6.000	1	1
76	9.000	3.000	2	2
77	15.000	6.000	2	2
78	10.000	−5.000	1	2
79	8.000	−2.000	1	1
80	9.000	1.000	2	2
81	3.000	−6.000	1	1
82	2.000	−1.000	1	1
83	9.000	7.000	2	2
84	10.000	1.000	2	2
85	15.000	5.000	2	2
86	10.000	−5.000	1	2
87	6.000	−4.000	1	1
88	11.000	5.000	2	2
89	2.000	−9.000	1	1
90	1.000	−1.000	1	1
91	12.000	11.000	2	2
92	9.000	−3.000	1	2
93	12.000	3.000	2	2
94	1.000	−11.000	1	1
95	8.000	7.000	2	1
96	15.000	7.000	2	2
97	2.000	−13.000	1	1
98	8.000	6.000	2	1
99	9.000	1.000	2	2
100	15.000	6.000	2	2
101	14.000	−1.000	1	2
102	12.000	−2.000	1	2

Table continues

Table 6-1   Continued

	Artificial Data	Artificial Delta-1	Increase/ Decrease	Median
103	8.000	−4.000	1	1
104	10.000	2.000	2	2
105	2.000	−8.000	1	1
106	13.000	11.000	2	2
107	1.000	−12.000	1	1
108	6.000	5.000	2	1
109	2.000	−4.000	1	1
110	9.000	7.000	2	2
111	3.000	−6.000	1	1
112	7.000	4.000	2	1
113	1.000	−6.000	1	1
114	4.000	3.000	2	1
115	14.000	10.000	2	2
116	8.000	−6.000	1	1
117	9.000	1.000	2	2
118	2.000	−7.000	1	1
119	8.000	6.000	2	1
120	12.000	4.000	2	2
121	10.000	−2.000	1	2
122	1.000	−9.000	1	1
123	11.000	10.000	2	2
124	14.000	3.000	2	2
125	12.000	−2.000	1	2
126	1.000	−11.000	1	1
127	14.000	13.000	2	2
128	4.000	−10.000	1	1
129	11.000	7.000	2	2
130	2.000	−9.000	1	1
131	9.000	7.000	2	2
132	8.000	−1.000	1	1
133	13.000	5.000	2	2
134	9.000	−4.000	1	2
135	5.000	−4.000	1	1
136	11.000	6.000	2	2

Table continues

Table 6-1   Continued

	Artificial Data	Artificial Delta-1	Increase/ Decrease	Median
137	12.000	1.000	2	2
138	6.000	−6.000	1	1
139	9.000	3.000	2	2
140	5.000	−4.000	1	1
141	11.000	6.000	2	2
142	9.000	−2.000	1	2
143	3.000	−6.000	1	1
144	4.000	1.000	2	1
145	12.000	8.000	2	2
146	13.000	1.000	2	2
147	6.000	−7.000	1	1
148	5.000	−1.000	1	1
149	15.000	10.000	2	2
150	2.000	−13.000	1	1
151	14.000	12.000	2	2
152	1.000	−13.000	1	1
153	6.000	5.000	2	1
154	5.000	−1.000	1	1
155	11.000	6.000	2	2
156	5.000	−6.000	1	1
157	4.000	−1.000	1	1
158	8.000	4.000	2	1
159	6.000	−2.000	1	1
160	2.000	−4.000	1	1
161	5.000	3.000	2	1
162	9.000	4.000	2	2
163	3.000	−6.000	1	1
164	1.000	−2.000	1	1
165	11.000	10.000	2	2
166	6.000	−5.000	1	1
167	11.000	5.000	2	2
168	7.000	−4.000	1	1
169	9.000	2.000	2	2
170	3.000	−6.000	1	1

Table continues

Table 6-1   Continued

	Artificial Data	Artificial Delta-1	Increase/ Decrease	Median
171	15.000	12.000	2	2
172	10.000	−5.000	1	2
173	12.000	2.000	2	2
174	3.000	−9.000	1	1
175	7.000	4.000	2	1
176	6.000	−1.000	1	1
177	13.000	7.000	2	2
178	3.000	−10.000	1	1
179	1.000	−2.000	1	1
180	6.000	5.000	2	1
181	1.000	−5.000	1	1
182	9.000	8.000	2	2
183	7.000	−2.000	1	1
184	1.000	−6.000	1	1
185	6.000	5.000	2	1
186	5.000	−1.000	1	1
187	8.000	3.000	2	1
188	12.000	4.000	2	2
189	5.000	−7.000	1	1
190	6.000	1.000	2	1
191	8.000	2.000	2	1
192	10.000	2.000	2	2
193	14.000	4.000	2	2
194	13.000	−1.000	1	2
195	15.000	2.000	2	2
196	10.000	−5.000	1	2
197	11.000	1.000	2	2
198	1.000	−10.000	1	1
199	2.000	1.000	2	1
200	6.000	4.000	2	1
201	•	•	•	•

Price Change	1	–6	11	–9	–2	–1	10	–1	–11	2	1	11	–2	–12	3
Coded Value	2	1	2	1	1	1	2	1	1	2	2	2	1	1	2

We continue the encoding process until we have encoded all of the *price changes*. Our final result should resemble Table 6-1, column 3. Now, we need to determine the number of *runs* in our coded data. A *run* is simply one or more sequential "1"s or "2"s. We will repeat the first 15 coded values from Table 6-1 below and indicate the sequential *runs* by alternate **bold** and regular type:

$$2\,1\,\mathbf{2}\,1\,1\,1\,\mathbf{2}\,1\,1\,\mathbf{2\,2\,2}\,1\,1\,\mathbf{2}...$$

The number of sequential *runs* of "1"s and "2"s based on the coded data in Table 6-1 are shown in Table 6-2. Now determine if this number of *runs* could occur by change or not using the formula below:

$$K = \frac{[3R - (2N + 2.5)]}{\sqrt{\dfrac{16N - 29}{10}}}$$

where R is the number of runs (137) and N is the total number of prices in our sample (200).

Using these values, this formula has the following form:

$$K = \frac{[3(137) - (2(200) + 2.5)]}{\sqrt{\dfrac{16(200) - 29}{10}}}$$

Table 6–2   Runs in Artificial Data

Prices in "Runs"	Decreases	Increases
1	41	46
2	23	16
3	4	5
4	0	2

K is the standard normal variable. If the value of K falls between
-1.96 and +1.96, the number of *runs* could have occurred by chance alone.
If the value of K is outside this range, then the number of runs probably
did not occur by chance alone; that is, a deterministic process may be at
work. If this is true, then you may be able to determine the underlying
rules that make this process work and use this information to make better
(more profitable) buy-sell decisions. In this example, our value of K is
0.477, well within this range, thus indicating that the number of *runs* in
our artificial data probably occurred by chance alone.

Real Data

Table 6-3 shows the daily price increases and decreases for the Standard
and Poor's Stock Index for 1988 (column 3). These data are encoded in the
same manner described above (a price increase is represented by a "2," a
decrease by a "1"). If you examine Table 6-3 (column 3), you will find that
the number of prices (N) is 252 and there are 134 runs (R). If you use these
values in the formula above, it will have the following form:

$$K = \frac{[3(134) - (2(252) + 2.5)]}{\sqrt{\dfrac{16(252) - 29}{10}}}$$

In this case, the value of K is -5.223, well outside the range described
earlier. This means that the *runs* of price increases and decreases in the
Standard & Poor's Stock Index are not random.

You can use a closely related technique to determine if there are a
predominance of price increases or decreases. Normally you would per-
form the test described only if the results of the test described above
showed that the runs of price increases or decreases was not caused by
chance alone. Use the following formula:

$$K = \frac{N - 2(S + 1)}{\sqrt{\dfrac{N + 1}{3}}}$$

where N is the total number of prices in our sample (252) and S is the
number of prices involved in *runs* of price increases or decreases, which-
ever is smaller.

Table 6–3

	S&P 500 Daily 1988	S&P 500 Daily 1988 Delta-1	Increase/ Decrease	S&P 500 Delta-1 Thirds
1	255.940	•	•	•
2	258.630	2.690	2	3
3	258.890	.260	2	2
4	261.070	2.180	2	3
5	243.400	−17.670	1	1
6	247.490	4.090	2	3
7	245.420	−2.070	1	1
8	245.810	.390	2	2
9	245.880	.070	2	2
10	252.050	6.170	2	3
11	251.880	−.170	1	2
12	249.320	−2.560	1	1
13	242.630	−6.690	1	1
14	243.140	.510	2	2
15	246.500	3.360	2	3
16	252.170	5.670	2	3
17	249.570	−2.600	1	1
18	249.380	−.190	1	2
19	252.290	2.910	2	3
20	257.070	4.780	2	3
21	255.040	−2.030	1	1
22	255.570	.530	2	2
23	252.210	−3.360	1	1
24	252.210	0	1	2
25	250.960	−1.250	1	1
26	249.100	−1.860	1	1
27	251.720	2.620	2	3
28	256.660	4.940	2	3
29	255.950	−.710	1	2
30	257.630	1.680	2	3
31	259.830	2.200	2	3
32	259.210	−6.20	1	2
33	257.910	−1.300	1	1
34	261.610	3.700	2	3

Table continues

Table 6–3   Continued

	S&P 500 Daily 1988	S&P 500 Daily 1988 Delta-1	Increase/ Decrease	S&P 500 Delta-1 Thirds
35	265.640	4.030	2	3
36	265.020	−.620	1	2
37	264.430	−.590	1	2
38	261.580	−2.850	1	1
39	262.460	.880	2	3
40	267.820	5.360	2	3
41	267.220	−.600	1	2
42	267.980	.760	2	2
43	267.880	−.100	1	2
44	267.300	−.580	1	2
45	267.380	.080	2	2
46	269.430	2.050	2	3
47	269.060	−.370	1	2
48	263.840	−5.220	1	1
49	264.940	1.100	2	3
50	266.370	1.430	2	3
51	266.130	−.240	1	2
52	268.650	2.520	2	3
53	271.220	2.570	2	3
54	271.120	−.100	1	2
55	268.740	−2.380	1	1
56	268.840	.100	2	2
57	268.910	.070	2	2
58	263.350	−5.560	1	1
59	258.510	−4.840	1	1
60	258.060	−.450	1	2
61	260.070	2.010	2	3
62	258.070	−2.000	1	1
63	258.890	.820	2	3
64	260.140	1.250	2	3
65	258.510	−1.630	1	1
66	265.490	6.980	2	3
67	266.160	.670	2	2
68	269.430	3.270	2	3

Table continues

Table 6–3   Continued

	S&P 500 Daily 1988	S&P 500 Daily 1988 Delta-1	Increase/ Decrease	S&P 500 Delta-1 Thirds
69	270.160	.730	2	2
70	271.370	1.210	2	3
71	271.570	.200	2	2
72	259.750	−11.820	1	1
73	259.770	.020	2	2
74	259.210	−.560	1	2
75	257.920	−1.290	1	1
76	256.130	−1.790	1	1
77	256.420	.290	2	2
78	260.140	3.720	2	3
79	262.460	2.320	2	3
80	263.930	1.470	2	3
81	263.800	−.130	1	2
82	262.610	−1.190	1	1
83	261.330	−1.280	1	1
84	261.560	.230	2	2
85	263.000	1.440	2	3
86	260.320	−2.680	1	1
87	258.790	−1.530	1	1
88	257.480	−1.310	1	1
89	256.540	−.940	1	1
90	257.620	1.080	2	3
91	253.310	−4.310	1	1
92	253.850	.540	2	2
93	256.780	2.930	2	3
94	258.710	1.930	2	3
95	255.390	−3.320	1	1
96	251.350	−4.040	1	1
97	252.570	1.220	2	3
98	253.020	.450	2	2
99	250.830	−2.190	1	1
100	253.510	2.680	2	3
101	253.760	.250	2	2
102	254.630	.870	2	3

Table continues

Table 6–3   Continued

	S&P 500 Daily 1988	S&P 500 Daily 1988 Delta-1	Increase/ Decrease	S&P 500 Delta-1 Thirds
103	253.420	−1.210	1	1
104	262.160	8.740	2	3
105	266.690	4.530	2	3
106	265.330	−1.360	1	1
107	266.450	1.120	2	3
108	267.050	.600	2	2
109	265.170	−1.880	1	1
110	271.520	6.350	2	3
111	270.200	−1.320	1	1
112	271.260	1.060	2	3
113	271.430	.170	2	2
114	274.300	2.870	2	3
115	274.450	.150	2	2
116	269.770	−4.680	1	1
117	270.680	.910	2	3
118	268.940	−1.740	1	1
119	271.670	2.730	2	3
120	275.660	3.990	2	3
121	274.820	−.840	1	1
122	273.780	−1.040	1	1
123	269.060	−4.720	1	1
124	272.310	3.250	2	3
125	270.980	−1.330	1	1
126	273.500	2.520	2	3
127	271.780	−1.720	1	1
128	275.810	4.030	2	3
129	272.020	−3.790	1	1
130	271.780	−.240	1	2
131	270.020	−1.760	1	1
132	270.550	.530	2	2
133	267.850	−2.700	1	1
134	269.320	1.470	2	3
135	270.260	.940	2	3
136	272.050	1.790	2	3

Table continues

Table 6–3   Continued

	S&P 500 Daily 1988	S&P 500 Daily 1988 Delta-1	Increase/ Decrease	S&P 500 Delta-1 Thirds
137	270.510	−1.540	1	1
138	268.470	−2.040	1	1
139	270.000	1.530	2	3
140	266.660	−3.340	1	1
141	263.500	−3.160	1	1
142	264.680	1.180	2	3
143	265.190	.510	2	2
144	262.500	−2.690	1	1
145	266.020	3.520	2	3
146	272.020	6.000	2	3
147	272.210	.190	2	2
148	272.060	−.150	1	2
149	272.980	.920	2	3
150	271.930	−1.050	1	1
151	271.150	−.780	1	2
152	269.980	−1.170	1	1
153	266.490	−3.490	1	1
154	261.900	−4.590	1	1
155	262.750	.850	2	3
156	262.550	−.200	1	2
157	258.690	−3.860	1	1
158	260.560	1.870	2	3
159	260.770	.210	2	2
160	261.030	.260	2	2
161	260.240	−.790	1	2
162	256.980	−3.260	1	1
163	257.090	.110	2	2
164	261.130	4.040	2	3
165	259.180	−1.950	1	1
166	259.680	.500	2	2
167	262.330	2.650	2	3
168	262.510	.180	2	2
169	261.520	−.990	1	1
170	258.350	−3.170	1	1

Table continues

Table 6–3   Continued

	S&P 500 Daily 1988	S&P 500 Daily 1988 Delta-1	Increase/ Decrease	S&P 500 Delta-1 Thirds
171	264.480	6.130	2	3
172	265.590	1.110	2	3
173	265.870	.280	2	2
174	265.880	.010	2	2
175	266.840	.960	2	3
176	266.470	−.370	1	2
177	267.430	.960	2	3
178	269.310	1.880	2	3
179	268.130	−1.180	1	1
180	270.650	2.520	2	3
181	268.820	−1.830	1	1
182	269.730	.910	2	3
183	270.160	.430	2	2
184	269.180	−.980	1	1
185	269.760	.580	2	2
186	268.880	−.880	1	1
187	268.260	−.620	1	2
188	269.080	.820	2	3
189	272.590	3.510	2	3
190	271.910	−.680	1	2
191	271.380	−.530	1	2
192	270.620	−.760	1	2
193	271.860	1.240	2	3
194	272.390	.530	2	2
195	278.070	5.680	2	3
196	278.240	.170	2	2
197	277.930	−.310	1	2
198	273.980	−3.950	1	1
199	275.220	1.240	2	3
200	275.500	.280	2	2
201	276.410	.910	2	3
202	279.380	2.970	2	3
203	276.970	−2.410	1	1
204	282.880	5.910	2	3

Table continues

Table 6–3   Continued

	S&P 500 Daily 1988	S&P 500 Daily 1988 Delta-1	Increase/ Decrease	S&P 500 Delta-1 Thirds
205	283.660	.780	2	2
206	282.280	−1.380	1	1
207	282.380	.100	2	2
208	281.380	−1.000	1	1
209	277.280	−4.100	1	1
210	278.530	1.250	2	3
211	278.970	.440	2	2
212	279.060	.090	2	2
213	279.060	0	1	2
214	279.200	.140	2	2
215	276.310	−2.890	1	1
216	273.930	−2.380	1	1
217	275.150	1.220	2	3
218	273.330	−1.820	1	1
219	273.690	.360	2	2
220	267.920	−5.770	1	1
221	267.720	−.200	1	2
222	268.340	.620	2	2
223	263.820	−4.520	1	1
224	264.600	.780	2	2
225	266.470	1.870	2	3
226	266.220	−.250	1	2
227	267.210	.990	2	3
228	269.000	1.790	2	3
229	267.230	−1.770	1	1
230	268.640	1.410	2	3
231	270.910	2.270	2	3
232	273.700	2.790	2	3
233	272.490	−1.210	1	1
234	271.810	−.680	1	2
235	274.930	3.120	2	3
236	277.590	2.660	2	3
237	278.130	.540	2	2
238	276.590	−1.540	1	1

Table continues

Table 6–3   Continued

	S&P 500 Daily 1988	S&P 500 Daily 1988 Delta-1	Increase/ Decrease	S&P 500 Delta-1 Thirds
239	277.030	.440	2	2
240	276.520	−.510	1	2
241	276.310	−.210	1	2
242	275.310	−1.000	1	1
243	274.280	−1.030	1	1
244	276.290	2.010	2	3
245	278.910	2.620	2	3
246	277.470	−1.440	1	1
247	277.380	−.090	1	2
248	276.870	−.510	1	2
249	277.870	1.000	2	3
250	276.830	−1.040	1	1
251	277.080	.250	2	2
252	279.400	2.320	2	3
253	277.720	−1.680	1	1

In this case, the runs of price decreases is smaller and involves 115 prices, while the number of prices involved with runs of price increases is 137. If you use these values in the formula, it has the following form:

$$K = \frac{252 - 2(115 + 1)}{\sqrt{\dfrac{252 + 1}{3}}}$$

In this case, K has the value 2.178 which is outside the range described earlier, so there is a predominance of price decreases.

Prices or *price changes* can be categorized in a variety of other ways. For example, you can determine the median price or *price change* and determine if the runs of prices or *price changes* above or below the median price are significant.

We will use the artificial price data in column 1 of Table 6-1 as our data. As shown in Table 6-4, the median price is 8, so we will encode this data and use a "1" to indicate a price below the median and a "2" to indicate a price above the median. The encoded data for prices above and below the median is shown in Table 6-1, column 4. Determine if the *runs* of prices above or below the median occurred by chance alone by using the following formula:

$$K = \frac{N(R - 1/2) - 2(n_1)(n_2)}{\sqrt{\dfrac{(2(n_1)(n_2))(2(n_1)(n_2) - N)}{N - 1}}}$$

where N is the total number of prices in our sample (200), R is the number of runs (104), n_1 is the number of prices involved in runs below the median (105), and n_2 is the number of prices involved in runs above the median (95).

If you use these values, the formula has the following form:

$$K = \frac{200(104 - 1/2) - 2(105)(95)}{\sqrt{\dfrac{(2(105)(95))(2(105)(95) - 200)}{200 - 1}}}$$

Table 6–4   Artificial Data Summary

Mean	Std. Dev.	Std. Error	Variance	Coef. Var.	Count
7.915	4.388	.31	19.254	55.438	200

Minimum	Maximum	Range	Sum	Sum of Sqr.	# Missing
1	15	14	1583	16361	1

# < 10th %	10th %	25th %	50th %	75th %	90th %
18	2	4	8	12	14

> 90th %
14

In the formula, K equals 0.672, which falls within the range described above and thus indicates that the runs of prices above and below the median probably occurred by chance alone. Most statisticians also believe that if this test is not significant, then the prices or *price changes* have a normal (bell-shaped) distribution. This also implies that the distribution of prices is probably random.

The *price changes* for the monthly average of the Standard & Poor's Stock Index for 1947 to 1987 is shown in Table 6-5, column 2. In Table 6-6, note that the median *price change* is 0.49, so encode *price changes* below the median ("1") and above the median ("2") in column 3 of Table 6-5. If you examine Table 6-5, you will find that the number of *price changes* (N) is 492, while the number of runs (R) is 200, and the number of *price changes* above and below the median is 246 (n_1 and n_2). If you enter these values in the formula above, it has the following form:

$$K = \frac{492(200 - 1/2) - 2(246)(246)}{\sqrt{\frac{(2(246)(246))(2(246)(246) - 492)}{492 - 1}}}$$

where value of K is 4.098, which indicates that the runs above and below the median *price change* did not occur by chance alone and the price changes are probably not normally distributed.

You can also use this method with the prices of a stock rather than *price changes*. Table 6-7 shows the summary statistics for Security Pacific Corporation for 1988. Table 6-8 shows the prices for Security Pacific Corporation for 1988 (column 1) and these prices are encoded on the basis of median price (column 2). In this case, the number of prices (N) is 253, the number of runs (R) is 20, while the number of prices involved with runs below the median (n_1) is 132 and above the median (n_2) is 121. If you enter these values in the formula above, it has the following form:

$$K = \frac{253(20 - 1/2) - 2(132)(121)}{\sqrt{\frac{(2(132)(121)(2(132)(121) - 253)}{253 - 1}}}$$

In the formula, the value of K is 13.422, which indicates that the distribution runs of prices above and below the median price did not occur by chance alone and, therefore, the distribution of prices is probably not random.

It is also possible to categorize our data into three categories. The cumulative probability density function of *price changes* of the Standard &

Table 6-5

	S&P 500 Index	Delta-1	Delta-1 Median	Thirds <25,25-75,>75
1	15.210	•	•	•
2	15.800	.590	2	2
3	15.160	-.640	1	2
4	14.600	-.560	1	2
5	14.340	-.260	1	2
6	14.840	.500	2	2
7	15.770	.930	2	2
8	15.460	-.310	1	2
9	15.060	-.400	1	2
10	15.450	.390	1	2
11	15.270	-.180	1	2
12	15.030	-.240	1	2
13	14.830	-.200	1	2
14	14.100	-.730	1	2
15	14.300	.200	1	2
16	15.400	1.100	2	2
17	16.150	.750	2	2
18	16.820	.670	2	2
19	16.420	-.400	1	2
20	15.940	-.480	1	2
21	15.760	-.180	1	2
22	16.190	.430	1	2
23	15.290	-.900	1	1
24	15.190	-.100	1	2
25	15.360	.170	1	2
26	14.770	-.590	1	2
27	14.910	.140	1	2
28	14.890	-.020	1	2
29	14.780	-.110	1	2
30	13.970	-.810	1	1
31	14.760	.790	2	2
32	15.290	.530	2	2
33	15.490	.200	1	2
34	15.890	.400	1	2

Table continues

Table 6–5   Continued

	S&P 500 Index	Delta-1	Delta-1 Median	Thirds <25,25-75,>75
35	16.110	.220	1	2
36	16.540	.430	1	2
37	16.880	.340	1	2
38	17.210	.330	1	2
39	17.350	.140	1	2
40	17.840	.490	1	2
41	18.440	.600	2	2
42	18.740	.300	1	2
43	17.380	−1.360	1	1
44	18.430	1.050	2	2
45	19.080	.650	2	2
46	19.870	.790	2	2
47	19.830	−.040	1	2
48	19.750	−.080	1	2
49	21.210	1.460	2	2
50	22.000	.790	2	2
51	21.630	−.370	1	2
52	21.920	.290	1	2
53	21.930	.010	1	2
54	21.550	−.380	1	2
55	21.930	.380	1	2
56	22.890	.960	2	2
57	23.480	.590	2	2
58	23.360	−.120	1	2
59	22.710	−.650	1	2
60	23.410	.700	2	2
61	24.190	.780	2	2
62	23.750	−.440	1	2
63	23.810	.060	1	2
64	23.750	−.060	1	2
65	23.730	−.020	1	2
66	24.380	.650	2	2
67	25.080	.700	2	2
68	25.180	.100	1	2

Table continues

Table 6–5   Continued

	S&P 500 Index	Delta-1	Delta-1 Median	Thirds <25,25-75,>75
69	24.780	−.400	1	2
70	24.260	−.520	1	2
71	25.030	.770	2	2
72	26.040	1.010	2	2
73	26.180	.140	1	2
74	25.860	−.320	1	2
75	25.990	.130	1	2
76	24.710	−1.280	1	1
77	24.840	.130	1	2
78	23.950	−.890	1	1
79	24.290	.340	1	2
80	24.390	.100	1	2
81	23.270	−1.120	1	1
82	23.970	.700	2	2
83	24.500	.530	2	2
84	24.830	.330	1	2
85	25.460	.630	2	2
86	26.020	.560	2	2
87	26.570	.550	2	2
88	27.630	1.060	2	2
89	28.730	1.100	2	2
90	28.960	.230	1	2
91	30.130	1.170	2	2
92	30.730	.600	2	2
93	31.450	.720	2	2
94	32.180	.730	2	2
95	33.440	1.260	2	2
96	34.970	1.530	2	2
97	35.600	.630	2	2
98	36.790	1.190	2	2
99	36.500	−.290	1	2
100	37.760	1.260	2	2
101	37.600	−.160	1	2
102	39.780	2.180	2	3

Table continues

Table 6-5   Continued

	S&P 500 Index	Delta-1	Delta-1 Median	Thirds <25,25-75,>75
103	42.690	2.910	2	3
104	42.430	−.260	1	2
105	44.340	1.910	2	3
106	42.110	−2.230	1	1
107	44.950	2.840	2	3
108	45.370	.420	1	2
109	44.150	−1.220	1	1
110	44.430	.280	1	2
111	47.490	3.060	2	3
112	48.050	.560	2	2
113	46.540	−1.510	1	1
114	46.270	−.270	1	2
115	48.780	2.510	2	3
116	48.490	−.290	1	2
117	46.840	−1.650	1	1
118	46.240	−.600	1	2
119	45.760	−.480	1	2
120	46.440	.680	2	2
121	45.430	−1.010	1	1
122	43.470	−1.960	1	1
123	44.030	.560	2	2
124	45.050	1.020	2	2
125	46.780	1.730	2	2
126	47.550	.770	2	2
127	48.510	.960	2	2
128	45.840	−2.670	1	1
129	43.980	−1.860	1	1
130	41.240	−2.740	1	1
131	40.350	−.890	1	1
132	40.330	−.020	1	2
133	41.120	.790	2	2
134	41.260	.140	1	2
135	42.110	.850	2	2
136	42.340	.230	1	2

Table continues

Table 6–5   Continued

	S&P 500 Index	Delta-1	Delta-1 Median	Thirds <25,25-75,>75
137	43.700	1.360	2	2
138	44.750	1.050	2	2
139	45.980	1.230	2	2
140	47.700	1.720	2	2
141	48.960	1.260	2	2
142	50.950	1.990	2	3
143	52.500	1.550	2	2
144	53.490	.990	2	2
145	55.620	2.130	2	3
146	54.770	−.850	1	1
147	56.150	1.380	2	2
148	57.100	.950	2	2
149	57.960	.860	2	2
150	57.460	−.500	1	2
151	59.740	2.280	2	3
152	59.400	−.340	1	2
153	57.050	−2.350	1	1
154	57.000	−.050	1	2
155	57.230	.230	1	2
156	59.060	1.830	2	3
157	58.030	−1.030	1	1
158	55.780	−2.250	1	1
159	55.020	−.760	1	2
160	55.730	.710	2	2
161	55.220	−.510	1	2
162	57.260	2.040	2	3
163	55.840	−1.420	1	1
164	56.510	.670	2	2
165	54.810	−1.700	1	1
166	53.730	−1.080	1	1
167	55.470	1.740	2	2
168	56.800	1.330	2	2
169	59.720	2.920	2	3
170	62.170	2.450	2	3

Table continues

Table 6–5   Continued

	S&P 500 Index	Delta-1	Delta-1 Median	Thirds <25,25-75,>75
171	64.120	1.950	2	3
172	65.830	1.710	2	2
173	66.500	.670	2	2
174	65.620	−.880	1	1
175	65.440	−.180	1	2
176	67.790	2.350	2	3
177	67.260	−.530	1	2
178	68.000	.740	2	2
179	71.080	3.080	2	3
180	71.740	.660	2	2
181	69.070	−2.670	1	1
182	70.220	1.150	2	2
183	70.290	.070	1	2
184	68.050	−2.240	1	1
185	62.990	−5.060	1	1
186	55.630	−7.360	1	1
187	56.970	1.340	2	2
188	58.520	1.550	2	2
189	58.000	−.520	1	2
190	56.170	−1.830	1	1
191	60.040	3.870	2	3
192	62.640	2.600	2	3
193	65.060	2.420	2	3
194	65.920	.860	2	2
195	65.670	−.250	1	2
196	68.760	3.090	2	3
197	70.140	1.380	2	2
198	70.110	−.030	1	2
199	69.070	−1.040	1	1
200	70.980	1.910	2	3
201	72.850	1.870	2	3
202	73.030	.180	1	2
203	72.620	−.410	1	2
204	74.170	1.550	2	2

Table continues

Table 6–5   Continued

	S&P 500 Index	Delta-1	Delta-1 Median	Thirds <25,25-75,>75
205	76.450	2.280	2	3
206	77.390	.940	2	2
207	78.800	1.410	2	2
208	79.940	1.140	2	2
209	80.720	.780	2	2
210	80.240	−.480	1	2
211	83.220	2.980	2	3
212	82.000	−1.220	1	1
213	83.410	1.410	2	2
214	84.850	1.440	2	2
215	85.440	.590	2	2
216	83.960	−1.480	1	1
217	86.120	2.160	2	3
218	86.750	.630	2	2
219	86.830	.080	1	2
220	87.970	1.140	2	2
221	89.280	1.310	2	2
222	85.040	−4.240	1	1
223	84.910	−.130	1	2
224	86.490	1.580	2	2
225	89.380	2.890	2	3
226	91.390	2.010	2	3
227	92.150	.760	2	2
228	91.730	−.420	1	2
229	93.320	1.590	2	2
230	92.690	−.630	1	2
231	88.880	−3.810	1	1
232	91.600	2.720	2	3
233	86.780	−4.820	1	1
234	86.060	−.720	1	2
235	85.840	−.220	1	2
236	80.650	−5.190	1	1
237	77.810	−2.840	1	1
238	77.130	−.680	1	2

Table continues

Table 6–5   Continued

	S&P 500 Index	Delta-1	Delta-1 Median	Thirds <25,25-75,>75
239	80.990	3.860	2	3
240	81.330	.340	1	2
241	84.450	3.120	2	3
242	87.360	2.910	2	3
243	89.420	2.060	2	3
244	90.960	1.540	2	2
245	92.590	1.630	2	2
246	91.430	−1.160	1	1
247	93.010	1.580	2	2
248	94.490	1.480	2	2
249	95.810	1.320	2	2
250	95.660	−.150	1	2
251	92.660	−3.000	1	1
252	95.300	2.640	2	3
253	95.040	−.260	1	2
254	90.750	−4.290	1	1
255	89.090	−1.660	1	1
256	95.670	6.580	2	3
257	97.870	2.200	2	3
258	100.530	2.660	2	3
259	100.300	−.230	1	2
260	98.110	−2.190	1	1
261	101.340	3.230	2	3
262	103.760	2.420	2	3
263	105.400	1.640	2	2
264	106.480	1.080	2	2
265	102.040	−4.440	1	1
266	101.460	−.580	1	2
267	99.300	−2.160	1	1
268	101.260	1.960	2	3
269	104.620	3.360	2	3
270	99.140	−5.480	1	1
271	94.710	−4.430	1	1
272	94.180	−.530	1	2

Table continues

Table 6–5   Continued

	S&P 500 Index	Delta-1	Delta-1 Median	Thirds <25,25-75,>75
273	94.510	.330	1	2
274	95.520	1.010	2	2
275	96.210	.690	2	2
276	91.110	−5.100	1	1
277	90.310	−.800	1	1
278	87.160	−3.150	1	1
279	88.650	1.490	2	2
280	85.950	−2.700	1	1
281	76.060	−9.890	1	1
282	75.590	−.470	1	2
283	75.720	.130	1	2
284	77.920	2.200	2	3
285	82.580	4.660	2	3
286	84.370	1.790	2	2
287	84.280	−.090	1	2
288	90.050	5.770	2	3
289	93.490	3.440	2	3
290	97.110	3.620	2	3
291	99.600	2.490	2	3
292	103.040	3.440	2	3
293	101.640	−1.400	1	1
294	99.720	−1.920	1	1
295	99.000	−.720	1	2
296	97.240	−1.760	1	1
297	99.400	2.160	2	3
298	97.290	−2.110	1	1
299	92.780	−4.510	1	1
300	99.170	6.390	2	3
301	103.300	4.130	2	3
302	105.240	1.940	2	3
303	107.690	2.450	2	3
304	108.810	1.120	2	2
305	107.650	−1.160	1	1
306	108.010	.360	1	2

Table continues

Table 6–5   Continued

	S&P 500 Index	Delta-1	Delta-1 Median	Thirds <25,25-75,>75
307	107.210	–.800	1	1
308	111.010	3.800	2	3
309	109.390	–1.620	1	1
310	109.560	.170	1	2
311	115.050	5.490	2	3
312	117.500	2.450	2	3
313	118.420	.920	2	2
314	114.160	–4.260	1	1
315	112.420	–1.740	1	1
316	110.270	–2.150	1	1
317	107.220	–3.050	1	1
318	104.750	–2.470	1	1
319	105.830	1.080	2	2
320	103.800	–2.030	1	1
321	105.610	1.810	2	2
322	109.840	4.230	2	3
323	102.030	–7.810	1	1
324	94.780	–7.250	1	1
325	96.110	1.330	2	2
326	93.450	–2.660	1	1
327	97.440	3.990	2	3
328	92.460	–4.980	1	1
329	89.670	–2.790	1	1
330	89.790	.120	1	2
331	82.820	–6.970	1	1
332	76.030	–6.790	1	1
333	68.120	–7.910	1	1
334	69.440	1.320	2	2
335	71.740	2.300	2	3
336	67.070	–4.670	1	1
337	72.560	5.490	2	3
338	80.100	7.540	2	3
339	83.780	3.680	2	3
340	84.720	.940	2	2

Table continues

Table 6–5   Continued

	S&P 500 Index	Delta-1	Delta-1 Median	Thirds <25,25-75,>75
341	90.100	5.380	2	3
342	92.400	2.300	2	3
343	92.490	.090	1	2
344	85.710	−6.780	1	1
345	84.670	−1.040	1	1
346	88.570	3.900	2	3
347	90.070	1.500	2	2
348	88.700	−1.370	1	1
349	96.860	8.160	2	3
350	100.640	3.780	2	3
351	101.080	.440	1	2
352	101.930	.850	2	2
353	101.160	−.770	1	2
354	101.770	.610	2	2
355	104.200	2.430	2	3
356	103.290	−.910	1	1
357	105.450	2.160	2	3
358	101.890	−3.560	1	1
359	101.190	−.700	1	2
360	104.660	3.470	2	3
361	103.810	−.850	1	1
362	100.960	−2.850	1	1
363	100.570	−.390	1	2
364	99.050	−1.520	1	1
365	98.760	−.290	1	2
366	99.290	.530	2	2
367	100.180	.890	2	2
368	97.750	−2.430	1	1
369	96.230	−1.520	1	1
370	93.740	−2.490	1	1
371	94.280	.540	2	2
372	93.820	−.460	1	2
373	90.250	−3.570	1	1
374	88.980	−1.270	1	1

Table continues

Table 6–5   Continued

	S&P 500 Index	Delta-1	Delta-1 Median	Thirds <25,25-75,>75
375	88.820	–.160	1	2
376	92.710	3.890	2	3
377	97.410	4.700	2	3
378	97.660	.250	1	2
379	97.190	–.470	1	2
380	103.920	6.730	2	3
381	103.860	–.060	1	2
382	100.580	–3.280	1	1
383	94.710	–5.870	1	1
384	96.110	1.400	2	2
385	99.710	3.600	2	3
386	98.230	–1.480	1	1
387	100.110	1.880	2	3
388	102.070	1.960	2	3
389	99.730	–2.340	1	1
390	101.730	2.000	2	3
391	102.710	.980	2	2
392	107.360	4.650	2	3
393	108.600	1.240	2	2
394	104.270	–4.330	1	1
395	103.660	–.610	1	2
396	107.780	4.120	2	3
397	110.870	3.090	2	3
398	115.340	4.470	2	3
399	104.690	–10.650	1	1
400	102.970	–1.720	1	1
401	107.690	4.720	2	3
402	114.550	6.860	2	3
403	119.830	5.280	2	3
404	123.500	3.670	2	3
405	126.510	3.010	2	3
406	130.220	3.710	2	3
407	135.650	5.430	2	3
408	133.480	–2.170	1	1

Table continues

Table 6–5   Continued

	S&P 500 Index	Delta-1	Delta-1 Median	Thirds <25,25-75,>75
409	132.970	−.510	1	2
410	128.400	−4.570	1	1
411	133.190	4.790	2	3
412	134.430	1.240	2	2
413	131.730	−2.700	1	1
414	132.280	.550	2	2
415	129.130	−3.150	1	1
416	129.630	.500	2	2
417	118.270	−11.360	1	1
418	119.800	1.530	2	2
419	122.920	3.120	2	3
420	123.790	.870	2	2
421	117.280	−6.510	1	1
422	114.500	−2.780	1	1
423	110.840	−3.660	1	1
424	116.310	5.470	2	3
425	116.350	.040	1	2
426	109.700	−6.650	1	1
427	109.380	−.320	1	2
428	109.650	.270	1	2
429	122.430	12.780	2	3
430	132.660	10.230	2	3
431	138.100	5.440	2	3
432	139.370	1.270	2	2
433	144.270	4.900	2	3
434	146.800	2.530	2	3
435	151.880	5.080	2	3
436	157.710	5.830	2	3
437	164.100	6.390	2	3
438	166.390	2.290	2	3
439	166.960	.570	2	2
440	162.420	−4.540	1	1
441	167.160	4.740	2	3
442	167.650	.490	•	2

Table continues

Table 6–5   Continued

	S&P 500 Index	Delta-1	Delta-1 Median	Thirds <25,25-75,>75
443	165.230	−2.420	1	1
444	164.360	−.870	1	1
445	166.390	2.030	2	3
446	157.250	−9.140	1	1
447	157.440	.190	1	2
448	157.600	.160	1	2
449	156.550	−1.050	1	1
450	153.120	−3.430	1	1
451	151.080	−2.040	1	1
452	164.420	13.340	2	3
453	166.110	1.690	2	2
454	164.820	−1.290	1	1
455	166.270	1.450	2	2
456	164.480	−1.790	1	1
457	171.610	7.130	2	3
458	180.880	9.270	2	3
459	179.420	−1.460	1	1
460	180.620	1.200	2	2
461	184.900	4.280	2	3
462	188.890	3.990	2	3
463	192.540	3.650	2	3
464	188.310	−4.230	1	1
465	184.060	−4.250	1	1
466	186.180	2.120	2	3
467	197.450	11.270	2	3
468	207.260	9.810	2	3
469	208.190	.930	2	2
470	219.370	11.180	2	3
471	232.330	12.960	2	3
472	237.980	5.650	2	3
473	238.460	.480	1	2
474	245.300	6.840	2	3
475	240.180	−5.120	1	1
476	245.000	4.820	2	3

Table continues

Table 6–5   Continued

	S&P 500 Index	Delta-1	Delta-1 Median	Thirds <25,25-75,>75
477	238.270	−6.730	1	1
478	237.360	−.910	1	1
479	245.090	7.730	2	3
480	248.610	3.520	2	3
481	264.510	15.900	2	3
482	280.930	16.420	2	3
483	292.470	11.540	2	3
484	289.320	−3.150	1	1
485	289.120	−.200	1	2
486	301.380	12.260	2	3
487	310.090	8.710	2	3
488	329.360	19.270	2	3
489	318.660	−10.700	1	1
490	280.160	−38.500	1	1
491	245.010	−35.150	1	1
492	240.960	−4.050	1	1

Poor's 500 Stock Index 1988 is shown in Figure 6-2 (the method used to construct this histogram is described in detail in Chapter 2). This histogram is divided into approximately equal thirds (1 = -17.67 to -0.8; 2 = -0.79 to +0.8; and 3 = +0.81 to 8.74). Each individual *price change* is encoded as a 1, 2, or 3, as shown in Table 6-3, column 4. The number of *price changes* (N) is 252, while the number of runs (R) is 185. The number of prices involved in the lowest third (encoded as a "1") is 80, the middle third ("2") is 82, and the highest third ("3") is 90. The formula used to evaluate the data which has been categorized by dividing it into thirds has the following form:

$$K = \frac{n_i{}^1 - N(N - R + 1/2)}{\sqrt{\dfrac{n_i{}^2(n_i{}^2 + N(N + 1)) - 2(N)\,(n_i{}^2 - N^3)}{N - 1}}}$$

Table 6–6   S&P 500 Index Summary

Mean	Std. Dev.	Std. Error	Variance	Coef. Var.	Count
.46	4.202	.19	17.656	913.891	491

Minimum	Maximum	Range	Sum	Sum of Sqr.	# Missing
−38.5	19.27	57.77	225.75	8755.007	1

# < 10th %	10th %	25th %	50th %	75th %	90th %
49	−2.91	−.792	.49	1.825	3.99

> 90th %
48

Table 6–7   Security Pacific Corporation Summary Table

Mean	Std. Dev.	Std. Error	Variance	Coef. Var.	Count
34.6	3.43	.21	11.8	9.93	25

Minimum	Maximum	Range	Sum	Sum of Sqr.	# Missing
26.0	41.0	14.9	8759.	306248.	1

# < 10th %	10th %	25th %	50th %	75th %	90th %
25	30.0	32.0	36	37.0	39.0

> 90th %
23

Table 6–8

	Security Pacific Corporation 1988	Security Pacific Median		Security Pacific Corporation 1988	Security Pacific Median
1	26.070	1	33	31.010	1
2	28.000	1	34	31.030	1
3	28.040	1	35	30.040	1
4	28.030	1	36	31.030	1
5	28.000	1	37	32.010	1
6	28.020	1	38	32.060	1
7	27.040	1	39	32.020	1
8	28.020	1	40	32.050	1
9	28.020	1	41	32.040	1
10	29.010	1	42	33.000	1
11	29.020	1	43	33.030	1
12	30.040	1	44	33.000	1
13	29.060	1	45	32.010	1
14	30.020	1	46	32.030	1
15	31.030	1	47	31.030	1
16	30.070	1	48	30.030	1
17	30.070	1	49	30.010	1
18	30.060	1	50	30.030	1
19	31.010	1	51	30.040	1
20	32.020	1	52	30.030	1
21	33.000	1	53	30.070	1
22	33.000	1	54	30.040	1
23	32.050	1	55	30.000	1
24	31.070	1	56	30.000	1
25	31.060	1	57	30.000	1
26	31.030	1	58	29.040	1
27	31.040	1	59	28.060	1
28	31.040	1	60	28.000	1
29	31.050	1	61	28.070	1
30	31.040	1	62	28.070	1
31	31.050	1	63	29.060	1
32	31.010	1	64	29.060	1

Table continues

Table 6–8   Continued

	Security Pacific Corporation 1988	Security Pacific Median		Security Pacific Corporation 1988	Security Pacific Median
65	29.020	1	97	34.050	1
66	30.000	1	98	33.010	1
67	30.040	1	99	33.060	1
68	30.020	1	100	34.010	1
69	30.010	1	101	34.060	1
70	30.020	1	102	34.040	1
71	30.000	1	103	34.040	1
72	30.040	1	104	35.000	1
73	30.040	1	105	35.060	1
74	30.040	1	106	35.040	1
75	31.020	1	107	35.070	1
76	32.030	1	108	35.060	1
77	32.000	1	109	36.000	1
78	32.020	1	110	36.020	2
79	32.070	1	111	36.040	2
80	33.050	1	112	36.060	2
81	32.050	1	113	37.020	2
82	33.000	1	114	37.070	2
83	33.000	1	115	37.060	2
84	32.060	1	116	37.020	2
85	33.020	1	117	37.010	2
86	33.030	1	118	37.010	2
87	33.050	1	119	37.030	2
88	33.050	1	120	37.050	2
89	34.000	1	121	37.000	2
90	34.020	1	122	36.070	2
91	33.070	1	123	36.010	2
92	34.070	1	124	36.010	2
93	35.030	1	125	35.070	1
94	35.000	1	126	36.030	2
95	34.030	1	127	36.050	2
96	34.020	1	128	37.040	2

Table continues

Table 6–8   Continued

	Security Pacific Corporation 1988	Security Pacific Median		Security Pacific Corporation 1988	Security Pacific Median
129	37.030	2	161	36.070	2
130	37.030	2	162	34.020	1
131	37.000	2	163	35.010	1
132	36.070	2	164	36.010	2
133	36.000	1	165	36.000	1
134	36.020	2	166	35.040	1
135	36.060	2	167	36.040	2
136	37.020	2	168	36.020	2
137	36.070	2	169	35.060	1
138	37.020	2	170	35.040	1
139	37.020	2	171	36.030	2
140	37.010	2	172	36.050	2
141	36.060	2	173	37.020	2
142	36.060	2	174	37.060	2
143	37.020	2	175	38.020	2
144	36.000	1	176	38.030	2
145	36.060	2	177	38.020	2
146	37.070	2	178	38.070	2
147	38.010	2	179	39.030	2
148	38.060	2	180	39.030	2
149	38.070	2	181	39.010	2
150	38.070	2	182	39.020	2
151	38.070	2	183	39.060	2
152	38.070	2	184	39.050	2
153	38.030	2	185	39.020	2
154	37.010	2	186	39.010	2
155	37.010	2	187	39.000	2
156	37.000	2	188	38.050	2
157	36.010	2	189	38.070	2
158	36.050	2	190	38.040	2
159	37.000	2	191	39.000	2
160	37.020	2	192	39.010	2

Table continues

Table 6–8   Continued

	Security Pacific Corporation 1988	Security Pacific Median		Security Pacific Corporation 1988	Security Pacific Median
193	39.020	2	224	35.060	1
194	39.030	2	225	35.060	1
195	39.060	2	226	35.050	1
196	39.050	2	227	35.060	1
197	39.070	2	228	36.020	2
198	39.060	2	229	36.010	2
199	40.010	2	230	36.020	2
200	40.000	2	231	36.060	2
201	40.020	2	232	37.030	2
202	40.020	2	233	36.060	2
203	40.030	2	234	36.020	2
204	41.010	2	235	37.040	2
205	41.040	2	246	37.050	2
206	41.010	2	237	38.000	2
207	40.050	2	238	37.060	2
208	40.010	2	239	37.060	2
209	39.060	2	240	37.030	2
210	39.020	2	241	37.020	2
211	39.060	2	242	36.060	2
212	39.070	2	243	35.060	1
213	39.070	2	244	36.010	2
214	39.010	2	245	35.010	1
215	38.010	2	246	34.040	1
216	38.020	2	247	34.020	1
217	38.020	2	248	34.050	1
218	37.070	2	249	35.000	1
219	37.050	2	250	34.060	1
220	36.050	2	251	35.000	1
221	36.060	2	252	36.000	1
222	37.000	2	253	36.010	2
223	36.000	1	254	•	•

Figure 6–2

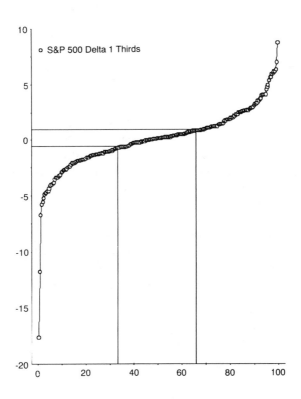

where:

	n_i	$n_i{}^2$	$n_i{}^3$
1	80	6400	512000
2	82	6724	551368
3	90	8100	729000
SUM	252	21224	1792368

If you enter the values above into the formula above, it has the following form:

$$K = \frac{21224 - 252(252 - 184 + 1/2)}{\sqrt{\dfrac{21224(21224 + (252)(253)) - 2(252)(1792368 - 16003008)}{252 - 1}}}$$

K has the value 0.742, which is within the range (-1.96 to +1.96), which indicates that the runs of *price changes* of the Standard & Poor's Stock Index, when it is categorized into thirds, probably occurs by chance alone.

You can also categorize our data in other ways and determine if the runs that occur would occur by chance or not. For example, you might want to know if runs of relatively small or large *price changes* occur by chance alone. Table 6-5, column 4 shows the monthly average *price changes* for the Standard & Poor's 500 Stock Index. The *price changes* in the table are divided into thirds, where the lowest third ("1") represents the *price changes* in the lowest quarter of *price changes* when they are ranked in order of size (–38.5 to –0.792). A "2" represents *price changes* in the middle 50% (from the 25th to the 75th percentiles or -0.791 to +1.825), and a "3" represents prices in the highest quartile (+1.826 to 19.27). The number of *price changes* (N) is 491, while the number of runs (R) is 142. The other values used in the formula are shown below:

		n_i	n_i^2	n_i^3
1		123	15129	1860867
2		245	60025	14706125
3		123	15129	1860867
	SUM	491	90283	18427859

If you place these values in the formula above, it will have the following form:

$$K = \frac{90283 - 491(491 - 142 + 1/2))}{\sqrt{\dfrac{90283(90283 + (491)(492)) - 2(491)(18427859 - 118370771)}{491 - 1}}}$$

The value of K in this case is –5.026 which is well outside of the range mentioned above. Thus, the distribution of runs when *price changes* are categorized in this manner is not random.

If you determine that the number of runs is significant (outside the range described above), then the number of runs is different from the number of runs that you would expect by chance alone. You can then examine the length of runs to determine if the distribution of run lengths differs from what would be expected by chance alone. This test works only if you have two categories, so we will use the data where we categorized runs above and below the median *price changes* in the Standard & Poor's 500 Stock Index for 1947 to 1987. The total number of *price changes* (N) is 492, while the number of *price changes* above the median and below the median is 246.

The probability of a *price change* above the median (p) is 246/492 or 0.5, and the probability of a *price change* below the median (q) is also 246/492 or 0.5. (*NOTE*: Generally "p" and "q" are not equal.) The expected number of runs of one *price change* above the median is (N)(p)(q), or (492) (0.5)(0.5), which equals 123. The expected number of runs of two *price changes* above the median is (N) $(p)^2(q)$, or (492) $(0.5)^2(0.5)$, which equals 62. The expected number of runs of three *price changes* is (N)$(p)^3(q)$, or (492)$(0.5)^3$(0.5), which equals 31. The expected number of runs of 1 to 12 *price changes* above the median are shown in Table 6-9, as are the observed number of runs of *price changes* above the median. We will compare these two sets of frequencies using Chi-square. The formula for Chi-square and the method used to calculate it are shown in Chapter 3. The value of this Chi-square is 99.540, which is highly significant. This means that the number of prices in each run is not random.

Persistence

Do price increases or decreases occur as isolated incidents or do they "stick" together as clusters? In other words, does a price increase, once it has occurred, tend to persist from day to day? One way to determine if there is *persistence* is to calculate Besson's Coefficient of Persistence, a measure that is commonly used in meteorology. The formula has the following form:

$$R = \frac{(1-p)}{(1-p_i)} - 1$$

where p is the probability of occurrence of an event like a *price change* increase and p_i is the probability that the event will occur after the event has occurred on the preceding day.

We will use the Standard & Poor's 500 Daily *price change* for 1988 where *price change* increases are encoded as a "2" and a decrease as a "1" (Table 3-18, column 3). If you examine these data, you will find that the probability of a *price change* increase (p) is 113/252 or 0.4484, and p_i is

Table 6–9   Chi-Square Test for Run Length

Run Length	Expected	Observed	Expected-Observed	(Expected-Observed)^2	(Expected-Observed)^2/ Expected	Σ
1	123	42	81	6561	53.34	53.34
2	62	25	37	1369	22.08	75.42
3	31	13	18	324	10.45	85.87
4	16	10	6	36	2.25	88.12
5	8	4	4	16	2.00	90.12
6	4	3	1	1	0.25	90.37
7	2	0	2	4	2	92.97
8	2	2	0	0	0	92.97
9	0.96	1	−0.04	0.0016	0.0017	92.37
10	0.48	0	.48	0.230	0.48	92.85
11	0.24	0	0.24	0.0576	.240	93.090
12	0.12	1	−0.88	0.774	6.45	99.540

46/252 or 0.1825. If you enter these values into the formula, it has the following form:

$$R = \frac{(1 - .4484)}{(1 - .1825)} - 1$$

where R equals -0.3253.

In order to determine if a given level of persistence is significant, we will use the following formula:

$$K = 1 \pm 1.96 \sqrt{\frac{pq}{N}}$$

where N is the number of prices or *price changes* in our sample, p is the probability of occurrence of a *price change* increase, and q is the probability of nonoccurrence of a *price change* increase.

Thus, p is 113/252 or 0.4484 and q is 139/252 or 0.5516. If we use these values in the formula, it has the following form:

$$K = 1 \pm 1.96 \sqrt{\frac{(.4484)\,(.5516)}{252}}$$

where K ranges from 0.9386 to 1.0614.

If R falls within these limits, then the observed level of persistence could occur by chance alone. If R exceeds these limits, then persistence occurred. A negative R, as occurred here, indicates that the occurrences and nonoccurrences tended to oscillate and thus did not persist.

What Does It All Mean?

If you use one of the runs tests described in this chapter and discover that the number of runs of prices is not statistically significant, then the underlying time series (prices or *price changes*) was generated by a random (and potentially independent) process. If this is so, then you cannot use these data to develop a reasoned trading strategy (see Chapters 3 and 4). On the other hand, if the number of runs of prices is statistically significant or if the prices persist, it means that the prices were not generated by a random (or independent) process. Therefore, it should be possible to use the techniques described in Chapters 3, 7, or 8 or other techniques that you have developed to discover the "rules" that generate the time series to develop more reasoned and profitable trading strategies.

Averaging   7

Background

Do you have a *signal* that you would like to use to determine when to buy or sell a particular stock or commodity? Do you sometimes miss this signal because it is masked by noise, such as random fluctuations or seasonal trends? If you believe that this *signal* is time-locked to some external event, such as the beginning or ending of a trading week or month, the behavior of some other stock or indicator, or an internal event such as a fixed number of price increases or decreases, then you can use a relatively powerful technique to detect your *signal* even in the presence of noise. This technique is called averaging. It was discovered and used by the scientists and engineers that were working on the development of RADAR during World War II.

You can use this technique with prices, *price changes*, or categories of prices or *price changes* (see Chapters 3 and 8). You can also use averaging to fine-tune your selection of moving averages.

We will construct our averaging histogram by labeling the vertical axis frequency and constructing a series of bins on the horizontal axis. The number of bins is determined by the time frame over which we are averaging. For example, if we are going to average by years on a monthly basis, we would need 12 bins, labeled 1 to 12 or January to December. If we are averaging on a weekly basis by days, we would need 5 bins, labeled 1 to 5 or Monday to Friday. To average by months on a daily basis, we would need to decide if we were going to use a calendar month (about 30 days), which would include spaces for weekends and holidays, or a trading month (about 23 days), which does not have spaces for nontrading days. It is important to realize that you can average over any time frame that you are interested in. For example, you can average over years, by months, or using 18 months rather than 12. The important thing to keep in mind is the potential relationship between your trigger and your signal.

Basic Technique

Once you have determined the time frame that you are going to average over and set up the appropriate number of bins, you will need a list of prices or *price changes* to average. We will treat the data in Chapter 2, Table 2-1 as if they were monthly average prices and the table contains data for about 16 years. To begin, line up the first 12 prices under the 12 bins. For example, the first price is 9, so write a 9 immediately below the "bin-Jan." The second price is 10, so we write a 10 immediately below "bin-Feb." Continue this process until the 12th price is reached, which is 4, so write a 4 immediately below the "bin-Dec." Then shift the list of prices to the left until we reach the 13th price, a 15. Then write a 15 below the 9 in "bin-Jan." The next price is 13 so write a 13 below the 10 in "bin-Feb" continuing this process of copying the 12 prices into the appropriate bins and then shifting the list of prices to the left until the last price is reached. In this case, the last price is a 10, so write a 10 at the bottom of the column below "bin-Dec." This column contains 16 prices, 4, 1, 15, 15, 1, 1, 10, 15, 6, 12, 8, 4, 5, 7, 6, and 10, as shown in Table 7-1. Each time you acquire an additional price, add it to the sum in the appropriate column and divide the sum by the number of prices in the column and replot the column on the chart.

There are a number of different ways to display our averaging histogram. The most traditional way is to find the mean of each column and display the means by column, as the relative height of the column. We do this by summing all of the individual prices in the column. For example, in "bin-Dec" there are 16 prices. They sum to 120 and when we divide the sum by the number of prices in the column (16), the average (mean) price is 7.5, as shown in "bin-Dec" in Figure 7-1. We can also display our averages with their associated standard deviations. The method for calculating the standard deviation and the meaning of the standard deviation is shown in Table 7-2. The means and standard deviations for our data are shown in Figure 7-2. We can also rank the prices in each column in our table from the lowest to the highest and determine which price is associated with each percentile (10%, 25%, 50% (median), 75%, or 90%). If we

Table 7-1

	Jan.	Feb.	March	April	May	June	July	August	Sept.	Oct.	Nov.	Dec.
1	9.000	10.000	4.000	15.000	6.000	4.000	3.000	13.000	12.000	1.000	3.000	4.000
2	15.000	13.000	1.000	4.000	8.000	13.000	4.000	2.000	12.000	9.000	12.000	1.000
3	4.000	14.000	1.000	15.000	6.000	11.000	12.000	8.000	14.000	11.000	2.000	15.000
4	11.000	8.000	4.000	8.000	15.000	14.000	12.000	5.000	12.000	10.000	9.000	15.000
5	12.000	13.000	2.000	6.000	13.000	9.000	5.000	15.000	11.000	14.000	11.000	1.000
6	7.000	5.000	6.000	14.000	8.000	2.000	4.000	5.000	8.000	13.000	2.000	1.000
7	8.000	12.000	6.000	9.000	15.000	10.000	8.000	9.000	3.000	2.000	9.000	10.000
8	15.000	10.000	6.000	11.000	2.000	1.000	12.000	9.000	12.000	1.000	8.000	15.000
9	2.000	8.000	9.000	15.000	14.000	12.000	8.000	10.000	2.000	13.000	1.000	6.000
10	2.000	9.000	3.000	7.000	1.000	4.000	14.000	8.000	9.000	2.000	8.000	12.000
11	10.000	1.000	11.000	14.000	12.000	1.000	14.000	4.000	11.000	2.000	9.000	8.000
12	13.000	9.000	5.000	11.000	12.000	6.000	9.000	5.000	11.000	9.000	3.000	4.000
13	12.000	13.000	6.000	5.000	15.000	2.000	14.000	1.000	6.000	5.000	11.000	5.000
14	4.000	8.000	6.000	2.000	5.000	9.000	3.000	1.000	11.000	6.000	11.000	7.000
15	9.000	3.000	15.000	10.000	12.000	3.000	7.000	6.000	13.000	3.000	1.000	6.000
16	1.000	9.000	7.000	1.000	6.000	5.000	8.000	12.000	5.000	6.000	8.000	10.000

Figure 7–1

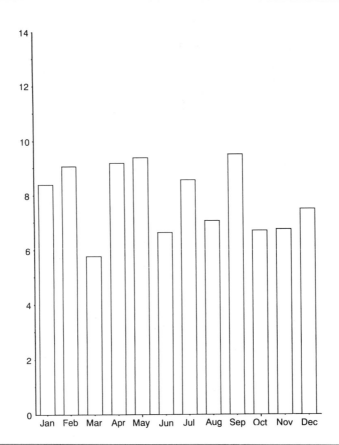

rank the prices in "bin-Jan," the result is 1, 2, 2, 4, 4, 7, 8, 9, 9, 10, 11, 12, 12, 13, 15, and 15. The median (50% of the prices fall above the median price and 50% below the median price) price is 9. The median prices are shown in Figure 7-3, where the median price is represented by the line in the middle of each box. The lower and upper end of each box represents the 25th and 75th percentile prices, respectively, while the lines outside the box represent the 10th and 90th percentiles.

While not precisely an average, there is another way to display this sort of data that can potentially provide useful information. Make the height of the column proportional to the sum of the individual monthly prices for each year and allow the relative height of each block (high-

Table 7–2   Standard Deviation

Note: The standard deviation is a measure of dispersion. A small standard deviation indicates that prices are relatively homogeneous, while a large standard deviation indicates that the prices vary widely. The formula for calculating the standard deviation is:

$$S.D. = \sqrt{\frac{\sum\limits_{n=1}^{16} (\text{mean-price})}{N - 1}}$$

Price	Deviations	(Deviations)^2	Σ
4	4 – 7.5 = –3.5	12.25	12.25
1	1 – 7.5 = –6.5	42.25	54.50
15	15 – 7.5 = 7.5	56.25	110.75
15	15 – 7.5 = 7.5	56.25	167.00
1	1 – 7.5 = –6.5	42.25	209.25
1	1 – 7.5 = –6.5	42.25	251.50
10	10 – 7.5 = 2.5	6.25	257.75
15	15 – 7.5 = 7.5	56.25	314.00
6	6 – 7.5 = –1.5	2.25	316.25
12	12 – 7.5 = 4.5	20.25	336.50
8	8 – 7.5 = 0.5	0.25	336.75
4	4 – 7.5 = –3.5	12.25	349.00
5	5 – 7.5 = –2.5	6.25	355.55
7	7 – 7.5 = –0.5	0.25	355.20
6	6 – 7.5 = –1.5	2.25	357.75
10	10 – 7.5 = 2.5	6.25	364.00
120			

Mean = 120/16 = 7.5

If we substitute the sum of deviations (column 4, row 16) and the number of prices (N = 16) into this formula, it has the following form:

$$S.D = \sqrt{\frac{364}{15}}$$

which equals 4.936.

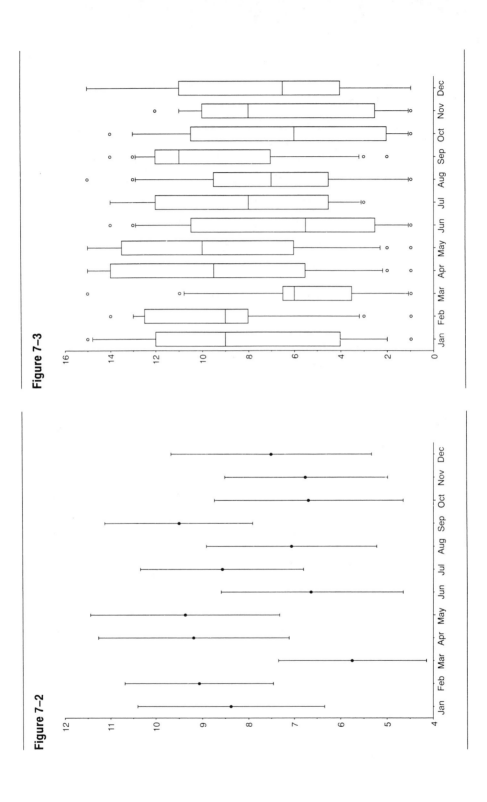

Figure 7-2

Figure 7-3

lighted by a different "fill") to represent the contribution of each price to the sum. This type of plot is shown in Figure 7-4.

We can also average categorized data using the method described in detail in Chapters 3 and 8. For example, we coded the price change data for our artificial data, where a price increase is encoded as a "2" and a decrease as a "1" (see Table 6-1, column 3, Chapter 6). We can display this data in the same manner as before, where the encoded data is tabulated in Table 7-3. The standard averaging plot is shown in Figure 7-5, while the mean and standard deviation plot is shown in Figure 7-6.

Real Data

The average monthly price of the Standard & Poor's 500 Stock Index for 1947-1987 is shown in Chapter 6, Table 6-5, column 1. We will use this data to collect an averaging histogram over years by months. The first price is 15.21, so write this value under the "bin-Jan" as previously described. The next price 15.80, so write this under the "bin-Feb" in our averaging histogram and continue this process until reaching the last price. The completed histogram should resemble the one shown in Table 7-4. The averaged plot is shown in Figure 7-7, the median plot in Figure 7-8, and the block plot in Figure 7-9.

Moving Average

If you are using the averaging technique to fine-tune your selection of a moving average, start with your best estimate of the duration of the moving average. For example, you might decide on a 20-day moving average. So, start your histogram with 20 bins and read your price data into it using the beginning of a cycle as the trigger. Once you have collected all of your data into your averaging histogram, calculate the mean price and the standard deviation of prices for each column. If you have chosen the optimum moving average, the relative height of the columns should mimic the effect of the moving average. One way to determine if you have an optimum moving average is to collect averages over several different time periods. For example, if you believe a 20-day moving average is optimum, you might collect it and a 15-day and a 25- or 30-day moving average. You can compare the mean and standard deviation for each column in each plot. The averaged plot that shows the optimum length moving average would have the smallest standard deviation values in each column of the plot.

Table 7–3

	Jan.	Feb.	March	April	May	June	July	August	Sept.	Oct.	Nov.	Dec.
1	2.000	1.000	2.000	1.000	1.000	1.000	2.000	1.000	1.000	2.000	2.000	2.000
2	1.000	1.000	2.000	2.000	2.000	1.000	1.000	2.000	1.000	2.000	1.000	2.000
3	2.000	1.000	2.000	1.000	2.000	2.000	1.000	2.000	1.000	1.000	2.000	1.000
4	1.000	1.000	2.000	2.000	1.000	1.000	1.000	2.000	1.000	1.000	2.000	1.000
5	2.000	1.000	2.000	2.000	1.000	1.000	2.000	1.000	2.000	1.000	1.000	2.000
6	1.000	2.000	2.000	1.000	1.000	2.000	2.000	2.000	2.000	1.000	1.000	2.000
7	2.000	1.000	2.000	2.000	1.000	1.000	2.000	1.000	1.000	2.000	2.000	2.000
8	1.000	1.000	2.000	1.000	1.000	2.000	2.000	2.000	2.000	2.000	2.000	1.000
9	2.000	2.000	2.000	1.000	2.000	2.000	1.000	1.000	1.000	2.000	2.000	1.000
10	2.000	1.000	2.000	1.000	2.000	2.000	1.000	2.000	1.000	2.000	2.000	1.000
11	1.000	2.000	2.000	1.000	1.000	2.000	1.000	2.000	1.000	2.000	2.000	2.000
12	1.000	1.000	2.000	2.000	1.000	2.000	1.000	2.000	1.000	1.000	2.000	2.000
13	2.000	1.000	1.000	2.000	1.000	2.000	1.000	2.000	1.000	2.000	1.000	1.000
14	2.000	1.000	1.000	2.000	2.000	1.000	1.000	2.000	1.000	2.000	1.000	2.000
15	1.000	2.000	1.000	2.000	1.000	2.000	1.000	2.000	1.000	1.000	2.000	1.000
16	2.000	1.000	1.000	2.000	1.000	2.000	2.000	1.000	2.000	2.000	2.000	2.000

Figure 7–4

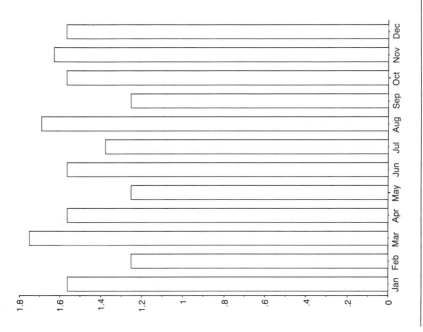

Figure7–5

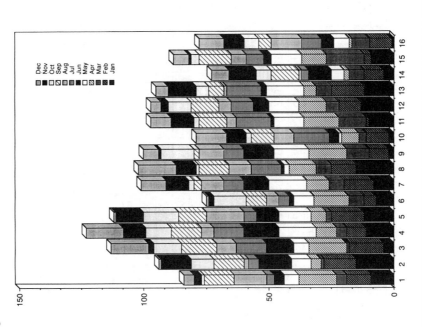

Table 7–4

	Jan.	Feb.	March	April	May	June	July	August	Sept.	Oct.	Nov.	Dec.
1	15.210	15.800	15.160	14.600	14.340	14.840	15.770	15.460	15.060	15.450	15.270	15.030
2	14.830	14.100	14.300	15.400	16.150	16.820	16.420	15.940	15.760	16.190	15.290	15.190
3	15.360	14.770	14.910	14.890	14.780	13.970	14.760	15.290	15.490	15.890	16.110	16.540
4	16.880	17.210	17.350	17.840	18.440	18.740	17.380	18.430	19.080	19.870	19.830	19.750
5	21.210	22.000	21.630	21.920	21.930	21.550	21.930	22.890	23.480	23.360	22.710	23.410
6	24.190	23.750	23.810	23.750	23.730	24.380	25.080	25.180	24.780	24.260	25.030	26.040
7	26.180	25.860	25.990	24.710	24.840	23.950	24.290	24.390	23.270	23.970	24.500	24.830
8	25.460	26.020	26.570	27.630	28.730	28.960	30.130	30.730	31.450	32.180	33.440	34.970
9	35.600	36.790	36.500	37.760	37.600	39.780	42.690	42.430	44.340	42.110	44.950	45.370
10	44.150	44.430	47.490	48.050	46.540	46.270	48.780	48.490	46.840	46.240	45.760	46.440
11	45.430	43.470	44.030	45.050	46.780	47.550	48.510	45.840	43.980	41.240	40.350	40.330
12	41.120	41.260	42.110	42.340	43.700	44.750	45.980	47.700	48.960	50.950	52.500	53.490
13	55.620	54.770	56.150	57.100	57.960	57.460	59.740	59.400	57.050	57.000	57.230	59.060
14	58.030	55.780	55.020	55.730	55.220	57.260	55.840	56.510	54.810	53.730	55.470	56.800
15	59.720	62.170	64.120	65.830	66.500	65.620	65.440	67.790	67.260	68.000	71.080	71.740
16	69.070	70.220	70.290	68.050	62.990	55.630	56.970	58.520	58.000	56.170	60.040	62.640
17	65.060	65.920	65.670	68.760	70.140	70.110	69.070	70.980	72.850	73.030	72.620	74.170
18	76.450	77.390	78.800	79.940	80.720	80.240	83.220	82.000	83.410	84.850	85.440	83.960
19	86.120	86.750	86.830	87.970	89.280	85.040	84.910	86.490	89.380	91.390	92.150	91.730
20	93.320	92.690	88.880	91.600	86.780	86.060	85.840	80.650	77.810	77.130	80.990	81.330

Table continues

Table 7-4 Continued

	Jan.	Feb.	March	April	May	June	July	August	Sept.	Oct.	Nov.	Dec.
21	84.450	87.360	89.420	90.960	92.590	91.430	93.010	94.490	95.810	95.660	92.660	95.300
22	95.040	90.750	89.090	95.670	97.870	100.530	100.300	98.110	101.340	103.760	105.400	106.480
23	102.040	101.460	99.300	101.260	104.620	99.140	94.710	94.180	94.510	95.520	96.210	91.110
24	90.310	87.160	88.650	85.950	76.060	75.590	75.720	77.920	82.580	84.370	84.280	90.050
25	93.490	97.110	99.600	103.040	101.640	99.720	99.000	97.240	99.400	97.290	92.780	99.170
26	103.300	105.240	107.690	108.810	107.650	108.010	107.210	111.010	109.390	109.560	115.050	117.500
27	118.420	114.160	112.420	110.270	107.220	104.750	105.830	103.800	105.610	109.840	102.030	94.780
28	96.110	93.450	97.440	92.460	89.670	89.790	82.820	76.030	68.120	69.440	71.740	67.070
29	72.560	80.100	83.780	84.720	90.100	92.400	92.490	85.710	84.670	88.570	90.070	88.700
30	96.860	100.640	101.080	101.930	101.160	101.770	104.200	103.290	105.450	101.890	101.190	104.660
31	103.810	100.960	100.570	99.050	98.760	99.290	100.180	97.750	96.230	93.740	94.280	93.820
32	90.250	88.980	88.820	92.710	97.410	97.660	97.190	103.920	103.860	100.580	94.710	96.110
33	99.710	98.230	100.110	102.070	99.730	101.730	102.710	107.360	108.600	104.270	103.660	107.780
34	110.870	115.340	104.690	102.970	107.690	114.550	119.830	123.500	126.510	130.220	135.650	133.480
35	132.970	128.400	133.190	134.430	131.730	132.280	129.130	129.630	118.270	119.800	122.920	123.790
36	117.280	114.500	110.840	116.310	116.350	109.700	109.380	109.650	122.430	132.660	138.100	139.370
37	144.270	146.800	151.880	157.710	164.100	166.390	166.960	162.420	167.160	167.650	165.230	164.360
38	166.390	157.250	157.440	157.600	156.550	153.120	151.080	164.420	166.110	164.820	166.270	164.480
39	171.610	180.880	179.420	180.620	184.900	188.890	192.540	188.310	184.060	186.180	197.450	207.260
40	208.190	219.370	232.330	237.980	238.460	245.300	240.180	245.000	238.270	237.360	245.090	248.610
41	264.510	280.930	292.470	289.320	289.120	301.380	310.090	329.360	318.660	280.160	245.010	240.960

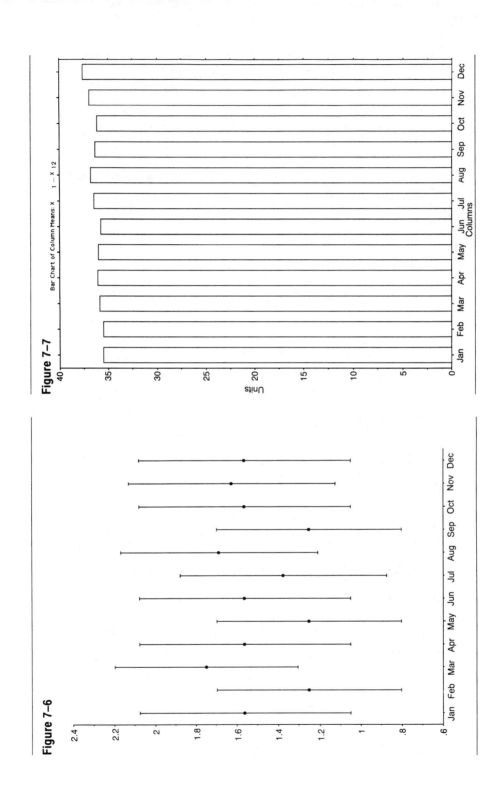

Figure 7–6

Figure 7–7

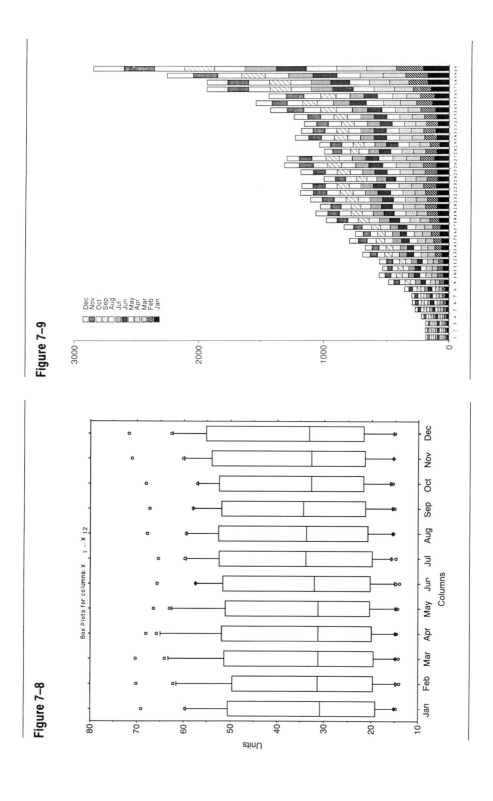

Figure 7-8

Figure 7-9

What Does It All Mean?

If you have a relatively large number of prices, then averaging provides a uniquely powerful tool to eliminate the effects of random noise (seasonal fluctuations, etc.). It also allows you to determine if the moving average you are using is the optimum moving average to generate the maximum number of meaningful signals. If your moving average is not optimum, averaging can help you find the optimum moving average.

Pattern Detection Techniques　　8

Background

Much of the work that technicians do, whether they realize it or not, is to seek patterns of activity in the past history of prices or *price changes* that will occur again in the future. These patterns of activity are time-locked to other events, such as significant increases or decreases in the price of a particular stock. These patterns act as a signal that these events are about to occur again. These signals tell a trader when to buy or sell a particular stock and make a profit or minimize a loss. Some traders look for traditional signals like the "head and shoulders top." Others wait for one moving average to cross another.

One problem with looking for these signals is that the time series that traders typically deal with are relatively complex and tend to be somewhat "noisy." Therefore, it is often relatively difficult to see the real signal and distinguish it from a false signal. One way to deal with this problem is to simplify the time series by categorizing prices or *price changes* (see Chapter 3) to minimize the effects of noise and maximize our ability to see patterns. It is important to note that we can use any method we choose to determine the categories.

For example, you might want to know if the temporal distribution of the highest or lowest 10% of the prices or *price changes* of a particular stock differs from the distribution of the middle 80%. Or you might want to know if the temporal distribution of prices or *price changes* above or below the mean or median are distributed randomly and/or independently.

Once you have decided on how to parse your time series, you must apply this criteria consistently. In addition to independence testing, you can also collect your categorized price into a variety of different histograms, such as densitogram, periodogram, the triggered price (change) histogram, or the temporal correlogram. You can also use these histograms to detect signals in your prices or *price changes* that will help you make profitable buy-sell decisions.

Densitogram—Basic Procedures

We will use the artificial "prices" in the left column at the bottom of Figure 8-1 as our basic data to illustrate how we generate a densitogram. We will collect these prices into a frequency histogram. If we are using paper and pencil, we will create a histogram with 10 bins on the horizontal axis, labeled 1 to 10. The vertical axis is labeled frequency. The first price is a "2," so increase the frequency of "bin-2" from 0 to 1. This is indicated by the small 1 immediately over this bin. The next price is a "10" so increase the frequency of "bin-10" from 0 to 1, as indicated by the small 2 over this bin. The next price is a "6" so increase the frequency of "bin-6" from 0 to 1. Continue this process of collecting the prices into this frequency histogram until we reach the last price, which is a "4." We will then increase the frequency of "bin-4" from 0 to 1, as indicated by the small 16 immediately over the bin. The frequency count in "bin-1" to "bin-10" is 1, 4, 1, 1, 1, 3, 0, 2, 1, and 2.

Now we can divide the histogram into parts. In Figure 8-1, we divided the histogram into unequal parts, as indicated by the heavy vertical lines on the histogram. Now we re-examine our original list of prices (left column) to determine to which third each belongs. The first price is a "2," which is located in the first third, so we encode it as a 1. The next price is a "10," which is contained in the third third, so we encode it as a 3. The next price is a "6," contained in the middle third, so we encode it as a 2. We continue this process until we reach the last price, a "4," which is located in the first third, so we encode it as a 1. In this example, we have seven 1's, four 2's, and five 3's.

We are now ready to generate the densitogram to determine how a particular price category is distributed in time. For example, we might want to know how sequential 1's are distributed. The number of bins in the densitogram is critical and has a significant impact on the shape (and meaning) of the densitogram, as described in detail below. In this example, we will use a densitogram with 11 bins. We lay the categorized price

Figure 8–1

2	1
10	3
6	2
3	1
6	2
2	1
1	1
10	3
6	2
9	3
2	1
5	2
8	3
8	3
2	1
4	1

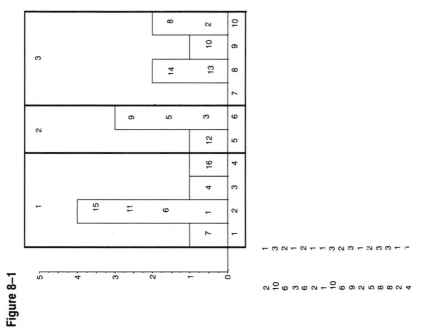

Figure 8–2

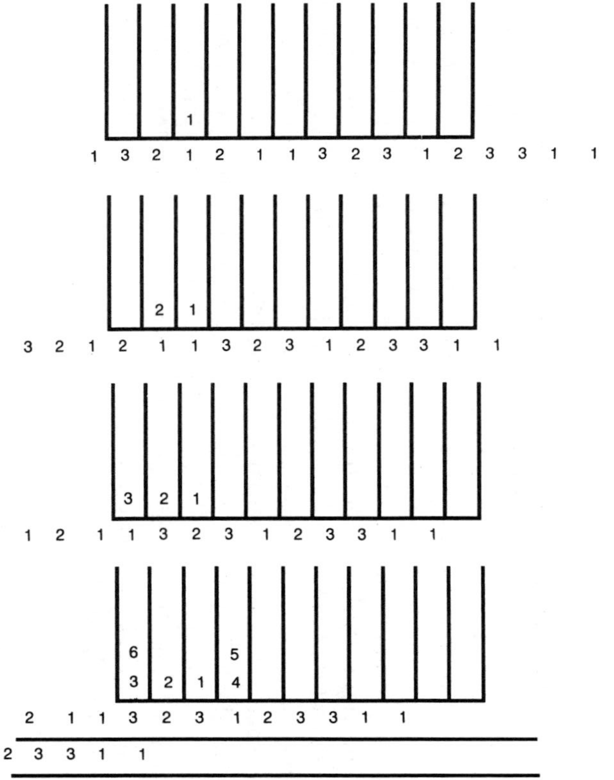

line below the densitogram, with the first "1" to the left of the first bin, as shown in Figure 8-2, top panel. Now we scan to the right on the categorized price line until we encounter the next sequential "1." When we find this "1," we increase the frequency of the bin from 0 to 1, as indicated by the small 1 in the bin. We then move the entire categorized price line to the left to the next sequential "1" (see Figure 8-2, panel 2). We scan the list to the right until we find the next sequential "1" and increase the frequency of that bin from 0 to 1, as indicated by the small 2 in that bin. We move the categorized price line to the left and rescan the price line until we reach the next sequential "1." Note that we are looking for the fourth sequential "1" in the categorized price line. We increase the frequency of this bin from 0 to 1, as indicated by the small 3 in that bin. We continue this process until we reach the last sequential "1." Since there are seven 1's in this artificial time series, the densitogram contains six counts, as shown in Figure 8-2, bottom panel.

Densitogram—Real Data

We will use the *price change* data for the Standard & Poor's 500 Stock Index for 1988 and divide the frequency histogram into four parts, as shown in Figure 8-3, where the categories are defined as follows: -$17.67 to -1.265 as a "1"; -1.264 to +0.16 as a "2"; +0.17 to 1.33 as a "3"; and 1.34 to 8.74 as a "4." The densitogram for a "1" to the first sequential "1" is shown in Figure 8-4, while the densitogram for a "2" to a "2," a "3" to a "3," and a "4" to a "4" are shown in Figures 8-5 to 8-7, respectively.

What information can we glean from these densitograms? We can see that the distribution of 1s, 2s, 3s, and 4's are probably not independent. There are two basic reasons for this assumption. First, if the serial distribution of 1's is independent, then the densitogram for a "1" to the next sequential "1" should be similar to the densitogram for a "2" to the next sequential "2" (or a "3" to a "3," etc.). If you examine Figures 8-4 and 8-5, you will note that the densitograms are not very similar. Second, you would expect that the densitogram for a "1" to the next sequential "1" should be relatively homogenous; that is, the relative frequency in each of the bins in the densitogram should be similar. Clearly, if you examine Figure 8-4, you can see that this is not the case. A "1" is much more likely to occur the day after a "1" has occurred (see "bin-1" in Figure 8-4).

This is even more striking if we look at higher order densitograms, such as the ones shown in Figures 8-8 and 8-9. For example, Figure 8-8 shows the densitogram for a "1" to the fifth sequential "1." If you examine

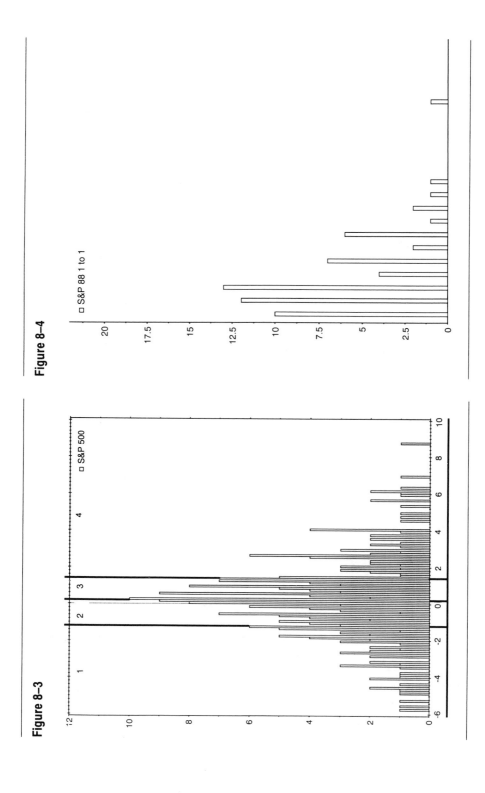

Figure 8–4

□ S&P 88 1 to 1

Figure 8–3

□ S&P 500

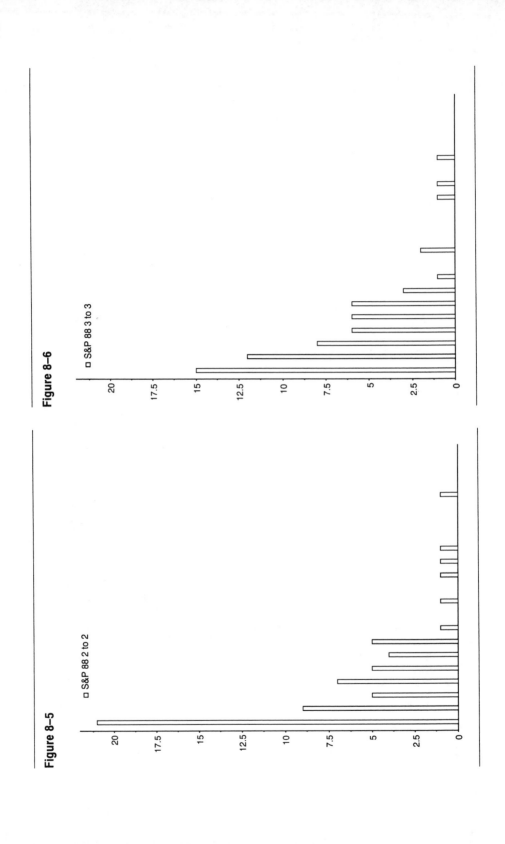

Figure 8-5

□ S&P 88 2 to 2

Figure 8-6

□ S&P 88 3 to 3

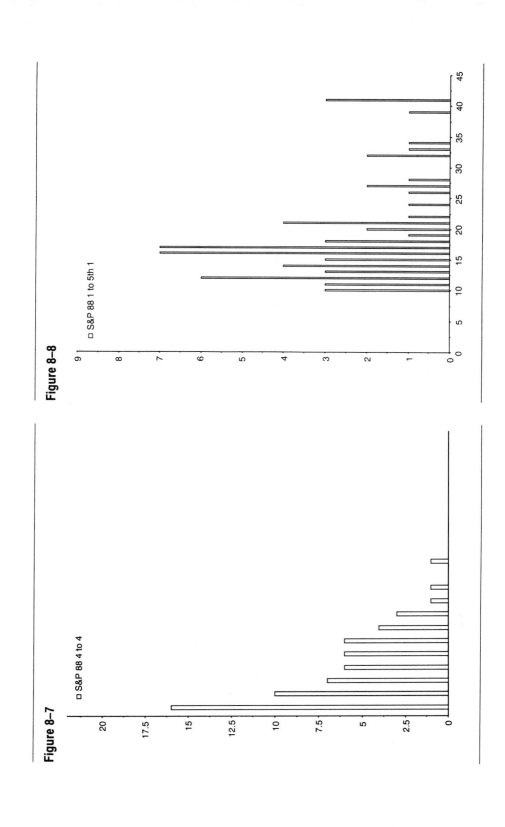

Figure 8-7

□ S&P 88 4 to 4

Figure 8-8

□ S&P 88 1 to 5th 1

Figure 8–9

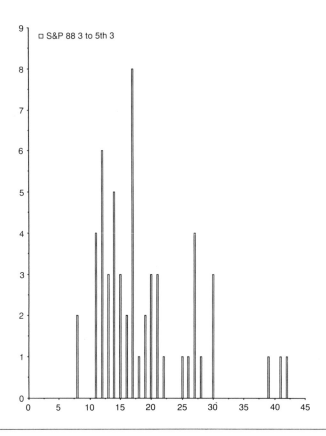

this figure, you will note that the distribution of 1s is not homogenous. In fact, although the densitogram is of a "1" to the fifth sequential "1," "bin-5" to "bin-9" do not contain any counts. The fifth sequential "1" only occurs after at least 10 days. The densitograms for a "1" to the fifth sequential "1" and a "3" to the fifth sequential "3" (Figure 8-9) are not similar. Again, both of these observations suggest that the relative distribution of 1s, 2s, etc., is not independent.

The frequency histogram delta-1 *price changes* for Comex silver in 1988 was divided into approximately equal thirds, where a "1" represents the lowest third of the *price changes* (–13160 to –110), while the middle third are encoded as a "2" (–105 to +90), and the highest third are encoded as a "3" (+95 to +8930). The paper and pencil version of densitogram for a

"1" to the next sequential "1" is shown in Table 8-1 (for the first six columns). The complete densitogram for a "1" to the next sequential "1" is shown in Figure 8-10, while the densitogram for a "1" to the sixth sequential "1" is shown in Figure 8-11.

We will use the delta-1 *price change* data for the Standard & Poor's 500 Stock Index for January 3, 1983 to September 15, 1988 to generate a series of densitograms. In this case, divide the frequency histogram in 10 approximately equal parts: "1" (–80.83 to –2.00); "2" (–2.07 to –1.19); "3" (–1.18 to –0.60); "4" (–0.59 to –0.20); "5" (–0.18 to 0.21); "6" (0.22 to 0.61); "7" (0.615 to 1.00); "8" (1.02 to 1.81); "9" (1.815 to 3.19); and "10" (3.20 to 41.84). The densitograms for a "1" to the next sequential "1," a "5" to the next sequential "5," and a "10" to the next sequential "10" are shown in Figures 8-12 to 8-14, respectively.

Periodogram—Real Data

The monthly averages for the Dow Jones Industrial for 1950 to 1985 are shown in Figure 8-15. We will collect the delta-1 "changes" into a frequency histogram and then divide the histogram in four equal parts, as described above, where a "1" represents the changes from $131.10 to $–12.10; a "2" (–11.29 to +4.16); a "3" (4.23 to 17.12); and a "4" (17.16 to 118.13). Rather than looking for patterns in individual changes, we will use digrams. In this case, a digram is defined as a "1" followed by a "1"; a "1" followed by a "2"; a "1" followed by a "3,"..., a "4" followed by a "4." We will generate the periodogram by determining the temporal distribution of each digram. The first digram is a 3,2. This digram occurs in the fourth place in the digram time line, in the ninth place in the digram time line, the thirteenth place, etc., as shown in Table 8-2.

We can use the periodogram in a number of different ways. For example, if the digrams are distributed independently, the mean or median place difference should be similar over digrams. If you examine Table 8-2, you will see that they are not. This suggests that the temporal distribution of digrams is not independent.

Triggered Categorized Price Histogram I—Basic Procedures

You can also trigger the collection of a histogram based on some signal that is external to the time series that you are examining. For example, you can trigger the collection of a histogram on the beginning of a trading week. In this case, you will need a histogram with five bins, labeled Mon.,

Table 8–1

	Column 1	Column 2	Column 3	Column 4	Column 5	Column 6
1	2	9	19	16	1	5
2	3	11	21	27	23	12
3	4	13	26	45	24	14
4	6	17	36	51	39	29
5	7	18	38	66	63	67
6	8	30	40	71	81	93
7	10	32	42	76	83	113
8	15	34	43	108	85	•
9	22	41	59	•	•	•
10	25	44	75	•	•	•
11	28	47	80	•	•	•
12	31	49	84	•	•	•
13	33	56	88	•	•	•
14	35	58	96	•	•	•
15	37	60	98	•	•	•
16	46	61	106	•	•	•
17	48	64	•	•	•	•
18	50	69	•	•	•	•
19	52	78	•	•	•	•
20	53	90	•	•	•	•
21	55	95	•	•	•	•
22	57	97	•	•	•	•
23	62	101	•	•	•	•
24	65	102	•	•	•	•
25	72	104	•	•	•	•
26	74	107	•	•	•	•
27	77	•	•	•	•	•
28	79	•	•	•	•	•
29	86	•	•	•	•	•
30	89	•	•	•	•	•
31	91	•	•	•	•	•
32	92	•	•	•	•	•
33	94	•	•	•	•	•
34	99	•	•	•	•	•
35	100	•	•	•	•	•
36	105	•	•	•	•	•

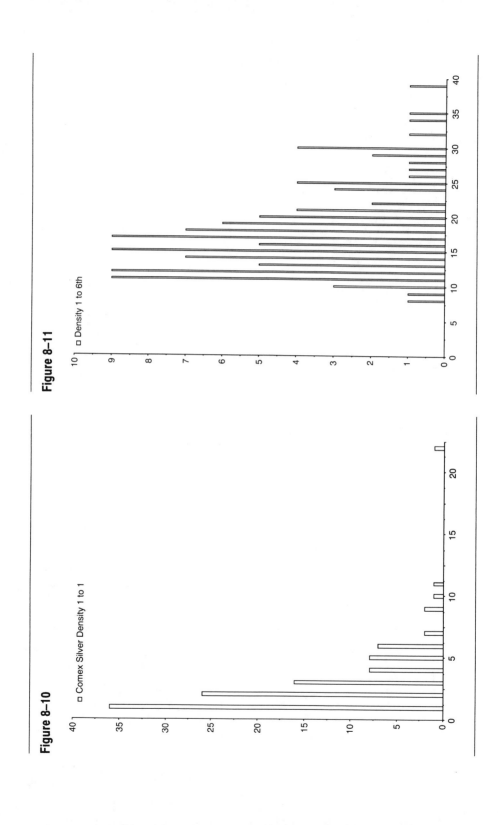

Figure 8–10

□ Comex Silver Density 1 to 1

Figure 8–11

□ Density 1 to 6th

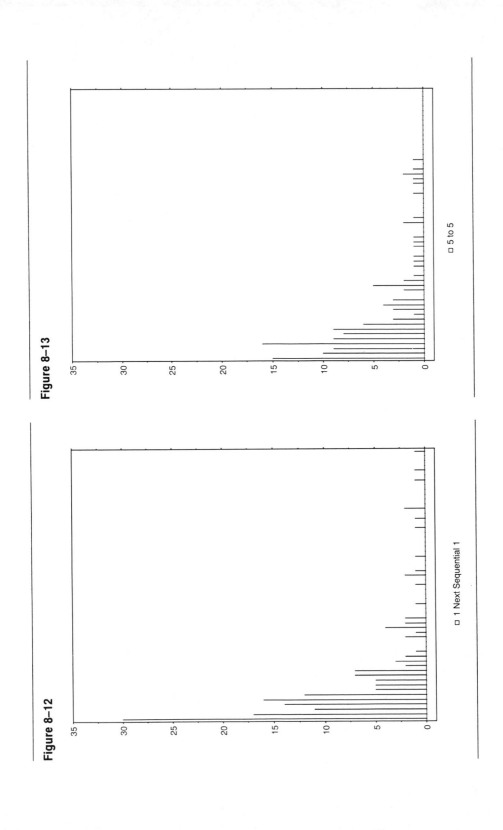

Figure 8–12

□ 1 Next Sequential 1

Figure 8–13

□ 5 to 5

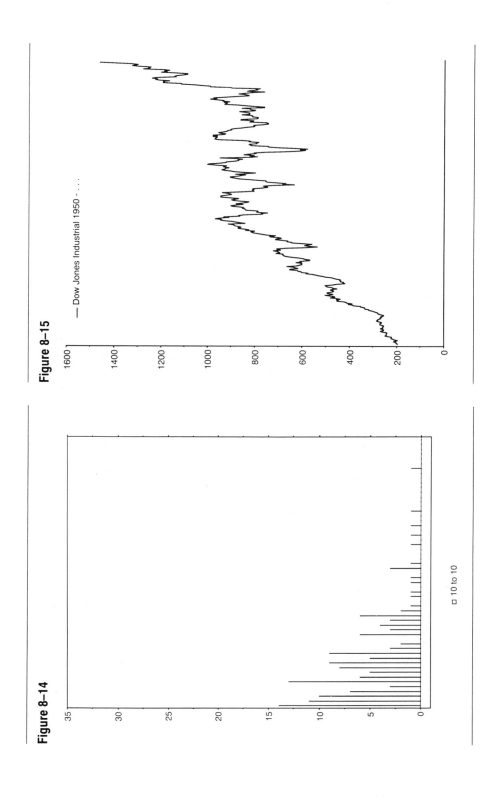

Figure 8–14

Figure 8–15

— Dow Jones Industrial 1950 - . . .

Table 8–2

	1, 2	1, 2	1, 3	1, 4	2, 1	2, 2	2, 3	2, 4
1	91	21	69	62	79	2	3	58
2	92	72	76	149	84	5	6	60
3	147	80	85	153	115	10	11	73
4	148	120	93	166	121	14	18	109
5	152	122	116	173	146	15	22	113
6	193	128	126	175	161	16	28	124
7	198	217	140	185	178	17	33	129
8	213	240	144	194	227	25	41	138
9	216	268	162	201	256	26	44	158
10	222	278	179	214	269	27	48	183
11	228	281	196	223	276	31	53	191
12	233	307	199	244	279	32	56	204
13	239	321	229	246	282	36	64	218
14	243	326	234	259	327	37	67	241
15	257	333	292	262	344	38	82	250
16	258	337	328	270	411	39	89	303
17	261	345	376	273	427	40	95	309
18	277	352	380	283	•	43	97	311
19	280	357	389	287	•	55	99	317
20	286	362	409	289	•	81	111	322
21	291	413	417	297	•	123	207	342
22	294	•	422	299	•	137	209	347
23	295	•	•	319	•	203	237	358
24	296	•	•	371	•	226	334	360
25	325	•	•	386	•	236	338	363
26	330	•	•	391	•	308	349	373
27	331	•	•	403	•	315	353	395
28	332	•	•	419	•	316	369	399
29	336	•	•	428	•	341	401	406
30	378	•	•	•	•	346	•	414
31	379	•	•	•	•	368	•	424
32	384	•	•	•	•	•	•	•
33	385	•	•	•	•	•	•	•
34	388	•	•	•	•	•	•	•
35	408	•	•	•	•	•	•	•
36	412	•	•	•	•	•	•	•

Table continues

Table 8–2   Continued

	3, 1	3, 2	3, 3	3, 4	4, 1	4, 2	4, 3	4, 4
1	20	1	7	65	61	59	74	133
2	68	4	8	70	71	63	103	154
3	75	9	12	87	119	66	105	159
4	90	13	19	102	125	88	130	176
5	127	24	23	104	139	108	134	219
6	143	30	29	107	174	110	150	224
7	151	35	34	118	184	114	155	247
8	165	42	45	132	192	160	164	251
9	172	47	46	163	195	177	167	252
10	197	52	49	169	215	202	170	263
11	200	54	50	188	232	225	186	274
12	212	57	51	210	242	255	189	284
13	221	78	77	231	245	275	205	300
14	238	83	86	254	260	302	211	301
15	267	94	100	265	285	310	220	312
16	272	96	101	339	288	314	248	313
17	293	98	106	350	290	340	253	355
18	306	112	117	354	298	343	264	364
19	324	136	131	382	318	348	266	365
20	329	145	135	393	320	359	271	366
21	335	157	141	•	351	367	304	374
22	370	182	142	•	356	372	323	396
23	377	190	156	•	361	394	392	397
24	390	206	168	•	375	398	404	415
25	402	208	171	•	383	400	•	420
26	418	235	180	•	387	426	•	425
27	•	249	181	•	407	•	•	429
28	•	405	187	•	416	•	•	430
29	•	410	230	•	421	•	•	•
30	•	423	305	•	•	•	•	•
31	•	•	381	•	•	•	•	•
32	•	•	•	•	•	•	•	•
33	•	•	•	•	•	•	•	•
34	•	•	•	•	•	•	•	•
35	•	•	•	•	•	•	•	•
36	•	•	•	•	•	•	•	•

Tues., Wed., Thurs., and Fri. We will use the artificial categorized prices shown in the right column at the bottom of Figure 8-1 as our data. In this case, assume that the first categorized price occurred on a Monday, the second on a Tuesday, etc., as shown in Figure 8-16. We line up the categorized time line under the bins. We will collect the triggered categorized price histogram for 1's. In the example shown in Figure 8-16, we increase the frequency of each bin where a "1" occurs. In this case, a "1" occurs on Monday and Thursday, so we increase the frequency in "bin-Mon." and "bin-Thurs." from 0 to 1, as indicated by the 1's in these bins. We now move the price line to the left by one full week and line up the second Monday with "bin-Mon." We increase the frequency of "bin-Mon." from

Figure 8–16

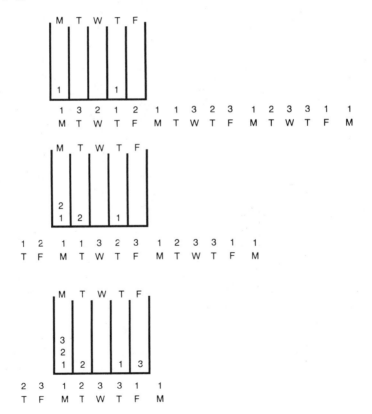

1 to 2, as indicated by the 2 in the bin and increase the frequency of "bin-Tues." from 0 to 1 (indicated by the small 2 in the bin). We continue this process until we reach the last week on the price line.

Triggered Categorized Price Histogram I—Real Data

We will use the delta-1 *price changes* for the closing prices for Sears in 1991 to generate a frequency histogram and then divide the histogram into unequal thirds, where a "1" represents the lowest 10% of the price changes (–$2.00 to –0.97), the middle 80% of the *price changes* are encoded as a "2" (–0.96 to +0.96), and the highest 10% are encoded as a "3" (+0.961 to 2.00).

We will generate a triggered categorized *price change* histogram using this categorized price line. We will collect the first "1" that occurs in each trading week in 1991. The resulting triggered categorized *price change* histogram is shown in Figure 8-17. The triggered categorized *price change* histogram for the first "3" in a trading week is shown in Figure 8-18. If you examine these figures, you will note that the temporal distribution of the highest and lowest 10% of *price changes* in a trading week is relatively homogenous. Although the distribution is homogenous, it is intriguing that the highest 10% *price changes* tend to occur at the beginning of the trading week, while the lowest 10% tend to occur towards the end of the trading week (Thursday).

It is important to note that you can use other types of time series besides prices or *price changes*. For example, you might want to know how changes in trading volume are distributed. We will use daily trading volume for Sears in 1991 to generate a "volume change" frequency histogram. We will divide this histogram into three unequal parts. The lowest 10% volume change is encoded as a "1" (–13582 to –3524 shares), a "2" encodes the middle 80% of volume change (–3328 to 2926), while the highest 10% are encoded as a "3" (3023 to 15814). The triggered categorized volume change histogram for the lowest volume of trading is shown in Figure 8-19, while the highest volume of trading is shown in Figure 8-20.

Triggered Categorized Price Histogram II—Basic Procedures

We can also use the characteristics of another time series as the trigger for the collection of a triggered categorized *price change* histogram. We will use the artificial prices from the right-hand column at the bottom of Fig-

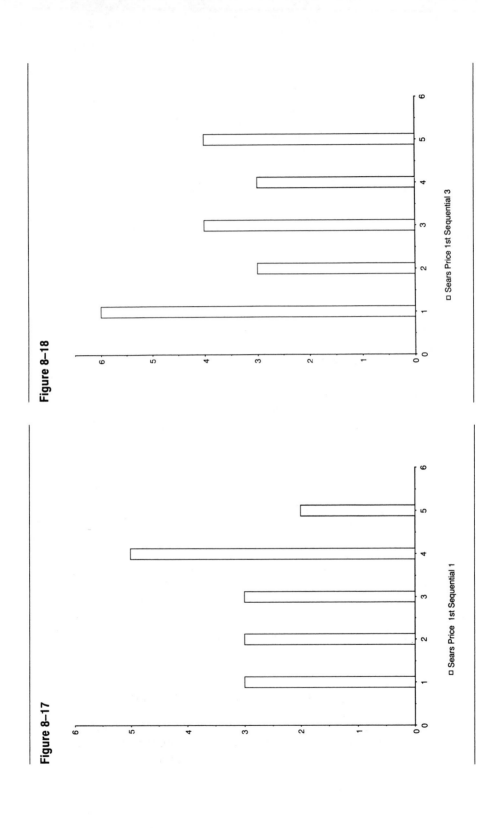

Figure 8–17

Figure 8–18

□ Sears Price 1st Sequential 1

□ Sears Price 1st Sequential 3

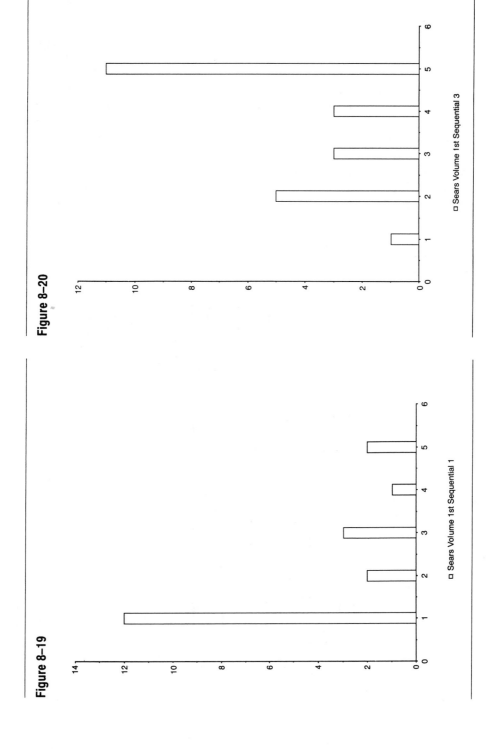

Figure 8-19

Sears Volume 1st Sequential 1

Figure 8-20

Sears Volume 1st Sequential 3

ure 8-1 as our categorized price time line, as shown in Figure 8-21. If you examine this figure, you will note that we generated another categorized price time line (the hollow numbers) that is time-locked to the original categorized price line. We will use this new categorized time series to trigger the collection of our triggered categorized *price change* histogram. In this example, we will trigger on a "4" in the trigger time series and collect the first sequential "1" that occurs in our original categorized price line. The first price in our trigger time series is a "4," so we look in our original price line for the first sequential "1." The first sequential "1" occurs at "bin-1," so we increase the frequency of this bin from 0 to 1, as indicated by the small 1 in the bin. Now, we move the price lines to the

Figure 8–21

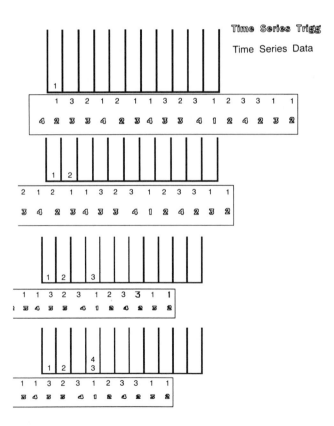

left until we encounter the next sequential "4" in our trigger price line. The first sequential "1" occurs at "bin-2." We increase the frequency of this bin from 0 to 1, as indicated by the small 2 in this bin. We continue this process until we reach the last "4" in the trigger price line, as shown in the lowest frame in this figure.

Triggered Categorized Price Histogram II—Real Data

In some cases, you might want to use each categorized price once and only once in generating your triggered categorized *price change* histogram. This will allow you to determine the precise temporal relationship between a categorized price in your trigger time series and a categorized price in your categorized price line. We collected the delta-1 closing prices for Comex gold and silver into two separate frequency histograms. We divided each frequency histogram into approximately four equal parts. We will use a "1" in the silver categorized price change line as the trigger and collect the first sequential "4" in the gold categorized *price change* line, using each "4" once and only once. The result is shown in Figure 8-22. If we trigger on a "4" in the silver price line and collect the first sequential "4" in the gold time line, using each "4" in the gold line once and only once, the result is shown in Figure 8-23.

Temporal Correlogram—Basic Procedures

We will use the categorized price lines in Table 8-3, column 1 and 2 to generate our temporal correlogram. We multiply the individual categorized prices in one of our categorized price lines by "10" (see column 3). Now we add the individual categorized prices in the first categorized price time line (column 1) to the individual categorized prices in the x10 price line (column 3), where the result is shown in column 4, which we use to plot the temporal correlogram (column 4). The resulting temporal correlogram is shown in Figure 8-24. It is important to note that each column in the temporal correlogram represents the relationship between two categorized prices.

Temporal Correlogram—Real Data

We will collect the delta-1 *price changes* for Comex gold and silver into a frequency histogram and then divide the histogram into unequal thirds.

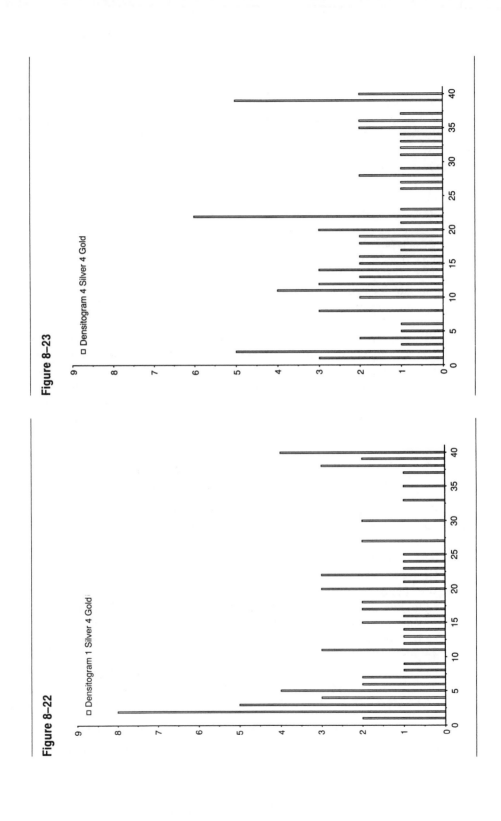

Figure 8–22

□ Densitogram 1 Silver 4 Gold

Figure 8–23

□ Densitogram 4 Silver 4 Gold

Table 8-3

	Time Series 1	Time Series 2	Series 2 × 10	Series 1 + (10 × Series 2)
1	1.000	2.000	20.000	21.000
2	3.000	1.000	10.000	13.000
3	2.000	3.000	30.000	32.000
4	1.000	3.000	30.000	31.000
5	2.000	2.000	20.000	22.000
6	1.000	1.000	10.000	11.000
7	1.000	2.000	20.000	21.000
8	3.000	2.000	20.000	23.000
9	2.000	3.000	30.000	32.000
10	3.000	2.000	20.000	23.000
11	1.000	2.000	20.000	21.000
12	2.000	1.000	10.000	12.000
13	3.000	3.000	30.000	33.000
14	3.000	3.000	30.000	33.000
15	1.000	1.000	10.000	11.000
16	1.000	2.000	20.000	21.000

The lowest third, encoded as "1," represents the lowest quarter *price changes* (gold –522 to –53; silver –13160 to –165); the middle third, encoded as a "2" represents the middle half of the *price changes* (gold -52 to +52; silver –160 to +180), while a "3" represents the highest 25% of the *price changes* (gold 53 to 485; silver 185 to 8930). Multiply the individual categorized silver prices by "10" and add it to the categorized gold price and plot the result. The resulting temporal correlogram is shown in Figure 8-25. If you examine the first column in this figure, you will note that it is an "11." This means that both silver and gold prices are in their lowest quarter. The second column is also an "11." The third column is a "32." This means that the price change of silver was in its highest 25% and the *price change* of gold is in its middle 50%. The relative distribution of pairs of categorized *price changes* is "1,1" (57); "1,2" (26); "1,3" (3); "2,1" (24); "2,2" (110); "2,3" (29); "3,1" (2); "3,2" (30); and "3,3" (51).

We can use the temporal correlogram to look at the relationship between volume and price for Sears in 1991. Divide the frequency histograms into approximately equal quarters. Encode the lowest 25% of price

Figure 8–24

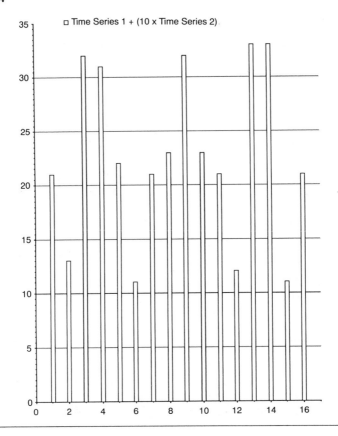

and volume as a "1" (price 22.03 to 26.04; volume 1731 to 4455); the next as a "2" (price 26.05 to 35.05; volume 4459 to 5576); the next as a "3" (price 35.06 to 37.07; volume 5591 to 7261); and the next as a "4" (price 38.00 to 41.07; volume 7462 to 20940). The volume (x10) + price temporal correlogram is shown in Figure 8-26.

Some investors believe that many stocks follow the "lead" of GM. We will compare the categorized price changes for GM with the categorized *price changes* for Sears and IBM. We will divide each frequency histogram into unequal thirds. The lowest third represents the lowest 25% of the *price changes* (GM –4.02 to –6.95; Sears –2.98 to –0.03; IBM –8.96 to –1.00) are encoded as a "1." The middle 50% of prices (GM –0.94 to +0.97; Sears –0.03 to +0.03; IBM –0.99 to +0.99) are encoded as a "2." The highest 25% of *price*

Figure 8-25

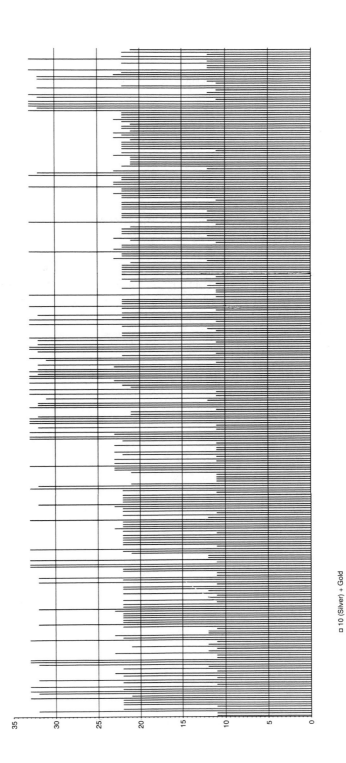

□ 10 (Silver) + Gold

changes (GM 0.98 to 4.03; Sears 0.04 to 3.00; IBM 1.00 to 4.04) are encoded as a "3." As indicated above, we multiply the GM category x10 and add it to the category of either Sears or IBM. The resulting temporal correlograms are shown in Figure 8-27 and 8-28, respectively.

What Does It All Mean?

The techniques described in this chapter can help you in two very different ways. First, they can supplement the methods described in detail in Chapter 3 and help you determine if your time series is independent or not. Second, if you discover that the sequential relationships of the prices or *price changes* of your stock, commodity, or index are dependent, then it should be possible to use a variety of techniques to identify "signals" that are time-locked to significant increases or decreases in the price of a particular stock. These signals tell a trader when to buy or sell a particular stock and make a profit or when to minimize a loss.

Figure 8–26

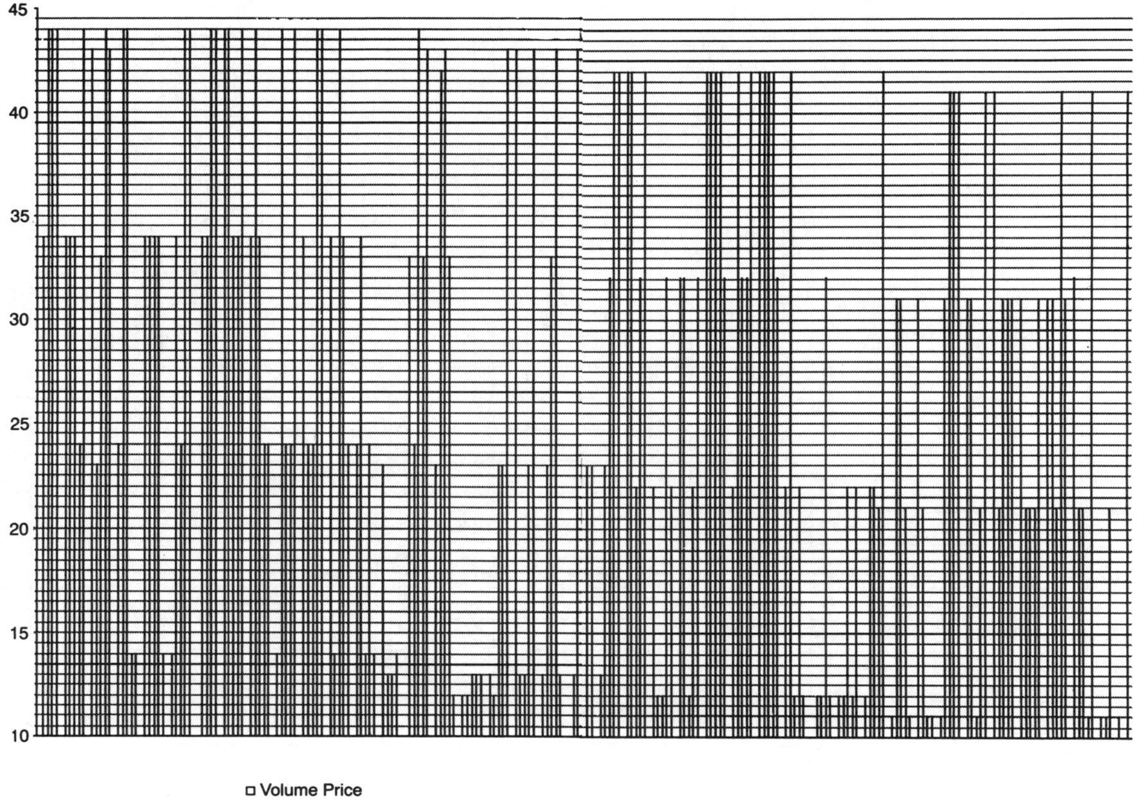

□ Volume Price

Figure 8–27   □ GM and Sears

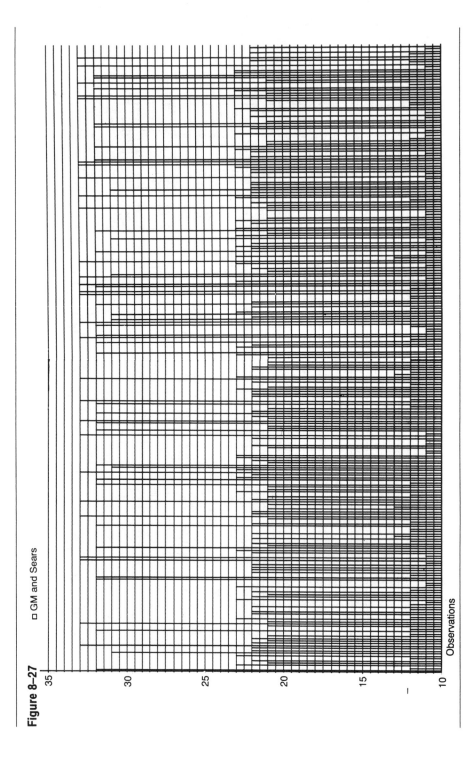

Observations

Figure 8–28

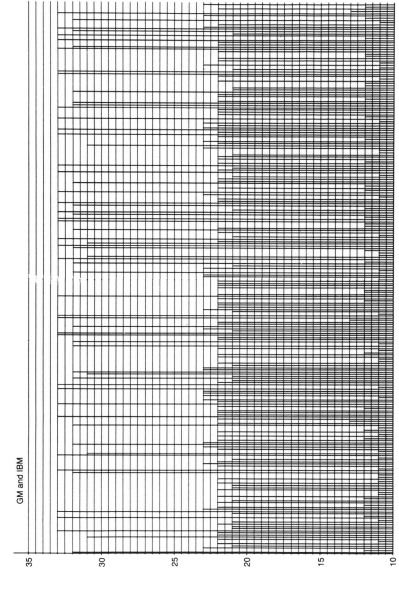

GM and IBM

Uncertainty and Risk   9

Many analysts allow risk and uncertainty to merge. But, while they are interrelated, they do represent two distinctly different concepts.

Risk attempts to quantify the relative probability of gain or loss. Risk is generally quantified in terms of variability of future returns. For the sake of illustration, assume that we live in a relatively simple world and we have only two choices of investment media: U.S. short-term government bonds, which yield 7%, or a new company that is trying to commercialize discoveries in quantum physics.

In the case of the government bonds, at least in theory (assuming that we do not have a major political, economic, or environmental catastrophe), we can estimate the return on our investment rather precisely. It will be 7%. Not more or not less. Because the return on the bond cannot vary, you can be relatively certain that you receive your original investment plus an additional 7%. Therefore, both your level of uncertainty and risk are minimal.

In the case of the quantum physics company, on the other hand, your potential return can range from -100% (you lose all of your investment) to 0% (that is, you get back your investment but do not make a profit) to 100% (that is, you get back your original investment plus an unknown but potentially large profit). In this case, your level of risk and uncertainty are maximal.

Modern analysts typically try to partition total risk into two principal components: systematic and random. Systematic risk is that portion of total risk that an individual firm has in common with the market as a whole and is "caused" by all of the factors that affect all stocks, such as political, social, and economic conditions. Generally, a large grouping of stocks, such as the Standard and Poor's 500 Stock Index is used as an analog of the entire market. One common measure of systematic risk is beta (W.F. Sharpe, *Portfolio Analysis and Capital Markets*, (McGraw Hill, 1970) and H. Markowitz, *Portfolio Selection: Efficient Diversification of Investments*, (Wiley, 1959)). This component of total risk can be minimized by diversification.

It is important to realize that the portfolio effect (diversification) works if the returns on individual stocks are negatively correlated. For example, in an expanding economy the returns on stocks "a" are high, while the returns on stock "b" tend to be low, while in a contracting economy (recession), these effects are reversed. Thus, when the two stocks are included in a portfolio, the returns on the portfolio tend to be relatively stable and to some extent, independent of the state of the economy. The greater the degree of negative correlation between the two stocks, the greater the reduction of the systematic risk.

On the other hand, if returns on stocks "a" and "b" are both high in an expanding economy and low in a contracting economy, then the returns on these two stocks are positively correlated. Clearly, the returns on this portfolio will vary with variations in the state of the economy. If the returns were perfectly correlated (an event that rarely happens in the "real" world), then the portfolio effect would be 0. That is, at least from the standpoint of minimizing systematic risk, there would be no benefit from having the two stocks in your portfolio.

If the correlation between returns on your stocks is 0, (this rarely happens in the real world), the returns from your two stocks are independent. In this case, you would obtain some benefit from diversification (owning both stocks "a" and "b"), but the magnitude of the benefit would be less than that obtained if the returns were negatively correlated. Theoretically, the standard deviation of the returns (see below) of the portfolio decrease with the square root of the number of stocks included in the portfolio. Typically, the effects of diversification plateaus at about 20 individual stocks. Adding additional stocks to the portfolio will have minimal effect(s) on decreasing systematic risk.

The other component of total risk, random risk, is that component of risk that is unique to a specific firm or industry (groups of firms involved in the same basic activity). This component of total risk is not affected by diversification.

Total risk is generally quantified in terms of the variance or standard deviation of expected returns. Because of the mathematical manipulations involved in calculating the variance or standard deviation, large deviations are given greater weight than small deviations. Another measure, average deviation, gives equal weight to both large and small deviations and thus is potentially a better measure of total risk.

It is important to realize that when you are dealing with expected returns, you are dealing with future events. Unless you happen to have a time machine or are a seer, you must use knowledge or intuition to make an estimate (guess) of what future returns will be. This is where uncertainty comes in.

Now you have a choice to make. You can use a simulation; that is, artificial data or you can use the past history of prices or *price changes*. If you decide to do a simulation using intuition or knowledge, you will need to determine the possible future returns that might be generated by your investment (r) and the probability of occurrence (p) of each of these possible future returns. Now multiply your estimates of future returns by the probability associated with each ($r_i p_i = r_i * p_i$) and then find the average probable return by summing over $r_i p_i$ and dividing the sum by the number of possible returns. Then calculate the variance, standard deviation, or average deviation to obtain an estimate of the risk associated with the investment.

On the other hand, you can use the past history of prices or *price changes* of your investment to make these estimates. If you choose to use the past prices or *price changes*, it is best to start with the most data points (prices) that you can acquire and manipulate. The number of possible data points is determined in part by how long the company has been in business and how you plan to do the analysis (paper and pencil, personal computer, mainframe computer, etc.). Once you have completed your initial evaluations using all of the data points available, it is best to repeat the evaluations using the most recent data points available and compare the results obtained. For example, if you have prices for the past 10 years, use this data, and then repeat using the data from the previous year and compare the results.

The first step is to determine if your time series of price or *price changes* is stationary or not, using the methods described in Chapter 2. If you discover that your price or price changes are not stationary, then you are dealing with maximum uncertainty. On the other hand, if you find that your time series is stationary then you have decreased the degree of uncertainty, because stationarity implies that the underlying rules that generated your time series did not change over time. Considerable additional research will need to be done to quantify the degree uncertainty is decreased by dealing with a stationary time series.

It is important to note that risk (as measured by variability of future returns) and stationarity can vary somewhat independently. That is, you can have two stocks that have similar variability, but one stock may be stationary and the other may not be. Since the uncertainty associated with a stationary stock is theoretically smaller than that associated with a non-stationary stock, you can vary your level of uncertainty while maintaining a relatively constant level of risk. You can also vary your level of risk while maintaining a relatively constant level of uncertainty. Since we can measure risk, as measured by variability of future returns, and uncertainty, as determined by whether our time series is stationary or not, (somewhat) independently, we have added an additional dimension to our stock evaluations.

If your time series is stationary, then the next step is to determine if your time series is independent or dependent using the methods described in Chapters 3, 5, 6, and 8. The techniques described in Chapter 3 are especially useful in this regard because they allow you to determine the duration of the "temporal window" during which the prices or *price changes* are not independent. Further, the techniques described in Chapters 3 and 8 will help you detect patterns of activity that might act as signals for making profitable buy-sell decisions. Most statisticians would concur with the notion that the degree of uncertainty associated with time series decreases when the sequential relationships of the individual prices or *price changes* diverge from independence. Since risk, as measured by variability of future returns, and uncertainty, as measured by divergence from independence, can be measured (somewhat) independently, you have added an additional dimension to your stock evaluation.

If a time series has been stationary and dependent in the past, it is relatively likely that it will continue to be in the present and possibly in the future. *It is vital that the reader understand that no one, no matter what they do, can consistently predict the future. All we can realistically do is use the best methods and techniques available to us to provide the best estimate of possible future returns and decrease the amount of uncertainty associated with them!*

Appendix   A

χ^2 **Critical Values for p = 0.05, 0.01 and 0.005 for Various Degrees of Freedom**

df	P = 0.05	P = 0.01	P = 0.005
1	3.84	6.63	7.88
2	5.99	9.21	10.6
3	7.81	11.34	12.84
4	9.49	13.28	14.86
5	11.07	15.09	16.75
6	12.59	16.81	18.55
7	14.07	18.48	20.28
8	15.51	20.09	21.96
9	16.92	21.67	23.59
10	18.31	23.21	25.19
11	19.68	24.73	26.76
12	21.03	26.22	28.3
13	22.36	27.69	29.82
14	23.68	29.14	31.32
15	25	39.58	32.8
30	43.77	59.89	53.67
60	79.08	88.38	91.95
120	146.57	158.95	163.64

The Chi-square critical values in this table were adapted from Natrella, Mary Gibbons, *Experimental Statistics*, National Bureau of Standards Handbook, 1991, U.S. Superintendent of Documents, Government Printing Office, Washington, D.C., 1963

Appendix   B

Skill or Luck?

Gambling, whether you do it in Las Vegas or in the backroom of your favorite club, is based almost totally on chance or luck. This is especially true if you are playing a game like lottery, roulette, slot machines, or craps (unless you happen to be a dice "handler," which can get you into a lot of trouble). It is less true of games like blackjack, which lends itself to card counting, or poker. But, even these games have a significant luck factor.

Most traders would like to believe that they are employing some level of skill when they make their buy-sell decisions. But are they? It is important to realize that you can make money on a game based totally on luck. Otherwise, gambling establishments would have long since gone out of business. Probability theorists and other experts generally agree that if you play a game based solely on luck, in the long run, you will lose.

Are your buy-sell decisions based on luck or skill? That is a difficult, but not impossible question to answer. Some years ago, meteorologists, who are often accused of guesses when they make their weather predictions, developed a simple formula which they call the "skill score" to determine if their forecasts are based on skill or luck. You can use this same formula to determine if your buy-sell decisions are based on skill or luck. The formula has the following form:

$$\text{Skill Score} = \frac{\text{Skilled }_{\text{Correct}} - \text{No Skill }_{\text{Correct}}}{\text{Total Decisions} - \text{No Skill }_{\text{Correct}}}$$

You can use this simple formula in the following manner. Write down each buy-sell decision that you make. At the same time, you need to make a "no-skill" decision, one based totally on chance. One simple way is to flip a fair coin. Let a head be a sell decision and a tail be a buy decision. At some time in the future, determine if your decision was correct or not. You can use any criterion that you like, such as whether or not you make any money or how much money, etc.

Using your criterion, determine if your decision, the no-skill decision, or both were correct. When you have collected 50 to 100 or more decisions, plug your numbers into the formula and make the calculations indicated. If your skill score is zero or negative, your decisions did not involve any skill, only luck. If on the other hand, your skill score is positive, some skill was involved. The magnitude of the number is a very crude indication of the amount of skill or luck involved.

Index

autocorrelation, 5, 78, 203, 206, 217, 218, 221, 222, 223, 224, 227-228
autocorrelogram, 206, 217, 218, 222-224, 227, 228
autocorrelogram correlation coefficient, 227
averaging, 275-288

Besson's Coefficient of Persistence, 271

category price transition matrix, 131, 133, 135, 137, 140
category price transitions, 140, 150, 151, 152, 153, 157
Chi-square, formula for, 38, 54
Chi-square test, 28, 64, 66, 87, 89, 90-91, 108, 110, 111, 125, 126-127, 130, 133, 135, 151, 157, 166, 271

densitogram, 290, 292, 296-297
differential spectrum, 86, 91, 93
digram transition matrix, 97, 107, 108, 117, 126, 133, 135, 162
Dow Jones Industrial Average, 62, 64, 66, 297

earnings multiplier(s), 1

filter rules, 5
Fourier transforms, 228

Gambler's Paradox, 85, 86, 112, 161

head and shoulders top, 289
histogram, frequency, 16, 18, 20, 21, 23, 26, 62, 87, 162, 166, 172, 173, 182, 197, 202, 204, 217, 218, 221-222, 275-276, 281, 290, 290, 292, 297, 304-305, 308-309

independence, 1-2, 5, 6, 85-164, 165, 184, 202, 203, 229, 289, 290, 292, 296, 297, 314

law of large numbers, 86, 165

Markov analysis, 140, 150, 151, 152, 153, 157
moving average, 78, 275, 281, 288, 289
moving-average plot, 9

noise, 206, 275, 288, 289

partitioning effect, 227
pattern detection techniques, 289-314

About the Publisher

PROBUS PUBLISHING COMPANY

Probus Publishing Company fills the informational needs of today's business professional by publishing authoritative, quality books on timely and relevant topics, including:

- Investing
- Futures/Options Trading
- Banking
- Finance
- Marketing and Sales
- Manufacturing and Project Management
- Personal Finance, Real Estate, Insurance and Estate Planning
- Entrepreneurship
- Management

Probus books are available at quantity discounts when purchased for business, educational or sales promotional use. For more information, please call the Director, Corporate/Institutional Sales at 1-800-PROBUS-1, or write:

Director, Corporate/Institutional Sales
Probus Publishing Company
1925 N. Clybourn Avenue
Chicago, Illinois 60614
FAX (312) 868-6250